*Joseph Ellicott and the
Holland Land Company*

A NEW YORK STATE STUDY

JOSEPH ELLICOTT, age 60, from an original painting by
A. G. D. Tuthill about 1820. This rendering was made
from a photograph of a daguerreotype printed in Orasmus
Turner, *Pioneer History of Western New York*. The likeness shows Ellicott's wispy hair, high forehead, direct-
looking eyes, pursed lips, and generous jowls. He is dressed
fashionably, wearing linen ruffles on the front of a well-
fitted coat.

Joseph Ellicott and the Holland Land Company

THE OPENING OF WESTERN NEW YORK

WILLIAM CHAZANOF

SYRACUSE UNIVERSITY PRESS

TO MY WIFE

WILLIAM CHAZANOF is professor of history at State University College, Fredonia, New York. He received the B.S. degree from State University College, Albany, the M.A. from Columbia University, and the Ph.D. from Syracuse University. He is especially interested in Colonial America and New York State history, and has written articles for journals in these fields.

Contents

ILLUSTRATIONS

Joseph Ellicott   *frontispiece*

Paul Busti   31

Acknowledgments

In the preparation of this book, I accumulated many obligations. It is not possible to thank each person by name for the help given me. Such a list includes librarians in colleges, historical societies, and city, county, and state-supported institutions. A sabbatical leave and two grants from The Netherland-America Foundation made it possible to study the large Holland Land Company Papers in Amsterdam, Holland. Two summer fellowships were most helpful: one from the Foundation of the State University at Fredonia, the other from the Research Foundation of the State University of New York. Because a great deal of research was done in Buffalo, the many courtesies of the staffs of the Buffalo and Erie County Historical Society and of the Buffalo and Erie County Library were appreciated. Professor Robert J. Rayback gave good direction in the incubation phases of this study. Professor George P. Zimmer, whose encouragement and interest were heartening, drew eight original maps with meticulous concern for accuracy. Professor Daniel Roselle, an office-mate for seventeen precious years, taught me so very much by example; he was invaluable in his editorial help, sage advice, and generous giving of his time. Professor Douglas H. Shepard helped to shape the Introduction and clarify the obscure. Mrs. Mary Notaro typed the entire manuscript with care and enthusiasm. My wife, Helen Wohl Chazanof, has a private niche. She read every word of the several drafts, offered sound critical judgments, and never lost faith in her husband. Special thanks go to my children, Esther and Jansen, for their patience.

Fredonia, New York
Summer 1970

*Joseph Ellicott and the
Holland Land Company*

Introduction

In December, 1800, a tired rider reached the eastern shore of Lake Erie. He dismounted, stretched his tall, robust frame, and looked around at the hamlet that would one day become Buffalo. Forty years old and accustomed to travel, Joseph Ellicott was happy to be back. During the past month's journey from Philadelphia, Ellicott had seen few familiar faces. Here at home, though, he knew just about everyone—indeed, all twenty-five residents of the settlement!

But that was in 1800. By 1820, a great change had occurred. The name of Joseph Ellicott was known to over 100,000 settlers in western New York, and now, at sixty years of age, he was on familiar terms with state governors and legislators at Albany and at Washington. Within two decades, this self-made man had established a career in New York State that was quite unusual, in fact extraordinary.

Today, Joseph Ellicott is almost forgotten, except for some small mementos western New York preserves in his honor. Buffalo named a street and a building after him. Chautauqua County has a town of Ellicott, Erie County a village of Ellicott, and Cattaraugus County a village of Ellicottville. Beyond this kind of recognition, Ellicott remains virtually unremembered.

This biographical study, necessary because no thorough one exists, focuses on the facts about a man little known but extremely important to the formation of western New York. The account follows Ellicott from 1800 to 1821, as he advances from surveyor to Resident-Agent of the Holland Land Company, a vital post of considerable influence. While the monograph provides material on the early development of western New York, at the same time it offers a case study on the uses of power on the frontier. As Resident-Agent, Ellicott's task is to sell at a profit the more than 3.3 million acres of Company land. From small beginnings in real estate, he comes to political power because, in order to sell the Company holdings, Ellicott *must* become involved with politics. Once caught in the political web, he then becomes enmeshed in the prosecution of the War of 1812, the internal squabbles of the Bank of Niagara, and the location of the western route of the Erie Canal. Through exceptional industry and shrewd maneuvering,

1

Ellicott by 1817 reaches a peak of economic and political power. Several circumstances, however, now combine to force his resignation as Resident-Agent and to topple him from his political pinnacle. His rise had been rapid, but so was the speed of his fall.

To be fully understood, Ellicott's life must be viewed from the perspective of his times. It was a world very different from now, a world in which Amsterdam was the Wall Street of western Europe. Without pretending to defend Dutch colonial policy, one of the miracles of the past four centuries has been how the Dutch reached such a level.

Beginning with few resources, a small population, limited land, 40 percent of which lay below sea level, the Netherlands won an eighty-year war (1565–1648) against mighty Spain and evolved into a powerful nation. The first step in Dutch growth was the herring industry, encouraged by the discovery in the late fifteenth century of a better method of curing fish. Then extending their coastal trade to the Baltic for grain and to Norway for timber and naval stores, they developed by 1600 a ship-building industry superior to all other countries. During the seventeenth century, a sea-carrying trade saw Dutch ships bring from Asia Japanese copper, Chinese silks and green tea, Persian carpets, Javanese coffee, and Malay tin. Although commerce was less heavy in the western hemisphere, this tiny country owned nearly half of Europe's shipping tonnage. Nor was this all. Highly skilled craftsmen also turned out cloth in Leyden, pottery in Delft, tapestry in Amsterdam, linens in Haarlem, while cutting diamonds in Antwerp (then a part of the Netherlands). By 1650, Holland had emerged as the principal European center for carriers, traders, manufacturers, and financiers. Dominating the oriental market, the nation likewise ranked first in several industries, handled much of the slave trade, and was an economic threat especially to Portugal, England, and France.

The Golden Century of the Netherlands was the seventeenth. Dutch affluence ranged beyond impressive bank balances and stately homes. In this century, the Dutch also produced first-rate creative talents such as the poet Vondel, the physicist Huygens, the painters Rembrandt, Hals, and De Hooch, the philosopher Spinoza, and the founder of international law, Grotius.

During the eighteenth century, the Netherlands lost its economic supremacy. The decline was not dramatic, but the slippage was fairly constant. Basically, the Netherlands lacked the raw materials for a permanent source of supply. But other factors hurt, too: the great strains of war against England and France in the seventeenth century, the increased burden of taxation, and the shrinking production from the industrial centers. Other nations, particularly England and France, caught up, imitated her industrial methods, and by developing their own commercial fleets became less dependent on Dutch carriers and traders.

Psychologically, too, the Dutch had exchanged their seventeenth-century daring in shipping and industrial investments for the less dynamic ventures of making loans to other countries. For the Dutch still had surprisingly strong financial muscles. As late as 1780, her bankers held some 40 percent of the British debt and had loaned to France about 25 million guilders (about $7 million). In addition, they made unexpectedly large advances to America, several in the 1780's, and by 1796 held the entire United States foreign debt of roughly $12 million. Federal bonds, state debts, and stock in canal-building like-wise attracted Dutch investors. The more important firms included Stadnitski, Vollenhoven, Schimmelpenninck, Van Staphorst, P. & C. van Eeghen, and W. & J. Willink—six houses that pooled some of their resources in 1792 to form the Holland Land Company. It was this Company that speculated in over 5 million acres in New York and Pennsylvania and hired Joseph Ellicott as Resident-Agent to sell its land in western New York. The export of Dutch capital then explains how, ultimately, the Holland Land Company and Joseph Ellicott came together.

For a broader perspective of Ellicott's times, though, the reader should examine the attitude of various groups toward land. In the American colonies, land tradition varied according to the different sections. In New England, with its surplus of rocks and shortage of fertile soil, the first settlers adopted a communal method of parceling out the precious real estate. Title to the land had been vested by the charter in the colonial legislature, which in turn made original grants of eight to ten square miles to each township. Here, the town proprietors in the town meeting made decisions on community organization and land distribution. At the center was the village common with the church, meetinghouse, minister's residence, school, and market place. The land near the village common was given to the proprietors, each of whom received a home lot of from two to five acres. Encircling the common were fields for planting and mowing that were divided into small plots and distributed by lot among the proprietors. What land remained belonged to the proprietors to be used in common for wood, pasturage, or whatever suited their needs. Newcomers were granted small plots and were permitted to participate in town meetings.

During the eighteenth century, the communal system of land administration disintegrated. Influential men were able to buy large parcels or wangle grants from pliant legislatures and resell them profitably to smaller settlers. Another basic change occurred when prosperous proprietors bought out the poorer ones. For both reasons, the seventeenth-century communal protections and unity eroded. The dispossessed New Englanders, driven to live on the frontier, hungrily eyed the fertile soil in western New York being sold by the Holland Land Company.

In the South, the land tradition took a different turn. At first the London Company had experimented with communal management. As sole owner of the land, the company used the settlers as servants: they worked as a cooperative unit, their harvests were collected into the company granary, and the company provided them with food and clothing. In theory, the surplus produce went to England to be sold for company profits. Through martial law and cruel punishments, the system was maintained but only for a short time. Communal management was abandoned and the Company introduced private ownership of land. Under the headright system, fifty acres were granted to anyone who remained at least three years.

Meanwhile, John Rolfe in 1612 introduced the tobacco crop and a second major change followed. With the abundant rolling lands, tobacco became profitable, the specialization bringing with it plantations, varying in size from one to six thousand acres. Labor shortage led to the use of slaves, and the plantation society was thus riveted on the South. Ecological differences had helped to shape the southern plantations as it had the New England townships.

A third approach to land distribution was the proprietary system. Under this method, a vast area was given to one or more so-called proprietors by the authority of the King. Charles II of England adopted the plan for two reasons. For colonial motives, he sought to outrun Spain for the contested land south of Virginia, and to push the Dutch out of New Netherland. And, for economic purposes, he found the system useful for paying off debts incurred during his exile under Cromwell.

As a buffer against Spain, the first proprietary grant of the Carolinas went in 1663 to eight of the King's associates. One year later, Charles II gave to his brother, the Duke of York, a princely domain of all the land between the Connecticut and Delaware Rivers. This area, previously New Netherland, was one of the war spoils wrested from the Dutch. The Duke of York promptly changed the name to New York and donated one part of his proprietorship, New Jersey, to two of his friends. The King's third grant was equally munificent. To cancel a debt of £16,000 (almost $40,000) owed by Charles II to William Penn's father, the King gave William the most valuable piece of land in all North America, Pennsylvania.

The colonial proprietary system was more frequently associated with the Middle Colonies than with the Carolinas. Yet, even with the contiguous Middle Colonies, land was divided differently in Pennsylvania than New York. William Penn recruited actively from all classes in Europe. Beckoning immigrants to the New World, he wrote of the low land prices for "fast fat earth," the "Natural Produce of the Country," the "sweet and clear" air, and the political and religious freedoms. As a result, the colony rose rapidly in population and prominence. So massive had been the King's grant that until the American Revolution the Penn family remained the proprietors of extensive lands.

New York traveled a different road. The Duke of York made no energetic efforts to attract settlers. Nor did the New York governors help, for several of them gave away huge estates on the frontier, thus partially blocking expansion. The big landowners, like Van Rensselaer, sought to enlarge their already sizable holdings rather than sell parcels to small settlers. Expansion westward was further discouraged by the powerful Iroquois who firmly controlled central and western New York. Until the American Revolution, the colony's population, economy, and assembly powers grew slowly.

Although the system of land distribution varied in each of the Middle Colonies, the basic concept of large single estates took root and was generally accepted. For example, the New York legislature in 1787 sold some 4 million acres of the North Country to Alexander Macomb without public protest. Similarly, when Robert Morris vended over 3 million acres of western New York to the Holland Land Company, it was a continuation of the proprietary tradition under which the Middle Colonies had been organized and developed. Thus the local land policy and Dutch economic development met to provide a field within which Joseph Ellicott could work out his destiny.

The focus thus far has been on the historical and economic context within which Ellicott functioned. But in addition, an analysis of his experiences as Resident-Agent of the Holland Land Company uncovers several underlying themes, each with its set of conflicts. The contest between man and nature in western New York is a microcosm of the three centuries of American expansion. The white man transforms the frontier west of the Genesee into permanent settlements, and as Frederick Jackson Turner recognized, "did indeed furnish a new field of opportunity, a gate of escape from the bondage of the past." Another motif is the struggle between the Few and the Many in New York politics. At first the settlers are at the mercy of the politicians of Canandaigua, but gradually the frontiersmen win their independence and with growing numbers increase their influence. A third struggle pits the European against the American traditions of social and economic organization. The frontiersmen adamantly insist on social equality and laissez faire rather than class rigidity and strong economic controls.

In effect, we are seeing some manifestations of the complicated interaction between various European and American traditions of social and economic organization. The conflicts of man against the wilderness and the Few against the Many were worked out at first with "European" methods of solution in an "American" setting. The third struggle of European against American traditions was affected heavily by the situation in the New World. The great distance from Europe, the slow communication, unbroken wilderness, land abundance, regional differences, and the cultural collision with the Indians—these among other factors helped shape the American solutions. All three themes merge into the attitude of different individuals and groups toward land.

The initial land tradition of the Dutch in America predates the creation of the Holland Land Company by some 170 years. In 1621, the States-General had granted an extensive trade monopoly to the Dutch West India Company. Conveying an immense area, the charter included New Netherland. Here, the Company fluctuated between trade and colonization but actually put much of its energies into the former. The land of New Netherland was regarded as Company property, and except for the ill-fated patroon venture, the bulk of the real estate remained in Company hands. Unable to attract many Dutch settlers, the Company came to regard land sales as far less important than trade. This commercial stress resembled many other Dutch ventures in Africa, Asia, and South America where the primary concern was trade, and not colonization, thus avoiding the problems of land disposition.

The Holland Land Company started in the path of its trade-oriented ancestors. Buying 3.3 million acres of land in western New York, the Company planned a quick disposal by selling the property in a few large blocks. Following Dutch tradition, the owners predictably shied away from involvement in small sales or long-term settlements. However, unforseen obstacles compelled the Company to alter its original designs. Some fifty years were needed before the Holland Land Company finally liquidated its holdings west of the Genesee. During that period, the sales were in small lots, and the Company was forced to take an active role in settlements.

The English land tradition, however, differed from the Dutch. Germane to the English was the fact they emphasized permanent settlements on small land plots, with opportunities for material gain. During the sixteenth century, Sir Humphrey Gilbert, his half-brother Sir Walter Raleigh, and the Hakluyts had strongly urged colonization rather than trade. A century later, Captain John Smith by example and by writing stimulated migration to North America. Smith used the usual arsenal of arguments: patriotism in the struggle against Spain and Portugal, religion "to convert those poore Salvages [sic] to know Christ," and history, citing "covetousnesse" for the fall of Rome and Turkey. He laid greatest stress, though, on the opportunities for a new, exciting, and materially rewarding life. Shunning a get-rich-quick and return to the Old World formula, he appealed to "father-lesse children, of thirteene or fourteen years of age, or young married people, that have small wealth to live on" to make permanent settlements and exploit the abundant resources.

On grounds similar to Smith, William Bradford explained the Puritan exodus from Leyden as due to nationalistic pride in their English birthright, a desire to spread Christianity, and the chances for a new, more prosperous way of life. John Winthrop reminded the Puritans, in a sermon from the deck of the ship *Arabella* that "wee shall be as a Citty upon a Hill." Examples to the world, they organized into small, homogeneous townships, making certain that each proprietor got his plot for settlement. By the end of the seventeenth century, a dozen English colonies dotted the landscape of North America, the settlers bringing with them the British tongue, laws, and institutions, all of which they quickly began to modify.

Joseph Ellicott became involved in both the Dutch and the English land traditions. Obedient to the masters of the Holland Land Company, he approved the idea of rapid sales to a few wealthy purchasers, and to this end he worked diligently. When this plan failed, he adopted the English tradition of longer range, smaller plot settlements. And it was that method which made his great successes between 1800 and 1821.

Who was this important, pivotal figure? Joseph Ellicott was in many ways quite ordinary. One of nine children, he had been raised in a comfortable home, felt close family ties, and enjoyed good health for many years. He had mastered an occupation of surveyor, was a practical businessman of good common sense, gained material independence, and did not become a burden to society. Ellicott had shortcomings. He was demanding of subordinates and to customers was often brusque to the point of rudeness. He was acquisitive to the verge of avarice and ignored some of the reasonable complaints for redress. This description can fit many men.

What then made Ellicott unusual? He was enormously industrious and applied his abundant energy to a few carefully selected goals rather than dissipating his vigor on many projects. He had, too, the rare facility of being able to do meticulous clerical type of work and at the same time achieve larger objectives. Thus, he could juxtapose his itemized and voluminous annual reports with the creation of new counties or the laying out of a canal route. He also had a capacity for growth. Starting out as an apprentice surveyor, Ellicott graduated to the positions of Chief of Survey of the Holland Company lands in western New York, to Resident-Agent, and to political leader of the purchase. When land sales were disappointingly small in 1801, he had the adaptability to recognize the interrelationship between business and politics. Although he preferred to limit his activities to business, Ellicott took an active part in broadening the suffrage, chartering a bank, and improving roads.

Ellicott was exceptional in another way. His life represents a case study of how one section of the West grew. The purchase in 1800 was very much a part of the West with its Indian culture based on hunting and fishing. During the transition from the nomadic Seneca life in the almost unbroken wilderness of western New York to the settled American society dependent on agriculture and trade, Ellicott was essential. Land had to be sold, local governments had to be established, taxes had to be raised, internal improvements had to be made, and safety for settlers and travelers had to be provided. These were problems that Ellicott as land agent tried to solve. Only then could the migrants use the roads and canals of western New York to carry them to the Northwest Territory, the Nebraska Territory, and over the Rockies to the Oregon and Washington Territories. In these western areas, the land agents had problems similar to those faced by Ellicott. A study of Joseph Ellicott, therefore, reveals in microcosm much of what happened in the settlement of the rest of the West.

I. The Great Survey

In 1794, Joseph Ellicott, a rugged six-foot-three surveyor, accepted employment with a combine of six Dutch banking houses. His task was to mark out some of the 1.5 million acres of land in northwestern Pennsylvania recently purchased by the wealthy Dutch financiers. To Ellicott, with ten years of experience measuring land on the frontier, the assignment seemed routine. However, what emerged was a close association with the Holland Land Company that, except for the year 1796, would continue without interruption until 1821. Begun in the Philadelphia office of the Dutch proprietors, this relationship would bring wealth, power, and fame to Joseph Ellicott. It would also have far-reaching effects on the history of western New York.

Prior to 1794, the Ellicotts had been typical of many families that left Europe and ventured to America. Joseph's ancestors were farmers, artisans, and millers, his generation being the first to become surveyors. Great-grandfather Andrew had come from Devonshire, England, where he had lived with his wife, belonged to the Society of Friends, and manufactured woolen goods. Why he left England is unclear, but one possible explanation was the business reverses he had suffered. Whatever the rationale, he left his wife in 1730 or 1731 and came to America with Andrew, the eldest son. Instead of a brief visit as planned, Andrew and his son settled down in Bucks County, Pennsylvania, bought fifty acres of land within five miles of Boylestown, and built a little log house. He never returned to his wife or the other two children.

Grandfather Andrew promptly fell in love and married Ann Bye in 1731. His grandmother, Joseph learned, was the daughter of a landed proprietor, a devout member of the Society of Friends, and a talented woman of considerable medical skill. She and his grandfather had five sons before Andrew died of pleurisy in 1741. Samuel Armitage, a neighbor appointed guardian of the fatherless five children, apprenticed one—Joseph's father—to a weaver, another to a carpenter, and a third to a blacksmith. The remaining two were too young to leave home.

Joseph's father, known simply as Jo, showed an exceptional apti-

9

tude for mechanics. His guardian had early recognized that Jo was "a smart, active boy, and a good weaver, but his mind ran wholly on the study of mechanics." Jo left weaving, worked for Samuel Bleaker repairing gristmills, and married Judith Bleaker, his employer's daughter. The young couple was so poor that they were forced to live with Jo's mother. Determined not to return to weaving, Jo persuaded his brothers and Samuel Armitage to build their own mill. Jo was the superintendent, the brothers all helped, and Armitage was the financier. The mill was built, and their business started to prosper.

Jo and Judith Ellicott had nine children, four boys and five girls. Joseph was born in Bucks County, Pennsylvania, on November 1, 1760. Andrew and David were older than Joseph, while Benjamin was five years younger. Sarah was the eldest sister, Letitia was two years younger than Joseph, Rachel was a twin to Benjamin, and Mary was the youngest.

Joseph was six years old when something happened that deeply affected the Ellicotts. His father, Jo, inherited a valuable property in England. Jo's father and grandfather had died; as next of kin surviving, he received his great-grandfather's estate. In 1767, Jo sailed to England, claimed the estate, and sold it for fifteen hundred pounds sterling, a considerable sum for those days. While in England, he indulged himself buying clocks, watches, and tools. When the now affluent Jo returned to Bucks County, people began to address him as Joseph Sr. He became the high sheriff of Bucks County and a member of the provincial assembly.

Jo devoted much of his new-found leisure to his hobby, the making of clocks. Of the many unusual timepieces his father built, young Joseph remembered one in particular. It was an ingenious astronomical and musical clock that Jo, with the aid of his fifteen-year-old son Andrew, completed in 1769. Standing eight feet high, the clock had four faces. One showed the planets moving accurately in their orbits. The second face indicated the time in seconds, minutes, hours, days, months, and years; it revealed the changes in the position of the moon. The third side had twenty-four tunes, dating back before the American Revolution. A small cylinder played a song every hour, and from the larger cylinder came a melody every three hours. By moving the pointer to a particular place, the clock played the selected tune. Among the songs heard were "Balance a Straw," "Plague on Those Girls," "Give Me Sweet Kisses," "The Lass with the Delicate Air," "The Pilgrim," and "God Save the King." At the fourth face was a window through which could be seen the complex mechanism. Judith Ellicott eventually gave the musical clock to her son, Joseph.

The industrious Ellicotts wanted more out of life than clockmaking. They were ambitious, venturesome, and unafraid to move. The higher standard of living made possible by Jo's inheritance whetted their appetites for greater material gain. Moreover, Jo's inheritance was a tidy stake for a larger enterprise.

Aware of the limited milling opportunities in Bucks County, Jo and his four brothers searched for a more attractive site. The five brothers, bound together by the early death of their father, remained close. Partners in the gristmill in Bucks County, they continued to operate as one unit. Jo and two of his brothers toured Maryland on horseback until they located what they wanted. It was a small meadow nestled among the roadless forests on the Patapsco River some ten miles from Baltimore. Not a stalk of wheat was being raised within miles of that location. Tobacco was the main crop, for the planters did not believe it feasible to grow wheat. Convinced otherwise, the Ellicott brothers, in 1772, bought 770 acres in two extensive tracts on the Patapsco River. That year, they began to erect a building.

Two years later, with the gristmill completed, the Ellicott clan moved to Maryland. The caravan included Jo, his wife Judith, their nine children, and Jo's two brothers. Remembering the hardships of his early life, Jo also brought along the six orphaned children of his deceased friend and former neighbor, William Evans. Jo's children and the Evans orphans got along well together, and eventually four of the children of each family intermarried. Three of the Evans boys married three of Jo's daughters, while Martha Evans became the wife of David, son of Jo.

Joseph, now fourteen, remembered the long and arduous trip in December, 1774, to their new home. Leaving Bucks County in wagons and carts, the caravan traveled to Philadelphia where they shipped down the Delaware River to Newcastle. There, they loaded their wagons, moved across the Peninsula, then took a boat down the Chesapeake Bay and up the Patapsco River. Reloading, they drove the carts and wagons the remaining mile to their final destination.

The Ellicotts literally carved a home out of the wilderness. The valley had been covered with huge trees which had grown untouched for centuries. The trees were of a large variety, with all sorts of oaks, hickory, maple, gum, ash, and chestnut. On the level ground were many kinds of shrubs that included dogwood, elder, spice wood, and red bud. Rabbits, squirrels, raccoon, pheasants, and partridges were in abundance. Less friendly were the wild cats who ventured out at night and destroyed pigs and poultry.

In their new location, the Ellicotts thrived. Tobacco growers, whose soil was wearing out, tried raising wheat and were successful. In 1774, the Ellicotts had their first customer who bought one hundred barrels of flour. Ellicott and Co., the name used by the brothers, became the greatest manufacturers of flour for export in that section of Maryland. Near the mill, Jo opened a general store, selling groceries, dry goods, and even satin and silks.

Joseph never forgot the lovely home his father built on the bluff overlooking the Patapsco. Located near the mills and the store, it was a mansion. The garden had rare plants and lovely shrubs, and in the center was a fountain that sent water streams some ten feet high. The inside of the house revealed the Quaker tastes of the occupants. The home was kept scrupulously neat and clean, the furniture designed for comfort rather than display. It was a happy home where the laughter was easy, and the family reunions numerous.

Jo's four sons had inherited the family talent for mathematics and science. None of the boys, however, became millers or clockmakers. Andrew, the eldest, lived an active public life. After a limited education, he returned to Bucks County in 1775 to marry Sara Brown, the daughter of a prominent Quaker. With the American Revolution entering a decisive phase in 1778, Andrew accepted a commission of captain, later major, in the Maryland militia. Military service violated the principles of the Society of Friends, but Major Ellicott insisted that the Quaker stand on defensive war was wrong. Whether he received a "minute of disownment" and his membership dropped from the Society of Friends for this transgression is not fully documented. In 1781, when the fighting ceased, the Major published an almanac that included among many items a recipe for pickling hams, a brief sermon on the text of the Book of Job, a list of justices of the New Jersey Supreme Court, and an editorial in support of the Patriots

Fascinated by mathematics, Andrew chose surveying as a career. Physically suited for the work, he stood over six feet tall and had a strong constitution. Despite a scanty formal preparation, he developed into an exceptionally able surveyor. The Major became known, too, as a competent scientist and a talented mathematician. It was as a surveyor, however, that he gained a national reputation and strongly shaped the vocational choice of his three younger brothers.

Andrew's career as a surveyor spanned more than a quarter of a century. He started in 1784 as a part of a group that extended the Mason and Dixon Line. The next year, he served on a commission that marked out the boundary of western and northern Pennsylvania, moved his family from the Patapsco River to nearby Baltimore, and taught mathematics at an academy in Baltimore. Andrew also found time to tutor his brothers Joseph, Benjamin, and David in the art of surveying. The Major had diverse interests. In 1786, for example, he was elected to represent Baltimore in the state legislature. That year, Andrew was further honored by being elected to the American Philosophical Society, for which he wrote a number of scientific papers.

Other commissions to survey land followed. In 1789, President Washington appointed Major Ellicott to fix the southwestern boundary of New York and thus settle the disputed ownership of Erie. Joseph and Benjamin helped Andrew with this survey, which established the Major's reputation. While he was in the area, Andrew made the "first actual measurements of the entire length of the [Niagara] river and of the falls and rapids from Lake Erie to Lake Ontario." His measurements of the river have since been accepted as correct. Shortly after, President Washington selected Andrew to lay out the federal capital which Major L'Enfant had designed. Andrew started work in 1791, brought in Joseph and Benjamin as assistants, and the three brothers did the bulk of the surveying. In 1794, Andrew helped to lay out another city, that of Erie in the northwestern corner of Pennsylvania.

Two years later came his greatest challenge. President Washington, for the third time, chose Andrew to do some surveying; he was to identify the frontier between the United States and the Spanish-owned lands to the south. His report was published as *The Journal of Andrew Ellicott,* a fascinating story that became one of America's classics. Returning to teaching in 1813, Major Ellicott went to West Point as a professor of mathematics, and there spent his remaining days.

David, Jo's second son who was two years younger than Andrew, lived a troubled life. He had married Martha Evans in 1777, and their four children all died in infancy. Martha was plagued by continued poor health that prevented her from performing her regular housework, yet was not sufficiently serious to keep her in bed. David also had financial difficulties. Unable to cope with all of his problems, David disappeared in 1787, not having informed anyone previously.

Seven years later, in 1794, Benjamin located David. By now Martha was dead, so David joined Joseph and Benjamin in surveying lands owned by the Holland Land Company. David continued to work for the Company until 1806. The following year, he went to Philadelphia with Joseph and settled his accounts with the Company. David then traveled to Maryland, where he paid off several debts, and mysteriously vanished. His disappearance in 1807 was a bitter blow to the closely knit brothers. David had always been mild mannered, sweet tempered, and agreeable. Joseph tried to locate him by contacting most of the post offices of the United States, but without success. Nothing was ever again heard from David Ellicott.

Joseph was Jo's third son, and his early years had been similar to those of his older brother Andrew. His formal education had been limited to the common school of a rural community. His skill in mathematics had also developed in the scientific climate of the congenial Ellicott home. And his teaching stint, too, had been short and in a Baltimore school.

Following Andrew's leadership, Joseph selected surveying as a profession. Andrew's teaching had been so effective that Joseph adopted his older brother's habits of painstaking and meticulous work. For fifteen years, Joseph surveyed land throughout the United States. In 1785, he assisted Andrew in marking off the western and northern borders of Pennsylvania. Four years later, he and Benjamin helped Andrew to lay out the western limits of New York State. Then, in 1791, Joseph struck out on his own. Timothy Pickering, the secretary of war, appointed him to run the boundary line between the State of Georgia and the land of the Creek Indians. This he did, but while working in Georgia, Joseph became seriously ill with yellow fever and almost lost his life. After he recovered, Joseph returned to the north where he joined Andrew and Benjamin in surveying the nation's capital.

By 1794, Joseph Ellicott had become an expert surveyor and had already revealed certain characteristics that would enhance his position. He had an independent and curious mind that digested his readings as thoroughly as it studied other men. Ellicott was short tempered, somewhat tactless, and strong willed with an inner drive that made him rather dictatorial. An exceptionally hard worker, he demanded the same intense industry from others working with him. Precise in his work habits, practical in outlook, he insisted on orderly operations. Joseph was as concerned with all the details related to surveying as he was with the act of measuring land itself. He kept a businesslike relationship with other men, for his great pride and reserve prevented him from becoming friendly with many people. To his family alone could he unburden his full feelings.

Joseph felt closest to Benjamin, youngest of the four Ellicott brothers. Five years younger than Joseph, Benjamin had been born in Bucks County, Pennsylvania on March 17, 1765. He had inherited his father's mathematical talent and was given an education similar to Joseph's. Impressed with Andrew's tutoring, Benjamin also adopted surveying as a profession. He was part of the brother team that fixed the boundary of southwestern New York in 1789 and laid out the federal capital in 1791. Benjamin resembled David in his tact, sweet temper, and charm. Physically, he was similar to Joseph, standing better than six feet tall with a sturdy frame. Benjamin and Joseph were both plain in their habits and frugal in their expenditures.

Joseph and Benjamin retained a very close relationship during their entire lives. They had common interests and attitudes. Both enjoyed surveying and were dependable, honest, keen businessmen. They invested their moneys together, although their profits were kept in separate accounts. Never married, the two bachelors lived together and were rarely separated.

The nine children of Jo and Judith Ellicott shared a feeling of togetherness. Although the four brothers and five sisters lived too far apart for frequent meetings, they apparently corresponded with one another regularly. They were genuinely concerned with each one's welfare. The coincidence of the three Ellicott girls marrying three Evans boys helped, also, to maintain this affection. Joseph and Andrew wrote long, detailed, and affectionate letters to each other. Never did Joseph forget that Andrew had given him his first start as a surveyor. During some lean years, when government pay came slowly, Joseph helped with cash. Benjamin and Rachel were twins who strengthened the wonder of their birth by an abiding affection for each other. In many ways, Benjamin and Rachel became Joseph's favorites.

By 1794, Joseph was emerging as head of the family. After his father died in 1780, he kept in close touch with his mother, looking after her needs until she died. Andrew and David were enmeshed in their own family problems. Joseph and Benjamin, however, early showed an ability to earn and save money. As Joseph's position improved, he gradually took over the family leadership. Lacking children of his own, Joseph frequently turned to the families of his brothers and sisters for the intangible comforts of a home atmosphere.

Joseph Ellicott was well prepared in 1794 for that new venture with the six Dutch banking houses. By training and experience, by ability, temperament, and ambition, Joseph had exactly the qualifications needed by the Dutch owners. He was on the threshold of an association that became a long-term relationship, a situation unforeseen even by the canny bankers of Holland.

Dutch investment in the United States had not come about suddenly. A number of Holland's capitalists had profited from loans which they had made during the American Revolution. The French Revolution had accentuated the interest of Dutch investors in the United States, because the wealthy Dutchmen feared the effects of the spread of this upheaval on their holdings in Europe.

There were two firms in Amsterdam that took a particular interest in American affairs. The house of Pieter Stadnitski and Son had been carrying on a thriving business as banker and broker in Amsterdam. The house of Nicolaas and Jacob Van Staphorst had been dealing with America since 1782 when it had taken a leading role in floating the first Dutch loan to the infant republic. As early as 1786, Stadnitski had been speculating in the securities of the American government. Dissatisfied with their experiences of dealing through brokers, Stadnitski and Van Staphorst united in 1789. Joining them that year were two other Dutch houses, P. & C. Van Eeghen and Ten Cate & Vollenhoven. The four Dutch banking houses now sent their own representative to America where he was the purchasing agent and also kept his clients informed about any changes in the financial condition of the United States.

The agent chosen to represent the four houses was Theophile Cazenove. A protégé of Pieter Stadnitski, Cazenove was jovial, personable, worldly, and also able to speak English. Signing his contract on November 30, 1789, he arrived in America early the next year. Cazenove continued to lead the good life to which he had become accustomed. He had a sensitive palate for fine food and for choice drinks. In the *Cazenove Journal, 1794,* he repeatedly identified the names of taverns, and evaluated the quality of their food and the convenience of their lodging. Cazenove traveled in grand style, riding in a coach and four, with an extra saddle horse, a valet, a coachman, and a postilion. His home on Market Street in Philadelphia became famous for the excellence of the dinners, and in a short time, he became friendly with American leaders in the fields of politics and finance.

Cazenove's employers had given him authority to invest some of their money, so he bought shares in the United States Bank as well as in state bonds. The government finances became so stable, however, that the opportunities for large profits through speculation diminished. Cazenove now put some money into canal building and in the Society for Establishing Useful Manufactures, but both investments failed. By 1791, the mania for land speculation was sweeping the nation, so he investigated the possibilities of investing money in land. While he debated the wisdom of such a move, two Dutch banking firms, W. J. Willink and Rutger Jan Schimmelpenninck, combined with the four houses in 1792.

A limited inquiry had made Cazenove enthusiastic about speculating in wild lands. His fervor was contagious, and the six houses authorized him to make several purchases, all in Pennsylvania and New York. Cazenove favored Pennsylvania because its law permitted aliens to own real estate. In 1792, he bought 1.5 million acres in northwestern Pennsylvania. New York, however, forbade aliens from owning land. Unable to overlook the glowing reports of fertile land at low prices, Cazenove circumvented the law by creating a board of American trustees to hold the land. Through the trustees, he bought, in 1792 and 1793, some 200,000 acres in the central part of New York and 3.3 million acres west of the Genesee River. Between 1792 and 1794, the Dutch bankers purchased over 5 million acres of land in New York and Pennsylvania.

Meanwhile, some members of the six houses were becoming uneasy about the extensive land purchases in America. To preserve harmony, the structure of the union of the six houses was changed into a stock company. This gave each of the six houses a greater flexibility in disposing of its shares. Details for this corporation were worked out in 1795, and, a year later, a company known as the *Hollandsche Land Compagnie,* more commonly identified as the Holland Land Company, came into existence.

Before any of the lands could be sold, accurate and detailed surveys of the holdings were essential. Theophile Cazenove, now designated as the Agent-General of the Dutch-owned properties, decided to survey the tract in northwestern Pennsylvania first. This took longer than anticipated. Sickness stalled the surveyors in 1793, and the following year, reports of Indian wars limited exploration of the frontier. Anxious to move more swiftly, the Agent-General put Joseph Ellicott in charge of the survey.

Cazenove's choice of Ellicott was a sound one. Joseph was an experienced surveyor who was also familiar with much of the terrain. Ten years earlier, he had helped to locate the boundary of western Pennsylvania. In 1794, he had been employed by Cazenove as one of the surveyors and had impressed the Agent-General with his industry and careful work.

His report to Cazenove of "certain lands in the six Districts" was characteristic of Joseph Ellicott. Running to fifty-eight pages, it was carefully organized, easily legible, thorough, and factual yet with occasional personal comments. Ellicott was a knowledgeable surveyor who readily identified the "White Oak, Ash, Beech, Basswood or Ilyum, Elm, Walnut, Hiccory, Mulberry, Crabb Tree, Plumb Tree, &

the Hawthorn." Nor did he miss the potential of the land, noting that *"real Vegetative soil* in few places exceeds two or three Inches in Depth." Joseph was also certain to remind his employer that the work of the surveyor was physically taxing, pointing out that on Saturday, June 7, "Being weary of travelling over a mountainous hilly & Miry road [we] concluded to lie by this day and wash our linnen." [1] Little did Ellicott or the Holland Land Company foresee that his stint in 1794 would be the start of twenty-seven years of employment with the Dutch proprietors.

Appointed chief surveyor in 1795, Joseph Ellicott spent the season of that year tramping through the Company holdings east of the Alleghanies. His brothers Benjamin and David served as assistants. Joseph took detailed and accurate notes of the land and, during the winter of 1795–96, prepared a full account for the Agent-General. The land was of poor quality, reported Ellicott, and this news was a deep disappointment to Cazenove. He had believed that the Pennsylvania holdings were more valuable than those in western New York.

Cazenove had made a blunder in buying the large tract in north-western Pennsylvania. Most of the land was covered by low moun-tains, and a great deal of the soil was unsuited for agriculture. To this day, the population of the region remains sparse. Had Cazenove sent an agent to make a confidential report before making the purchase, he would have quickly learned the true value of the land. Even the rather crude maps of that day suggested the character of the land. Why he bought the tract is a puzzle. A possible explanation was the mania for land speculation in 1792 that muddied the judgment of even shrewder businessmen than Cazenove. Whatever the reason, the investment led to heavy losses.

Cazenove now turned his attention to the Holland Land Company holdings in western New York. Here he had a different problem—how to get a clear title to ownership.

Western New York had gone through a long history that included several major changes in land ownership. Long before the six houses bought this tract, the Seneca Indians had lived there. During the American Revolution, however, this member of the Iroquois Confed-eracy had suffered a crushing defeat in the Clinton-Sullivan campaign and lost its ability to resist the white man's encroachments. When the war ended, the State of New York and the Commonwealth of Massa-chusetts each insisted that it owned the land in western New York.

Massachusetts traced its claim to the original charter. On Novem-ber 3, 1620, King James I had granted to the Plymouth Company title to all the land between the fortieth and the forty-eighth parallel that extended from sea to sea. A portion of this territory was ceded by the Plymouth Company to the Massachusetts colony in 1628 and was confirmed a year later by King Charles I. The charter of 1628 was vacated in 1684, and another one was granted by William and Mary in 1691. This charter included the lands from 42°2′ to 44°15′ that ranged from the Atlantic to the Pacific Ocean. Western New York extended south to the 42° and almost reached the 44° to the north. On this basis, Massachusetts claimed the land in western New York.

New York also cited royal decree as proof of ownership. In 1664, King Charles II had given to his brother James, Duke of York, the Dutch possession of New York, including the present State of New Jersey. The land extended from the west side of the Connecticut River to the east side of the Delaware River. The royal grant was later confirmed by treaty with Holland. The Duke of York thus acquired land which was also claimed by Massachusetts.

The overlapping land claims were resolved in two steps. The first was taken rather easily. The land beyond the present boundary of western New York was ceded to the United States. This was done by New York in 1780 and by Massachusetts five years later.

The second step was more complex. Ownership of the 19,000 square miles east of the present boundary of western New York was hotly disputed. Massachusetts based her claim under the royal charter of 1628, while New York claimed the land by virtue of her protectorate over the Iroquois Six Nations. To settle the controversy, ten representatives from Massachusetts and New York worked out a compromise at a conference at Hartford, Connecticut, in 1786. New York acknowledged the right of the Commonwealth of Massachusetts to preemption of the soil, that is the right of first purchase from the Indians of all the land in western New York except for a mile-wide tract along the Niagara River. Specifically, this area comprised 6 million acres that lay west of a line drawn north from the eighty-second milestone on the Pennsylvania north line and extending through Seneca Lake to Sodus Bay on Lake Ontario. In return, Massachusetts recognized the political sovereignty of the State of New York over this same area.

Two years after this treaty, Massachusetts sold all of its land in New York, east and west of the Genesee, to two land speculators, Oliver Phelps and Nathaniel Gorham. These men agreed to pay $1 million (£300,000) in three annual installments to Massachusetts for the 6-million-acre territory. Before Phelps and Gorham could sell

factor, perhaps, was his appointment one month before the meeting as Chief of Survey; his task was to lay out the Company lands west of the Genesee, once the title had been properly transferred.

The discussions were proceeding on a pacific note until some one began selling whisky to the Indians. What resulted was a three-day drunken orgy which ended only with the timely intervention by Farmer's Brother; he managed personally to "stave in the heads of the casks." [7]

The conference was now resumed. Red Jacket, Farmer's Brother, and Cornplanter, realizing the implications of the sale, refused to sign away the lands. The sessions were stormy, and both sides seemed to be reaching an impasse. Morris now tried a new tactic. A promise of sixty cows won over the Seneca women. An old approach, bribery, brought support from key Seneca sachems. Morris made immediate pledges to Red Jacket $600, Cornplanter $300, Farmer's Brother $100, Billy $100, and, Little Beard $50. In addition, annuities were guaranteed to Cornplanter $250, Red Jacket $100, Farmer's Brother $100, Billy $100, and Pollard $50.[8] Thus were the Senecas persuaded to give up their ancient claims to most of western New York.

On September 15, 1797, fifty-two Seneca leaders and Thomas Morris, as attorney for his father, signed the momentous Treaty of Big Tree at present-day Geneseo, New York. According to the terms, the Senecas would retain as their reservations a little less than 200,000 of the original 4 million acres. The Morris agents had fought hard to limit further the Indian holdings to 100,000 acres but failed. In the final negotiations, the Senecas agreed to sell their enormous piece of real estate "for the sum of one hundred thousand dollars." [9] The money was to be invested in Bank of the United States stock which would be held in the name of the President of the United States; dividends would be paid the Indians semi-annually. In a confirming note to the Senecas, Secretary of War James McHenry reiterated the treaty details, adding that Joseph Ellicott "has been employed to lay off the Reservations" set aside for the Indians.[10] With the signing of the Treaty of Big Tree, Robert Morris officially transferred to the Holland Land Company what had been conditionally agreed upon in 1792 and 1793: the three tracts of 1.5 million, 1 million, and 800,000 acres, for a grand total of 3.3 million acres.

Although the Company had had no legal right to participate in the meeting, the Dutch capitalists had become heavily committed. They had promised a sizable sum to get the meeting held and to obtain a clear title to the land. And the agents did more than observe. With

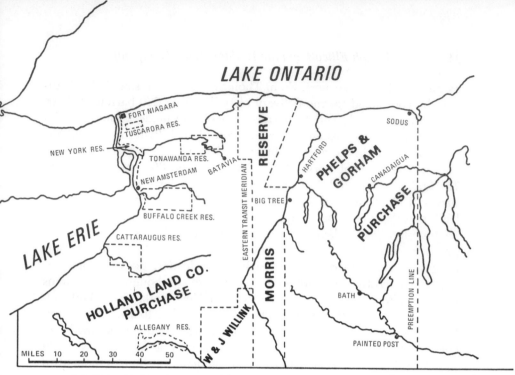

LAND HOLDINGS IN WESTERN NEW YORK — 1804

Company approval, they promised a reward of $1,000 to each of the three interpreters and $2,000 to the agent of the federal government to the Six Nations, if the Indians did not retain more than 200,000 acres to themselves.

The Treaty of Big Tree was signed sooner than expected, so Ellicott immediately set out to do some preliminary exploration in preparation for the formidable task ahead. During the fall of 1797, he toured the boundaries of the Company land. He surveyed the south shore of Lake Ontario to the mouth of the Niagara River, and from the southwest beach of Lake Erie to the western boundary of New York. He also prepared a topographical map of this survey. It had not been an easy journey. The last part of the trip had been made in foul weather, and he had walked nearly two-hundred miles through snow. By the middle of November, a physically exhausted Ellicott had completed the preparatory survey.

With a clearer idea of his needs, Ellicott spent the entire winter of 1797–98 in Philadelphia preparing for the expedition. Paid eight dollars a day, he was given complete authority by Cazenove. He planned to employ a party of 150 men—surveyors, draftsmen, cooks, ax men, and camp keepers. From Thomas Morris, the son of the financier, he contracted for the delivery of bulk items: 270 barrels of flour, 100 barrels of pork, and 15 barrels of beef. He made a long and detailed list of articles essential for a season of such living in the wilderness. Some of the equipment included 5 boats, 2 ox teams, 35 pack horses, 100 pairs of horse shoes, 200 blankets, 30 regimental tents, 70 "falling" axes, and 150 pairs of shoes. To keep a record of the survey, Ellicott ordered 6 large folio blank books, 2 "grosses" of black lead pencils, 1,000 Dutch quills, and 1 gross of binding." [11]

Joseph Ellicott planned the survey as carefully as a general prepared for a military campaign. Dividing the men into smaller groups, he gave specific instructions to each group leader. Because transportation was costly and time consuming, Ellicott bought many items from suppliers located nearer to western New York. From Philadelphia, a stream of letters was mailed to New York, Albany, Fort Schuyler, Queenston, and Canandaigua. Deliveries had to be made to coincide with rendezvous plans of each survey group. It was a big job, yet Ellicott was as meticulous with the details as he was thoughtful about the large items. For example, his estimate of the cost of the articles was $7,336, while the wages of the employees for six months in 1798 was calculated at $16,830.

The choice of survey instruments posed a unique problem. The purchase was bounded in part by meridians, lines running north and south. To guarantee absolute accuracy in identifying the meridian, astronomical measurements had to be made. And to do this, a transit instrument, rather than the surveyor's compass, was essential. The transit instrument is a telescope mounted on a tripod which provides the stability and accuracy missing in the conventional compass. According to Ellicott, at the time there was in the country but one portable transit instrument. That was being used by Joseph's old brother, Andrew, who was laying out the boundary between the United States and the Spanish lands to the south. Special portable transit instruments, therefore, were built, and they seemed to have been constructed by Benjamin, Joseph's younger brother. [12]

Cazenove gave Ellicott only the most general instructions. The Agent-General was fully aware of the importance of the project, referring to it as "le grand arpentage," the great survey. Cazenove respected and trusted Ellicott's judgment, and in May, 1798, wrote to him: "To your vigilance alone the direction, Management and superintendence of this great and import Survey is trusted." As Chief of Survey, Ellicott was to lay out the 3.3 million acres of Company land purchased from Morris. Based on the recent Treaty of Big Tree, Joseph was to arrange with the Seneca Indians the specific boundaries of their reservations. He was also to subdivide all the Company lands "into towns of six miles square, with a map of each town accompanied with field Books descriptive of the land, waters, Mill seats, Plains, Valeys, mines, minerals etcs." [13]

Ellicott continued to work closely with brothers Benjamin and David. They had helped Joseph in the survey of the Company lands in western Pennsylvania and now assisted him in western New York. Joseph, however, felt a special affection for Benjamin. An example of this intimacy was his answer to Cazenove's request to name a successor if something prevented Joseph from completing the great survey. "In that case," he answered, "I could wish my brother Mr. Benjamin Ellicott should act in my place, from a conviction that he is fully competent to performed [sic] every thing in that line with as much facility as I am able to do it myself." [14] Cazenove did just that, designating Benjamin as Joseph's successor should that become necessary.

In the spring of 1798, Ellicott headed a party of 130 men who plunged into the forests to begin the project. The high standards that brother Andrew had taught Joseph were now imposed by Ellicott upon his subordinates. He refused to depend on merely marking the various trees, for these imprints too often disappeared in a short while. Instead, Ellicott used permanent stone marks; these were set up along the boundaries of the Company lands, the Indian reservations, and the lines for townships. He showed an almost passionate concern for the accuracy of the survey. At the time, the country lacked a national standard for the measurement of a foot. Ellicott, therefore, collected a number of rulers, determined the average of their lengths, and used that figure for one foot length. To perpetuate his standard of measurement, he attached a brass twelve-inch ruler to the cover of every field book.

Ellicott's concern for detail also appeared in the careful system he introduced for taking field notes. He instructed each surveyor to identify himself and his assistants on the first page of every volume of field notes. By simple inspection, he wanted the reader to see easily the hills, plains, valleys, size of rivers, distances, and quality of the land. An index book was also constructed to facilitate locating particular field books.

The great survey took longer than Ellicott had envisioned. Originally planned for one season, it stretched into three. Officially, the survey started March, 1798. Benjamin Ellicott led one group at Williamsburgh near Genesee Falls, while John Thompson had charge of another band at Buffalo. Ellicott was busy, traveling between Canandaigua and Buffalo, keeping track of the groups, making key decisions, and exhorting the men to greater effort.

His first objective was to establish the boundaries of the Indian reservations. Most of this was done the first season. Except for the Tuscaroras, who refused to allow a survey in 1798, the men measured and laid off Indian reservations at Cattaraugus, Tanawanta (Tonawanda), Buffalo Creek, and several smaller places. Ellicott was particularly pleased with the survey of the Buffalo reservation. Aware of the importance of owning the east end of Lake Erie, he had managed to get it excluded from the Indian reservation. To Cazenove, he confided happily that this section was "one of the Keys to the Companies land." [15]

The next task was to lay out the eastern boundary of the purchase. This proved difficult. First, it was essential that both the Company and Robert Morris agree on the exact boundary that separated their properties. A joint survey was needed. To effect this, Ellicott went to Canandaigua where he met with Major Adam Hoops, a surveyor employed by Morris. Hoops, however, refused to send a surveyor or approve a boundary that the Company would lay out. From June 4 to June 14, there occurred a series of meetings and then an exchange of letters, all in Canandaigua, which an outsider would have found comical. Annoyed, discontented, and impatient to get on with business elsewhere, Ellicott reined in his normally quick temper. Finally, he persuaded Hoops to accept some principles as a basis to start the survey in the southwest corner of the Phelps and Gorham purchase.

Two days after his trying business at Canandaigua had ended, Ellicott was in Williamsburgh to set that party in motion up the Genesee River. Conferring with his brother Benjamin, who was in charge of the group, Joseph designed a plan of survey that would utilize the Genesee River for much of the travel northward. A boat was purchased, and Ellicott departed for Buffalo, leaving Benjamin to start this phase of the big survey. However, the plan to travel by boat failed. After Benjamin's party ascended the river about ten miles, they found the water too shallow and rapid. The water route was abandoned, and Benjamin had to buy a wagon and open a wagon road from Williamsburgh north. It was July 5 when Benjamin's part of the survey at long last began.

Benjamin's group pushed northward steadily. They followed a routine of camping in the woods, pitching their tents, transporting their provisions, and surveying the lines. Then, they struck their tents, moved to another place, camped, and repeated the process. At each mile, a stone was set up and properly lettered. By December 3, the group had surveyed ninety-four miles and had finally reached Lake Ontario. Marking the specific boundary point on Lake Ontario was delayed until a double check could be made of the interior lines. Otherwise, the second objective, surveying the eastern boundary of the purchase, had been achieved.

Ellicott, however, was keenly disappointed that the entire survey had not been completed in 1798. He had worked the men hard, keeping them in the woods until December 7. By then, the snowfall was so deep and the weather so cold that it became impractical to continue. There had been unexpected delays. His troubles with Major Hoops and his miscalculations of the feasibility of using the Genesee River as a roadway north had caused a full month's delay. In September, several of the workers had been taken ill with fever and ague. Many of the pack horses got distemper, and several were lost in a short time. Although new recruits and fresh horses were soon gained, the time loss could not be made up.

Part of Ellicott's disappointment stemmed from his great desire to please Cazenove. In his report, he stressed the achievements, rather than the work yet to be done. The major and most intricate part of the big survey had been completed. What tasks remained were relatively small—laying out patches of Indian reservations, identifying the eastern boundary at Lake Ontario, and surveying the southwestern corner of the Company's land.

One way to court favor with the Dutch owners was by strict attention to costs, and this came naturally to the business-minded Ellicott. He kept careful accounts of all disbursements, large and small. His reports to Cazenove were studded with regrets at unexpected costs. But Ellicott did more than express regrets. He cited that in 1798 trade had stagnated, that jobs were scarce, and as a consequence the men worked harder. Trade did not improve in 1799, so he reduced salaries. Pay for surveyors was cut from three dollars a day to one dollar and fifty cents. Chain bearers, axemen, packhorsemen, and boatmen had their monthly wages dropped from fifteen to twelve dollars. However, the salaries of the two group leaders, Benjamin Ellicott and John Thompson, remained at four dollars and fifty cents and four dollars a day respectively. And Joseph's pay continued at the rate of eight dollars a day.

One more task remained, putting together a comprehensive report of the findings of the big survey. Ellicott started to organize the report during the winter of 1798–99. Getting an adequate store of provisions, he spent that winter in a cabin somewhere on the Genesee road in western New York. After the pressing summer of 1798, Ellicott welcomed the solitude, describing the "situation well adapted for that purpose; being out of reach of all Society, I have nothing to attend to but the business." [16] When the survey was finally completed, he spent many months preparing a full and detailed report. In cold statistics, the big survey had started in March, 1798, had ended October, 1800, and had cost the Holland Land Company precisely $70,-921.69½.

The great survey was finished, and Ellicott had achieved many things. He had marked out the boundaries of the Company land, he had subdivided the territory into townships of six miles square, and he had organized these districts into ranges. At the same time, he had taken careful notes regarding the land—the quality of the soil, the topography of the various sections, and locations suitable for future settlements. Ellicott's report showed great care and exactness, and made clear to the Company that its tract of land in western New York was extremely valuable. The next step taken by the Holland Land Company was important—the selection of a skillful agent to sell this attractive property at a good profit.

II. Many Applicants, Few Buyers

The Holland Land Company understood the significance of choosing the right agent, and was equally aware of the importance of devising a sound plan for selling the land. The agent and the policy were like two sides of the same coin. Candidates and proposals, therefore, received careful and lengthy study. From 1792, the year of the preliminary sale, until 1800, when Ellicott had completed the great survey, the Dutch owners had discussed policy, consulted candidates, and studied their plans.

They conferred with men already active in selling land to the east of the purchase. James Wadsworth, a cousin of Jeremiah who represented the federal government at the Treaty of Big Tree, made a favorable impression. Having migrated from Connecticut to Big Tree (Geneseo) in 1790, Wadsworth had become a large landowner in his own right and an agent for several speculators who owned land in that area. His suggestions to "avoid all considerable expenses, . . . to sell rather at low prices than to give long Credits, and to make the purchase of these Lands an object to rich individuals and Societies" suited the economy-minded directors.[1] Paul Busti, Cazenove's successor, was so pleased that he offered Wadsworth "a temporary agency over the lands" west of the Genesee which Wadsworth limited "for the ensuing year only."[2] The Company, however, rejected Wadsworth as permanent agent. His terms were too high, and he was already committed to so many affairs that he could not give full-time service. Moreover, the accusation by Thomas Morris impugning Wadsworth's honesty shook the upright Busti. Charles Williamson, the experienced land agent in charge of the nearby Pulteney Estate since 1791, proposed that the Holland Land Company spend large sums of money on the development of the territory in order to encourage a more profitable future sale. Williamson had already disbursed about $1 million on the Pulteney land, building roads, constructing a theater, laying out a race track, and erecting a sumptuous hotel. The Company quickly eliminated Williamson from the list of contenders; it wanted to make a quick profit, rather than spend money for larger, long-range gains. Thomas Morris refused to set down his thoughts on paper because he was suspicious that his advice might be used without compensating him. What little he suggested resembled the ideas of Williamson, so Morris' candidacy was rejected.

Despite Ellicott's preoccupation with surveying the Company lands in western New York, he found time to submit his plans. Like Wadsworth, he emphasized that the Company should spend as little money as possible in the development of the land. Let private investors, rather than the Company, put capital in the land, he urged; surely there would be many individuals who would be willing to invest money in such a sound project. He suggested that the Company spend money on essentials alone: the opening of a few main roads, the erection of a grist and sawmill, the raising of a house and office for the agent, the construction of a tavern in which to house potential customers, and the building of a blacksmith shop, equipped with irons and tools.

In the three sets of plans he had offered, Ellicott elaborated on his ideas. Foreseeing easy sales but difficult collections, he proposed that the Company help the settlers by accepting payments in cattle, hogs, and grain. Such a system would encourage the settlers to clear the land for farming and to erect a gristmill nearby. Ellicott included suggestions for settlement. Aware that many of the applicants would want small lots, he preferred that the Company sell much of the land in large, wholesale parcels. To attract larger purchases, he recommended a substantial reduction in price. Ellicott also stressed that every tract purchased be settled. Only those who had paid the full sum would be exempt from this condition. As a last recommendation, Ellicott advised the Company to reserve sizable parcels of good land and thus avoid being left with lots of poor quality. The reserved land would thereby increase in value as the settlements grew up around the Company holdings. Ellicott's proposals revealed his clear thinking, lucid expression, practical outlook, and sound balance between details and broad plans.

Although he had no experience in the selling of land comparable to that of the other candidates, Ellicott gained considerable support from the Company officials. He had already displayed certain traits and abilities that the Company weighed heavily in his favor. He had spent most of his life on the frontier and would feel at home in western New York, which in 1800 was in a primitive state. An expert surveyor, he had observed the techniques by which some of the other large landowners handled the sales of their properties and could apply this knowledge to the purchase. As a result of his careful survey in

PAUL BUSTI, painted by St. Memin. This rendering was
made from a reproduction of a photograph in the Holland
Land Company Papers at the City Archives in Amsterdam,
Holland. Limited because of the profile view, it does reveal
Busti as well groomed, wearing a tailored coat with stylish
ruffles.

western New York, Ellicott also knew the land and its topography
better than did any of the other candidates who sought the job. In addition to this, Cazenove and Paul Busti had learned that Ellicott
had managed Company funds with care and complete honesty during
the great survey. Of some weight, too, was the fact that the unmarried
Ellicott had devoted all of his time unstintingly to serve the Company,
and he had not shown any marital ambitions that would make heavy
demands on his time. Finally, Joseph Ellicott's great common sense—
perhaps more than any other qualification—convinced the Dutch proprietors to appoint him as their Resident-Agent in western New York.

On November 1, 1800, in Philadelphia, Joseph Ellicott and Paul
Busti signed the carefully written contract that was to mark the begin-

ning of Ellicott's long career as Resident-Agent of the Holland Land
Company. Ellicott, now forty years old, signed only for himself. Busti,
however, placed his signature on behalf of the directors of the Company—five men who bore the stately names of Willink, Van Staphorst,
Van Eeghen, Vollenhoven, and Schimmelpenninck. Thus was created
a business and social relationship between Ellicott and Busti that was
to last for more than a score of years.

Paul Busti had come into the Holland Land Company through
proven ability and family connections. Born on October 17, 1749, in
Milan, Italy, and educated in that country, Busti took a job in Amsterdam working in his uncle's bank. He acquired an enviable reputation for business acumen, industry, and scrupulous honesty. A
brother-in-law of Ten Cate, the head of one of the six Dutch banking
houses that had formed the Holland Land Company, Busti was persuaded to join the Company in 1796 as an assistant to Theophile
Cazenove. Cazenove's carelessness had disturbed the ledger-conscious
Dutch owners. He kept almost no accounts and even confused the
Company funds with his own. The Company, however, had to move
cautiously with Cazenove, for he was in the midst of delicate negotiations to extinguish Indian land titles in western New York. Busti
arrived in Pennsylvania in February, 1797, and for two years assisted
Cazenove until the latter went back to Europe. The Company then
appointed Busti as Agent-General, granting him "full power and authority" to represent the Dutch owners and, if necessary, to defend
them in state and federal courts. From 1799 until his death in July,
1824, Busti had complete charge, managing all the Company holdings
from his Philadelphia office.

The terms of the contract signed by Busti and Ellicott were carefully drawn and characteristically circumspect. The position of Resident-Agent was for six years and paid a sliding salary. Ellicott would
receive $1,500 a year so long as the area under control remained at
300,000 acres. The annual salary would increase in proportion to the
acreage under his control. In addition, he would receive a commission
of 5 percent on all sales under his jurisdiction. The Company would
spend up to $2,500 for a residence and an office for Ellicott. At the
date of his retirement, Ellicott was to be given two bonuses from the
Company: 1,000 acres of land, and 1 percent of all the unsold property under his control. The Company, in return, expected Ellicott to
sell the land, to work only for the Dutch proprietors, and to enrich
the stockholders.

During his twenty-year tenure as Resident-Agent, Ellicott's contract was renewed several times and its terms revised. In 1810, for example, his 5 percent commission was satisfied by the transfer of about 30,000 acres to Ellicott. The 1810 contract also limited the bonus to be given Ellicott at the time of his retirement to 6,000 acres, rather than the original 1 percent of all the unsold property. In 1811, Ellicott's annual salary was increased to $5,000, but he was given a 2 percent commission upon receipts rather than the previous 5 percent upon sales. This partially reduced his income. The Dutch owners reckoned that during Ellicott's first ten years as Resident-Agent, he received about $11,500 annually. During the last ten years, his yearly income decreased to about $7,000.

Once appointed to the position of Resident-Agent, Ellicott left Philadelphia on November 5, 1800, eager to get on with the business of selling land. En route, he kept Busti informed of his activities and explained the various delays that occurred. From Albany, on November 26, he wrote to Busti about his need to wait for the printers. It was essential to have stationery, handbills to advertise the Company land, and Articles of Agreement to be made with each sale. The weather, too, was inclement. By December 17, Ellicott reached Canandaigua where he learned happily that land sales in that area were brisk. Just three days after Christmas in 1800, he arrived at New Amsterdam (Buffalo).

Ellicott's journey from Philadelphia to New Amsterdam pointed up the contrasts in urban and frontier living. By 1800, Philadelphia was the largest city in America with a population of seventy thousand. It had been fortunate. With a prosperous economy that had been relatively unaffected by the Revolution, the City of Brotherly Love clung to its lead in imports and exports over all other urban centers until the middle 1790's. It had also the most extensive and varied industry in the nation, with almost half of the country's banking capital in Philadelphia. The streets were laid out at right angles to one another, had curbs, and were covered with small stones; the sidewalks were of brick and had been put down a foot higher than the roads. Philadelphia was just completing a major project for tapping the Schuylkill River from which water was brought by steam pumps into a central reservoir, and from there distributed throughout the city. The engineering feat was a topic of conversation among the Friends, dressed somberly, their broadbrim hats kept tightly on their heads, never to be removed in deference to any person. The reservoir also interested the Amish, Mennonites, Schwenkfelders, and Moravians, some of whom tended to isolate themselves from the general population. Philadelphia was affluent and cosmopolitan, its residents proud of the publishing house, the literary association, and the library.

In 1800, the major rival to Philadelphia and the second-largest city in America was New York. With a population of 60,000, New York City had the potential of becoming the metropolis of the United States. It had an ideal location, a deep, large, protected harbor, easy channels of communication with the interior by water, and a skilled, industrious, flexible population. In 1800, New York was a mixture of British and Yankee sailors, of Irish and German laborers, of Scottish traders, of free Negroes and Negro slaves. The urban workers toiled ten to fourteen hours a day, according to the season, while the doctors, lawyers, and other professional men worked almost as long. From Long Island and from upper Manhattan, the farmers came into New York City to market their potatoes, fruits, or poultry. The city dwellers crowded the southern tip of Manhattan Island, for the area north of present-day Fourteenth Street was practically unoccupied or else farm land. By 1800, New York had outdistanced its urban competitors in exports and imports. As proud as Philadelphians, New York City residents cited other achievements: the abandonment of corporal punishment, the limitation of death sentences to the committal of three capital crimes, and the creation of a penitentiary system.

Outside New York City, the state was predominantly agricultural. The fertile Hudson Valley was still a feudal domain of the Schuylers, the Van Rensselaers, and other Dutch families. From Albany, a thin strip of farmed land ran west along the Mohawk River. To the north and to the east of Albany, cultivated lands reached out toward Quebec and Vermont. Otherwise, the state's outposts were at Oswego and Niagara. The farmers, however, were already pushing into the Genesee Valley.

From New York City, stretching one hundred fifty miles up the Hudson and into the interior of the state was Albany. Like New York, Albany had suffered during the American Revolution, having had a substantial number of refugees, wounded soldiers, and Tory conspirators. Yet, Albany had certain advantages. Located on the west bank of the Hudson, it was the gateway for the rich region to the west; for many years, Albany had been the center for a profitable fur trade. In 1797, it had also become the state capital. When John Maude, an observant British traveler, visited Albany in June, 1800, he was impressed with "the neighborhood very busy hay making." Never had Maude seen "the wild grape and wild strawberry in such profusion." [3] Moreover, he found the prices reasonable. Beef cost six to nine cents a pound, butter sold for twenty cents a pound, and twenty eggs fetched twelve and one-half cents. Despite its assets, Albany had progressed slowly. In 1800, its population was roughly 5,300, about one-sixth of New York City.

When Ellicott headed for western New York in November, 1800, the differences between cities like Philadelphia, New York, and Albany and the less populated areas stood out sharply. The Resident-Agent, apparently, left no notes of his trip. Fortunately, John Maude, who covered the same territory in the summer of 1800, recorded his experiences. Maude had lived in the United States at intervals between 1793 and 1803. By habit, he jotted down observations on the spot and in the same evening carefully transcribed the day's events in a journal. Maude's comments corresponded factually with the reports written by several other travelers who journeyed through western New York at about the same time. The journal, therefore, is a dependable case study of what travelers saw of the state in 1800.

John Maude was an alert tourist. Over relatively good roads, the stagecoach took him from Albany to Utica. En route, he stopped at Schenectady long enough to note it had 150 to 200 houses and an educational institute called Union College. Incorporated in 1795, Union College owned a library of 1,000 volumes and, in 1800, catered to 37 students. Maude set down, too, what he had eaten for breakfast: a loin of veal, ham, strawberries, cheese, coffee, tea, tarts, and preserved apples. Utica had some 60 houses and Schwartz's Hotel, which Maude recorded tersely: "excellent house, miserably kept." [4]

Travel from Utica to Buffalo was mainly on horseback. In the township of Manlius, Maude learned about the state policy of setting aside the military tract there as a land bonus for war veterans. He discovered that speculators had bought much of these 1.5 million acres at cheap prices, adding judiciously: "Tis true the Soldiers sold their patents many times over—perhaps once a week." [5] In the Syracuse area, New York permitted any one to produce salt from the Salt Lake provided he paid the state four cents for every bushel of salt made. Geneva impressed Maude. The town had grown from three or four families in 1792 to at least sixty in 1800. It was at Geneva that Maude had several enjoyable visits with Charles Williamson, the agent of the Pulteney lands. The trip from Geneva to Canandaigua was made through heavy timbers, rich soil, and bad roads. Maude recalled ruefully that "the mosquitoes of this swampy district were of a stouter race than any I had yet encountered, and to my utter astonishment, I found them capable of drawing blood through a thick leather riding glove." [6]

In many ways, Canandaigua was an outpost, a springboard for

those about to continue to Buffalo. Canandaigua and Geneva had been about the same size in 1792, each having a few farm houses and some log cabins. By 1800, Canandaigua had pulled ahead and now had ninety families, the residents including Thomas Morris, Nathaniel Gorham, and Oliver Phelps. Situated on high ground, the village had one principal street that extended from the lovely Canandaigua Lake in a straight line for over a mile. Carefully laid out, this spacious street had thirty lots on each side, each lot containing forty acres. The county seat of Ontario County, Canandaigua had a court house which was also used by the Presbyterian congregation for services. The village was the site of the land office of Phelps and Gorham, the first land office in western New York and possibly one of the first in the United States.

In 1800, Canandaigua was the northern point of entry into the Genesee country. The land between Canandaigua and the Genesee River was being settled, but slowly. West of the Genesee River, however, in the region where the Holland Land Company had its holdings, the area was virtually unoccupied.

When Joseph Ellicott accepted the position of Resident-Agent in 1800, travelers in western New York had been using the Indian trails. Practically no other roads existed on the purchase. The single exception was the road which DuQuesne, the French leader, had built in 1753 to connect Lake Erie with Chautauqua Lake. This route became known as the Old Portage or French Road and joined Mayville, the Chautauqua County seat, with the town of Westfield on Lake Erie.

With western New York heavily wooded, the tourists found their journeys in this area slow, disagreeable, and hazardous. In his excursion to Niagara Falls in 1799, Charles Williamson described the territory as "settled for about twelve miles; but after that, for about sixty-five miles to Niagara River, the country remains a wilderness." One year later, the missionary David Bacon, who worked among the Indians in western New York, took a trip from East Bloomfield to New Amsterdam with his wife and brother. The minister's brother noted the traveling conditions and recorded: "There was no wagon road, only a path through the woods, sometimes rather obscure, the trees marked to show the way." John Maude summed up the situation succinctly: "excellent land, execrable roads." And Timothy Dwight, the president of Yale College and a seasoned traveler, experienced his share of difficulties in passing through western New York in 1804: "The stumps and roots were innumerable, and singularly perplexing and dangerous," he complained. "The mud, through most of the distances, was knee-deep; and often so stiff as to make it impossible for a horse to extricate himself without extreme labor." [7]

Travel through western New York in 1800 was unquestionably poor, but a journey by stagecoach in the more settled areas brought discomforts, too. The American coach at this time carried nine persons inside and one passenger who occupied the low seat beside the driver. The nine people inside sat in rows facing the front of the vehicle. Three filled the front seats, three more occupied the places in the middle row—using for a back-rest a broad leather strap that passed across the entire coach—and the last three sat in the rear row. The front and rear seats had solid back supports whereas the center row had less secure spinal comfort. Sometimes, the leather strap became unhooked and, when this occurred, the three in the middle seat fell back so that their heads struck the stomachs of the passengers in back of them. Not until 1807 did the state legislature even grant a franchise for regular stagecoach service in western New York.

An examination of the Company lands west of the Genesee provided clues about future settlements. The surface of the northern section of the purchase was remarkably level, there not being a single hill of any height between the Genesee River and New Amsterdam (Buffalo). The land in the southern half, however, was generally rugged, broken, and in parts mountainous. The most common species of trees were sugar maple, beech, oak, ash, and elm, with the oak plants growing in the more fertile parts. The soil was suitable for raising corn, wheat, rye, and other varieties of grain. Living in western New York in 1800 was dangerous. Rattlesnakes were frequently seen, and bears, wolves, elk, and foxes wandered mainly in the southern sector. Deer, mink, otter, and muskrats were abundant. What impressed travelers were the great numbers of black and red squirrels that scampered through the woods.

Before 1800, the area around New Amsterdam had gone through several changes. In the seventeenth century, two major events had occurred. Destroying the Erie Indians in a savage battle, the Senecas took over control of the region in 1654. And twenty-five years later, the first white man appeared in New Amsterdam. Under the direction of Henry de Tonty, a lieutenant of La Salle, the ship, the *Griffon*, was constructed a few miles above the Niagara Falls. Tonty anchored the *Griffon* near what later became known as Squaw Island, within the present limits of Buffalo. Sailed and towed through the rapids, the *Griffon* became the first ship to enter Lake Erie. The Niagara route, henceforth, became one of the main courses to the west. Recognizing the importance of the territory, the French, in 1726, erected Fort Niagara at the mouth of the Niagara River. During the French and Indian War, however, when Britain defeated France, Fort Niagara was destroyed. Great Britain was also aware of the strategic importance of the region and, in 1764, built Fort Erie; it was located at the mouth of Lake Erie on the northwestern side. But the area continued to be a place to traverse, and few pioneers remained. Only after the American Revolution did interest mount for a more permanent settlement.

New Amsterdam was a sparsely populated hamlet in 1800. Five years earlier, the Duke La Rochefoucauld-Liancourt, a French nobleman, had visited New Amsterdam and described it as "a small collection of four or five houses, built about a quarter of a mile from the Lake."[8] By 1798, the hamlet had a blacksmith shop, a silversmith shop, a half-dozen houses, and a population of about twenty to twenty-five that did not include the Senecas who lived near the village. In 1800, four residents from New Amsterdam paid a tax to the town of Northampton of $4.55. When Ellicott became Resident-Agent, the hamlet had no schoolhouse or place of worship. The Holland Land Company owned virtually all the land in the village. New Amsterdam had not yet been surveyed nor had any streets been laid out. Ellicott persisted in calling the area New Amsterdam, but the name never stuck. The inhabitants preferred calling it Buffaloe Creek until it was shortened to Buffalo. Whatever the name, New Amsterdam in 1800 was a pioneer community, few in numbers, primitive in equipment, but ideal in location.

When Ellicott reached New Amsterdam in December, 1800, the area was so underdeveloped he had to wait for suitable quarters to be built. This he anticipated, for he had sold 150 acres to Asa Ransom in 1799 on the condition that Ransom would build an inn for travelers. Ransom, a goldsmith, paid $2 an acre, gave a down payment of $10 in cash, and owed a balance of $290. He met his commitment, erecting a large two-story house of "hewn logs 46 feet in length," and covering it with a roof of "good white pine shingles." Inside was a fireplace and a commodious kitchen. Adjoining the house was a stable large enough to house "several Span of horses." Late in January, 1801, Ellicott moved into Asa Ransom's house and took over a part of the dwelling for an office. He remained with the Ransoms until early in 1802 when he changed his residence to the small village of Batavia.[9] There he established the main Company office in western New York.

Even before he had established himself in his temporary headquarters in New Amsterdam, Ellicott had received a great number of inquiries regarding the purchase of land. When he officially opened his office for business, many applicants appeared. However, these potential buyers came mainly to shop rather than to purchase. As a result, in 1801, he made but sixty-seven sales of $26,343.54 worth of land, and he collected only $625.14½ advance in cash. Most of the settlers who did buy land had a limited amount of cash, so they purchased small lots; they then proceeded promptly to build homes and clear their small parts of the forest. But the numerous sales that Ellicott had counted on failed to materialize.

Disappointed, Ellicott reexamined the problems of selling land. Originally, the Company and Ellicott had hoped to sell the lands in large parcels and thus liquidate the holdings within twenty years. When Ellicott realized that this could not be done, he decided to concentrate on disposing the land in smaller sections and thus attract a larger number of buyers from among the landless families. In settling the purchase, Ellicott also saw other advantages to selling to families, rather than to individual speculators. The numerous hard-working settlers, he realized, would hew their wood, draw their water, build their homes, and push back the forest. As the number of settlements increased, western New York would cease to be a frontier. It would attract people who wanted to purchase land that was less expensive than in the East. All this, Ellicott reasoned, would bring more business and greater profit to the Holland Land Company. On the other hand, the speculator and the wealthy aristocrat would only retard the development of western New York. So whenever Ellicott considered the investment of Company money on land improvements, he used two important criteria for such a decision: the extent that such an expense would encourage responsible settlers to buy land; and the sum that such a task would require.

Agent-General Paul Busti was informed of Ellicott's plan, but he nevertheless demanded a clearer explanation of his failure to sell more lands during his first year. In an effort to spell out more clearly to Busti the justification for his temporary setback, Ellicott enumerated the factors that hindered his success. That first year, the infamous "Genesee fever" afflicted many settlers; this "uncommon sickness," he pointed out, gave western New York bad publicity and discouraged migration. Ellicott also felt that the average of $2.30 per acre charged by the Company contrasted sharply with the price of $.12 an acre for land in upper Canada. In addition, the settlers accused the Resident-Agent of reserving the best lands for the Company while selling the poorest to the settlers. Ellicott and the residents also agreed that the farmers' produce brought low prices, that the markets were remote from the farms, and that the scarcity of money discouraged the buying of land.

Still unconvinced, the cautious Busti now sent Jan Lincklaen on a fact-finding tour of western New York. Lincklaen was a good choice because he had learned a great deal about land sales on the frontier. Coming from Holland to Philadelphia in June, 1791, he had taken several trips into central and western New York to investigate tracts that the Company might buy. And since 1793, he had been in charge of selling the 114,000 Company-owned acres in the Cazenovia area, a post smaller yet similar to Ellicott's.

Lincklaen took Busti's assignment seriously. He spent the summer of 1802 traveling through the purchase, noting the general over-all progress and testing Ellicott's explanation for the low land sales. Then, in a thirty-three-page report, he disclosed his findings to Busti. Buffalo consisted of two stores, two taverns, and about "a dozen other Build-ings." To Lincklaen, Buffalo was "the handsomest spot which I have seen on the Holland Purchase." Then he added prophetically: "It is supposed likewise, that in time it will command a Great proportion of the trade on the Country." At Batavia, the village had two taverns, one a two-story building, the other a log house; a two-story log house occupied by Ellicott; and, "two or three Log Houses besides." Batavia had, too, "a very good sawmill with a substantial Dam" and a nearly completed three-story court house.[10]

Lincklaen got on well with Ellicott. The Resident-Agent was "open and candid" and spoke frankly on the problems of land sales. After a thorough study, Lincklaen agreed with Ellicott. The prices were high "compared to nearby lands and conditions," and the Company policy of withholding some properties from sale did discourage potential customers.[11]

In addition to these grievances, Ellicott identified three major prob-lems which, he concluded, reduced the land sales. The first was the poor transportation facilities, for no roads existed except the moccasin-worn Indian paths. The second dealt with the long distance that the residents of western New York were forced to travel in order to reach the county seat, Canandaigua, where officials recorded deeds and mort-gages. The final problem pertained to the county taxation of Company lands, which reduced the profit of sales. These three problems, Ellicott reported to Busti, were at the heart of the failure to sell land. Busti concurred with his Resident-Agent and urged him to work with the settlers in taking appropriate action.

Ellicott and the settlers agreed completely on the first problem—a need for roads. Without thoroughfares over which the farmers could drive their wagons to market, the sale of their produce was almost impossible. This was a serious matter because the settlers planned to liquidate their debts to the Company by selling part of their crops. Many of them had managed to scrape up the 5 percent down payment that Ellicott required for a sale, but, beyond that sum, they had very little money. In addition, the lack of roads discouraged potential customers from risking their limited capital in land west of the Genesee; for they saw no way of earning sufficient money to pay for such a purchase without a highway on which to transport the crops that they raised. Furthermore, the roadless expanse of heavy forest, without settlements, deterred families from buying land on the purchase. Thus, Ellicott faced the knotty problem of providing the settlers in western New York with better transportation.

While everyone on the purchase agreed on the need for roads, they differed with each other in regard to the manner of construction. The question arose as to who would pay the expenses that such thoroughfares entailed. To construct highways through the forest cost a great deal of money. Further, these roads required maintenance to prevent shrubs and saplings from covering the original highways; this also increased the expenses. Neither the state legislature nor the county board of supervisors considered road-building as one of its functions, and the townships lacked the funds necessary for such work. The settlers on the purchase reasoned that the Holland Land Company would reap the greatest profits from the highways, so they looked to the Resident-Agent to take action. Ellicott felt the sharp horns of this dilemma: he wanted to spend as little money as possible, yet he felt confident that roads would increase land sales by attracting more settlers and by making it easier for the residents to get to market.

Avoiding taking a stand on whether or not the Company would shoulder the full cost of road-building, the Resident-Agent sought other solutions to the road problem. In 1801 General James Wilkinson, of the United States Army, asked Ellicott to mark out a military road between Lake Ontario and Lake Erie. Seeing an opportunity for getting the army to spend money on the construction of a road that would be equally good for civilian purposes, Ellicott quickly complied with this request. Within two months of his recommendations, Ellicott reported to Busti that the army expected to complete a road one hundred feet wide that would pass through at least eight miles of the Company's land. By August of that year, Ellicott announced to Secretary of War Henry Dearborn that the road-builders had completed nearly twelve miles of the highway. However, considering the large territory of western New York, the army highway of twelve miles served only a small area, and the formidable task of proper transportation facilities remained.

Still searching for some answer to the problem of roads, Ellicott experimented with a scheme that would keep the Company cost low. He offered to individual settlers who opened roads one-third of the amount of their labor in cash and the other two-thirds in land. Ellicott signed many such contracts in 1801, but few of the residents fulfilled their agreements. His plan failed due in part to negligence, sickness, and the great poverty that forced the settlers to devote their full time to clearing the lands for themselves. By this process, Ellicott managed to start several roads, though none was completed. Two of these radiated from Batavia: one went west toward Buffalo, and the other ran north toward Queenstown, Canada. Despite the efforts of the Resident-Agent, the lack of adequate transportation facilities continued to hamper the settling of western New York.

Ellicott became convinced that only the government had the financial resources to construct the necessary highways. He arrived at this belief by a rather unique process of elimination. Since he thought it undesirable to spend much of the Company's money on road-building, and since he discounted the willingness of private investors to undertake the building of turnpikes, he concluded that only the government could do the job.

This solution, however, depended on the Resident-Agent's finding an answer to the question: what level of government should do the work? The Jeffersonians had serious misgivings about the federal government spending money on intrastate internal improvements. The county government lacked the resources, for at this time one county—Ontario—covered all of western New York and did not have the necessary taxable wealth. The town government had less income than did the other governments. The state government, alone, had the money and unquestioned authority to build roads on the purchase; however, it would not enthusiastically support such projects because there was very little precedent for state road-building. Moreover, the western area was too sparsely populated to warrant heavy state expenditures.

Ellicott was greatly concerned also with the long distance from his office at Batavia to Canandaigua, the county seat. Despite the fact that Batavia was nearer Canandaigua than Buffalo, some forty-five miles still separated the county seat from Ellicott's main office, and the Resident-Agent found his journeys to Canandaigua formidable. Yet,

COUNTY ORGANIZATION - 1800

as part of the land sales, such trips had to be made; for only at the county seat were deeds and mortgages recorded, wills probated, and land transferred legally.

To solve this second problem, Ellicott concluded that western New York needed a new county. If the government created a county whose territory covered only the land west of the Genesee, his journeys to Canandaigua would end, or at least these trips would be shorter. Such a remedy would be impossible under the present organization, for Ontario County covered an area east of the Genesee, as well as all of the land west of that river. The idea of dividing Ontario County had not come to Ellicott suddenly. When he chose Batavia as the Company seat, he already had in mind the establishment of a new county. The answer to this problem of access to the county seat, like Ellicott's solution to the building of roads, obviously required governmental action.

Ellicott was also acutely concerned with the third problem—the taxation of the Company's lands. Shortly after he took office, he had received tax bills from the County of Ontario. This angered Ellicott, for the bills arrived at a time when he had shown no profit from land sales. After his initial rage gave way to reflection, he realized the gravity of this problem. These taxes increased his already embarrassing deficit; more serious was the fact that, once the Company remitted the money, the county would expect subsequent payments. Ellicott was therefore bitterly opposed to county taxes.

If the Resident-Agent refused to pay the taxes, however, litigation would surely follow; and should the court decide against the Company, the Dutch owners would be compelled to remit the money, as well as the customary 14 percent interest charge for neglecting such remittances. While Ellicott tried to decide what to do, other forces exerted pressure on him to pay the money. In a special letter, the county treasurer requested that Ellicott remit the taxes. Also, the people to whom the county treasurer owed money urged Ellicott to send the money so that the county treasurer could in turn pay them.

The amount of the taxes, however, exceeded the income from the land sales, and the question of payment or nonpayment now became a matter of survival for Joseph Ellicott and the Holland Land Company. In 1801, Ellicott had collected $625.14½ for land sales, but the taxes that same year amounted to $4,231. Desperately, Ellicott sought ways to avoid paying the tax. He combed the law books for some loophole, but in vain. He then asked the advice of eminent lawyers like David A. Ogden, the Company's legal counsel in New York City. "The whole of these Proceedings have been irregular," replied Ogden, "and . . . the Company would be justified in contesting the payment." [12] However, the Company counselor offered no specific suggestions for action.

After an exhaustive search for some way to avoid payment, Ellicott finally realized the futility of continuing his opposition. Moreover, he had become increasingly aware that his resistance to such a levy was bringing the Company poor publicity. Therefore, he accepted the advice of his Canandaigua lawyers and discharged the obligation. Ellicott, however, continued to be sensitive on the subject of taxation. When he felt that the Company in 1801 had been assessed for more land than it owned, he again became incensed. In truth, the assessors had erred, for they charged the Company for some 4.5 million acres of land, rather than for the more accurate sum of 3.3 million acres. The assessors later acknowledged the mistake and accepted the latter figure. At another time, Ellicott suspected that the Company land had a higher assessment rate than the surrounding property. After he carefully examined the relative assessments, he changed his mind. Not only did the Resident-Agent therefore resign himself to pay the taxes, but by 1802, he reluctantly admitted to Busti that these taxes "will not likely decrease." [13]

Although Ellicott had unwillingly submitted to the payment of taxes, he sought to participate in the allocation of this revenue. He made a careful analysis of the county budget, and then complained that the board of supervisors favored the area east of the Genesee over that of western New York in budgetary expenditures.

His remonstrances, however, did not remedy the situation. The Resident-Agent learned that the Ontario County Board of Supervisors kept a tight control over the distribution as well as the collection of its funds. Furthermore, the supervisors were popularly elected officials and were responsible only to the voters, most of whom lived east of the Genesee. Ellicott had no way to influence the Ontario County Board of Supervisors in its taxation policies. If he wished to have a voice in the matters of revenue, he had to circumvent the board. Such a move required political activity.

As Ellicott analyzed his problems—the lack of roads, the long distance from Canandaigua, and the unfair system of taxation—he realized that political action was the only solution for all three. He had arrived at this decision reluctantly, because political participation would add another burden to his already heavy load of reports, surveys, collections, and the many time-consuming details attached to his work. Yet, if he wanted greater profits, the Resident-Agent had to assume a more active political role. Thus did Joseph Ellicott decide to enter the field of politics.

III. Reluctant Politician

"I give you my full and complete absolution for the sin you have committed," in entering political life, Agent-General Paul Busti generously wrote to Joseph Ellicott on December 6, 1803.[1] It was a pardon that proved to be as logical as it was gracious, for it was Ellicott's decision to enter politics that was one of the basic factors responsible for the success of the program of the Holland Land Company.

Ellicott's first political target was nothing less than the creation of a new county. He regarded the division of Ontario County as a highly desirable change. The creation of a county west of the Genesee would eliminate his uncomfortable and time-consuming journeys to Canandaigua for county business. Locating a new county seat in Batavia, which in 1803 was the heartland of the Company's purchase, would help to pump new life into the area and enhance considerably the value of Company property. Most important of all, a new county would elect its own board of supervisors which would represent the voters in western New York, and Ellicott hoped that such a board would favor better roads and lower taxation. A new county, he was convinced, would help to increase the sales and profits of his employers.

Although this was Joseph Ellicott's initial venture into politics, he already held well-formulated political convictions. He was a strong Jeffersonian who shared the frontiersman's hostility to the allegedly aristocratic Federalists. When questioned about his political ideas, he stoutly defended his Jeffersonian principles and did not hesitate to expound his beliefs in a blunt and outspoken manner.

The tide was running with the Jeffersonians. The election of Thomas Jefferson in 1801 had ended Federalist control of the presidency. Not even the shrewdest men of the day, however, could foresee how far-reaching were the election results. It started the alliance of southern planters and northern big-city bosses, a partnership that has dominated the Democratic party to this day. It strengthened the principle of local sovereignty which would help bring on the sectional Civil War sixty years later. It turned the United States toward the West where the so-called destiny of the nation lay. And, it stimulated

46

humanitarian forces that would add dignity and worth to the common man.

The traditional view that democracy evolved with the election of Republican Jefferson has undergone great modification. A careful study of the times revealed that the ideological struggle between democratic-minded Jeffersonians and patrician-inclined Hamiltonians has been much exaggerated. In 1800, the United States, in contrast to Europe, was a classless society. Domestic servants, for example, were described as "help." [2] American children stood less in awe of their parents, and women often went about unchaperoned. The federal constitution specifically prohibited the granting of titles. Much before the election of Jefferson, then, Americans were determined not to create an aristocracy.

Likewise, the conditions of life in the United States worked against an aristocracy. In colonial days, some sizable fortunes were accumulated, but few if any were vast or permanent. Moreover, whatever fortunes were amassed did not prevent others from similar material acquisition. Even in the South, with its landholding base, society was surprisingly fluid for the white man. Land wore out, mobility was considerable, and "dynasties" were difficult to establish.

Politics in America were equally fluid. It is true that the Federalists did represent social, political, and economic privilege which Republicans impugned. The Federalists identified themselves as "gentlemen," and by dress, manner, speech, and profession formed a group that differed from the Republicans. To the Federalists, democracy was rule by the mob, and they sought stability after the American Revolution. Not all the Federalists, however, were rich men, and not all agreed with the policies of Hamilton. Many a small farmer in upstate New York, western Pennsylvania, and Virginia was a Federalist without aristocratic convictions. He might be a Federalist because he idolized Washington, or liked the federal constitution, or opposed the seemingly excessive freedom of Republicanism. In the 1790's, the party label stirred lively competition. However, there was no absolute cleavage between Federalist and Republican, nor was there an inflexible identity between party and policy.

In a real sense, Thomas Jefferson fitted the stereotype of what Joseph Ellicott and other Republicans wanted America to be. Jefferson was a virtuous husbandman at a time when the great majority of the population lived in rural areas, and the freeholding farmers comprised the great proportion of the American people. Furthermore, Jefferson was an ardent expansionist. American democracy in 1800 implied constant change and an expanded economy; the people were flexible, restless, and acquisitive. Marcus Cunliffe, the British historian, colorfully summed up the drives of American society in 1800 as "a perpetual discontent, an itch to try the cards at the next table, the view from the next ridge." [3] On March 4, 1801, Thomas Jefferson, whose Declaration of Independence encouraged "a perpetual discontent," delivered his beautifully phrased inaugural address. Defining democratic principles in terms of majority-minority relations, Jefferson encouraged Americans to seek "the view from the next ridge."

At the time of Jefferson's inauguration, politics in New York state reflected the nation in its lack of genuine ideological differences. The political parties in New York did not correspond to definite classes, for no party was thoroughly homogeneous in its composition. As in most of the nation, the state had a fluid society, high in social mobility and imprecise in class distinction. New York had its respected aristocrats and its degraded types. However, the vast majority of the people, whether living in the city or the country, fitted in the category of the flexible middle class.

Another alleged similarity between state and national politics was the traditional classification of the Federalists and the Republicans in terms of aristocratic and democratic. Historical evidence of state politics seems to disprove this conventional interpretation. For example, George Clinton, a Republican and New York's first and only governor from 1777 to 1795, had many laudable achievements. Yet this Republican behaved undemocratically in the election of 1792. John Jay, his Federalist opponent, was winning when Clinton's men invalidated ballots from three counties. Thus Clinton "filched" the election.[4] Another case was that of John Jay, Clinton's successor as governor between 1795 and 1801. Jay did not fit the stereotype of the leader from the superior class who looked down on the mass of society. During his two terms, he was nonpartisan in his appointments; few officials were dismissed because of political affiliation. Moreover, he urged the democratic measure of maintaining the common schools. And, under Jay's leadership, the Federalists pushed through a law in 1799 that provided for the gradual abolition of slavery in New York.

During this time, there was greater interest in state than in national politics. Most political leaders preferred to hold state offices over federal ones. Such partiality can be found in many instances. John Jay resigned as Chief Justice of the United States Supreme Court in 1795 to become governor of the state. DeWitt Clinton vacated the office of United States senator in 1803 to accept the appointment of mayor of

New York City. Daniel Tompkins relinquished his seat in Congress in 1804 to take the post of associate justice of the New York Supreme Court.

Political parties in New York state were made up of heterogeneous groups of men who banded together to elect certain candidates to office. Because this was their primary goal, party activity was seasonal. Intent on electing particular candidates, political organizations were highly personalized. Elections rarely turned on matters of principle, but revolved rather around chosen figures. The death of a leader often brought dissolution to the political party. So fluid was the situation that political factions constantly formed, disintegrated, and re-formed.

The plasticity of state politics could be clearly seen in Albany. In 1797, politics consisted of the Clintons, the Livingstons, and the Schuylers. Assessing the situation, James Parton, the historian, made the famous quip: "The Clintons had power; the Livingstons had numbers; the Schuylers had Hamilton." Disappointed at being passed over in political appointments, the Livingstons now split with the Federalists, joined the Clintons, and ran Robert R. Livingston for governor against Jay in 1798. The Schuyler and Federalist influence reached a peak in 1799 and declined the following year because of two serious setbacks: Hamilton's badly timed attack on Adams that split the party, and Jay's refusal to seek a third term as governor. Meantime, Aaron Burr's star rose among the Republicans. In 1800, Burr had given valiant and decisive aid to Jefferson, using the Society of Tammany to help carry New York. Catapulted to the vice-presidency, Burr became a serious threat to the Clintons and Livingstons. When George Clinton won his seventh term as governor in 1801, the power of the Republicans was divided among three factions—the Clintons, the Livingstons, and the Burrs.

For different reasons, the Clintons, the Livingstons, and Jefferson set out to reduce Burr's influence. The motive most bandied about related to Jefferson's election. When the Federalists had supported Aaron Burr during the electoral stalemate in 1801, it cast suspicion on him, a man already known as a slippery intriguer. In this situation, however, Burr had apparently behaved honorably, and the accusation became a smoke screen to hide less honorable purposes. Never comfortable with Burr, Jefferson distrusted him and probably believed the rumors about his deal with the Federalists. DeWitt Clinton, the young and vigorous leader of his faction, was talented, ambitious, and ruthless. Jealous and apprehensive of Burr's power, Clinton was determined to undermine him. The Livingstons, friendly to Burr, but ambitious for office, were easily won over by Clinton and Jefferson.

Surrounded by powerful enemies, Aaron Burr was isolated, a man marked for political ruin. Hamilton, leader of the Federalists, was relentless in harassing Burr. The Republican attack was a sorry spectacle. Jefferson subtly deferred to Governor Clinton in distributing federal patronage. But the Governor's nephew, DeWitt Clinton, dominated the Clinton faction, and he and Jefferson teamed up in favoring the Livingstons. Clinton's followers shared the spoils of office with the Livingstons. Jefferson appointed Chancellor Livingston as minister to France. DeWitt Clinton arranged that Edward Livingston be chosen mayor of New York City; Brockholst Livingston, judge of the supreme court; Morgan Lewis, brother-in-law of Edward Livingston, chief judge of the supreme court; Thomas Tillotson, another brother-in-law of Edward Livingston, secretary of state in New York; and Smith Thompson, son-in-law of Gilbert Livingston, judge of the supreme court. William Stewart, brother-in-law of Governor Clinton, was named district attorney of Tioga and several other nearby counties; Sylvanus Miller, a Clinton lieutenant, was appointed surrogate of New York County; and DeWitt Clinton held successively the offices of United States senator from New York and mayor of New York City when that position became vacant. Few appointments went to any known follower of Aaron Burr. Clinton had made a clean sweep of the federal and state appointive offices. The Federalists had introduced the spoils system, but DeWitt Clinton taught them how extensively it could function.

This was the political situation that prevailed in 1802 when Joseph Ellicott, Resident-Agent of the Holland Land Company, entered politics. Ellicott staunchly supported the Republicans, but realized that he was too inexperienced to rely exclusively on his own judgment in concrete political affairs. Aware of the thorny thicket of Republican factionalism, he sought the guidance and suggestions of more experienced individuals.

Since the responsibility for dividing the county lay in the domain of the state legislature, Ellicott asked advice from those of his associates who were familiar with state politics. Paul Busti, Ellicott's immediate superior, concurred with him that such a county was desirable and possible. David A. Ogden, the Company's counselor, was optimistic about the possibilities of effecting such a project. Dudley Saltonstall, Ellicott's lawyer from Canandaigua, recommended that Ellicott himself travel to Albany to lobby for the new county rather than forward a petition.

Armed with these suggestions, Joseph Ellicott started the move for the division of Ontario County. First, he instructed Saltonstall to draw up a petition for a new county which would cover only the land west of the Genesee. Then, although he was reluctant to make the uncomfortable trip to Albany, Ellicott yielded to its necessity. He planned to meet David Ogden in Albany and to work with him there in perfecting their plans.

In all such activities, the Resident-Agent informed Busti of his actions and the Agent-General gave his approval. Benjamin Ellicott, for example, reported to his brother Joseph that Busti "was anctious for the division of the County and wishes you to use your influence to procure it if possible." [5] Busti also directed Ogden to support Joseph Ellicott in Albany, advising him that the Company would grant concessions in the form of money and buildings, if the legislature approved a new county. In his instructions, Busti authorized Ogden to "make the volunteer offer of the Holland Company to contribute a sum of $1,000 besides the usual contributions for erection of the Court and gaol. You may even propose that the building of the Courthouse will be made the private expense of the Company." [6]

In return, David Ogden counseled Ellicott on the procedure and tactics for lobbying in Albany. When the Resident-Agent reached the New York State capital, he was to "call on the leading members of the Legislature, and became acquainted with them, particularly the *Republican* Members." Knowing the Jeffersonian convictions of the Resident-Agent, Ogden suggested that Ellicott "had better intrust to my care the *Federal* Members." In regard to individuals, he informed Ellicott that the Resident-Agent would receive letters from Ezra L'Hommedieu and E. Watson. L'Hommedieu, Ogden described, as "a Senator from the Southern District and a man of considerable influence, and property, of your Politics, an Honest man, and disposed to what is Right; he is a friend of mine, and I am well assured will do all in his power to serve us." While Watson was not in the legislature, Ogden explained to Ellicott that he was "an industrious man, has considerable influence over the Lieut. Governor and others, and I think will be of service, and for this reason employ him—we must employ him." David Ogden also urged Ellicott to secure the support of Ambrose Spencer. "Mr. Spencer, the Attorney General, *is a politician;* to secure *your interest,* he will take great pains; he can be of essential service, and therefore you must not omit making use of the advantages, that your growing influence and situation must naturally give you, over the politics of the Western part of the State; he will immediately perceive the policy of obliging you, and will become an active partisan." Finally,

Ogden pointed out that Peter B. Porter, the Ontario County clerk, would probably resist the creation of a county because it would diminish the income of his office; he therefore recommended that Ellicott call on Porter in an effort to win his support. Confident that their lobbying would succeed, Ogden concluded: "On the whole, I have little doubt that our exertions will be successful, if we proceed with *caution* and *industry*, particularly, when I reflect that the measure we are advocating is just and proper, and that we shall probably secure the leading men of both parties." [7]

Despite Ogden's optimism, there was some opposition to Ellicott's plan to divide the county. James Wadsworth, for example, who had failed to obtain the position of Resident-Agent and who owned much land near the Genesee River, favored a new county but opposed Ellicott's proposal for the division. Wadsworth wanted the eastern boundary of the projected county to run between Canandaigua and the Genesee, rather than alongside of the river itself. He envisaged that the county seat would be located at Hartford (Avon) and not at Batavia; and, since Hartford was nearer to the Wadsworth land holdings, he would profit by the establishment of such a new county. Under the Wadsworth plan for division, the new county board of supervisors might also favor the sale of Wadsworth's property, and thus indirectly delay the development of the Holland Land Company's program of sales. Ellicott therefore felt that such a new county as Wadsworth proposed would perpetuate, and not correct, his problems.

It was Ellicott's good fortune, however, that Wadsworth was away from Albany at the time that the legislature voted on the Resident-Agent's plan for the new county. Because of Ellicott's and Ogden's careful preparation, the legislature on March 30, 1802, passed Ellicott's bill. Genesee County was created with Batavia the county seat.

In the establishment of the new county, a variety of tactics was employed, including bribery to the extent of $200. Busti paid the bill for the "$200 gratification at Albany," and asked only that Ellicott keep a separate account of his expenses at the state capital. [8] Watson had received part of this sum, but later he compelled Ogden to give him an additional $50. David Ogden explained this squeeze to Ellicott: "I found it necessary in order to satisfy W——n [*sic*] to pay him $50 in addition to the sum which you delivered him in my letter. He drew on me for the same and I thought it best to pay his draft. He declared if the thing is known it will be Ruinous to him and has made me promise most sincerely that I will not communicate his agency in the Business to any Person; as his service may be useful in the future, you will of course keep this business secret. This sum I have charged to your account." [9] In addition to the use of bribery, Ellicott promised that the Company would later support the legislators of the Republican party, if they would vote for his bill.

While Ellicott was delighted that the legislature had finally created Genesee County, he did not yet feel completely secure. His concern stemmed from the fact that the Governor, who belonged to the powerful Council of Revision, had had a disagreement with one of the Holland Land Company agents. The Council of Revision at that time possessed constitutional authority to veto any law within ten days of its passage, and Ellicott feared that Governor George Clinton might urge its members to oppose the law in retaliation. Ellicott, therefore, took steps to avert this possibility. He visited Governor Clinton and did his best to mitigate any ill-feelings which the Governor might have harbored against the Company. It was only after the required ten days following the passage of the law had elapsed that Ellicott relaxed, secure in the fact that no one could now contest the creation of Genesee County.

The division of Ontario County greatly pleased Paul Busti and he praised Ellicott generously for his role in its creation. In glowing terms, the Agent-General thanked the Resident-Agent for his prudence, loyalty, and decisiveness in the establishment of Genesee County. Due to the subsequent split between these two friends, an excerpt to Busti's letter of appreciation to Ellicott deserves quoting:

> We are indebted to Your foresight, and to Your Sagacious Conduct for the Salutary effects, which this arrangement has for the proprietors. You were the first, who, revolted by the vexations and injustices of the Commissioners of Ontario County, have formed the plan to detach the lands of the Holland Comp. from it, which were unmercifully taxed for the benefit of a Small corner of the County. From the Very beginning of Your administration, your attention was bent on getting them out of the reach of these rapacities; in this you were Sincerely assisted by Mr. Ogden, but without your influence with the Governor, and the Council of Revision, I am afraid that the business would have failed.[10]

On his part, Joseph Ellicott graciously maintained that Busti's shrewd offer to erect a court house and jail at Company expense helped to get the bill through the legislature.

Turning from his lobbying activity in Albany, Ellicott next concerned himself with the organization of the new county. Only through a friendly board of supervisors could he solve his remaining two problems: the construction of better roads and the reduction of taxes. The Ontario County tax increase in 1802 spurred Ellicott to greater action to start the operation of the governing agencies of Genesee County. If this were not done, the unfriendly supervisors of Ontario County would continue to rule western New York. It was imperative, Ellicott pointed out to Busti, "to see the County of Genesee first organized and fairly out of the clutches of these unprincipled Fellows." [11]

The first step in the organization of Genesee County was the erection of a court house and county jail at Batavia, for the law that had created the county had also specified that such construction be completed before appointments could be made and elections held. The Holland Land Company had promised the legislature to construct both buildings, the adequacy of which was to be determined by the governor of the state.

Ellicott proceeded to do everything that he could to hasten the construction of the required buildings. In the process, he met some unexpected obstacles. First, a tornado caused some damage, and later the sawmill broke down. The latter problem prevented him for a month from getting the necessary timbers. Finally, in March, 1803, the carpenters completed their work, and Ellicott had overcome the initial obstacle to the organization of Genesee County.

Governor George Clinton then appointed three commissioners and authorized them to certify that the Company had erected the required court house and jail and to accept these buildings legally on behalf of Genesee County. To perform this task, the Governor selected Lemuel Chipman, Richard Stoddard, and John Thompson as commissioners; the approval of two of these three men could make the transfer official. To speed up this legal consequence, Ellicott urged Stoddard, an old employee of the Resident-Agent, to contact Chipman as quickly as possible so that both commissioners could judge the adequacy of the buildings without delay. Stoddard complied with Ellicott's request, and the two commissioners "prevailed on Mr. Chipman" to approve unanimously the court house and jail.[12] The Governor then accepted the certification of the commissioners.

With the Governor's acceptance of the court house and jail, Ellicott involved himself in the next move for the organization of Genesee County: the appointment of officials to transact county business. The filling of these offices, however, lay in the province of the Council of Appointment, and this organization functioned with open political partiality.

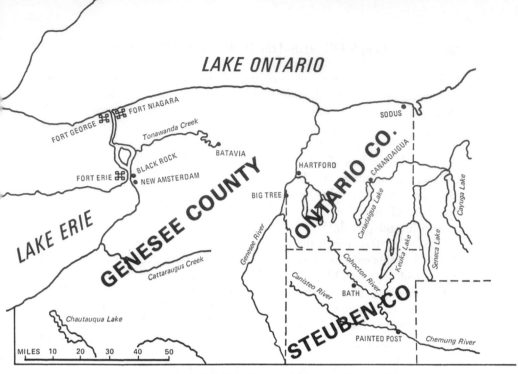

COUNTY ORGANIZATION — 1802

By 1803, the Council of Appointment had evolved into an important machine that dispensed political patronage, despite the fact that John Jay, the father of the New York State Constitution of 1777, had originally designed the council simply to limit the appointive power of the governor. Under this constitution, the governor nominated most of the appointive candidates for state, county, town, city, and village offices, but the council had the power to approve or disapprove the nominations. Since five members made up the council—the governor, who belonged *ex officio*, and four state senators—any three allied senators on the council were able to control the governor's appointments and thus wield considerable influence.[13]

The power of the Council of Appointment was particularly great in New York State because the voters elected comparatively few officials and many posts were filled by appointment. Qualified voters cast ballots for the governor, lieutenant-governor, members of the state legislature, and state treasurer; but they elected only the aldermen in the cities and chose only the supervisors in the counties. The constitution, on the other hand, empowered the council to make numerous appointments on all levels of government. On the state level, these positions included the adjutant-general, state printer, comptroller, collector of customs, surveyor of customs, inspector of prisons, superintendent of schools, port wardens, harbor masters, judges of the state supreme court, and circuit judges. For the counties, the council selected the surrogates, judges, district attorneys, sheriffs, clerks, and coroners. In the cities, the council assigned the mayors; for the towns, it chose the justices of peace; and it also appointed officers in the state militia. In addition to these powers, the council controlled many sinecures; for example, it selected "scullers of staves and headings," "packers of beef," and a bewildering variety of inspectors of flour, pearlash, and potash.[14]

In 1792, the appointments of the council numbered more than 1,200, and this sum increased steadily. As the patronage grew, the fight to control the assembly, which selected the four senators on the council, intensified. This struggle became even more accentuated in 1801, when the Constitution of 1777 was amended so that additional power was granted to the senators on the Council of Appointment. Now these senators could nominate, as well as approve the appointments of candidates.[15]

From 1800, the Republicans had gained a series of striking victories in the state legislature. Winning the elections in 1800, 1801, and 1802, they got control of the assembly, and with that, dominated the Council of Appointment. Although the council members were not "eligible to the said Council for two years successively," [16] the Republicans rotated enough of their followers to keep firm control of this substantial patronage-dispensing machine. Becoming increasingly known as Democrats, the Republicans won a smashing triumph in 1803 when they increased their total to eighty-three seats in the assembly while the Federalists dropped to only seventeen. In that year, George Clinton was governor, the Council of Appointment was in Republican hands, and DeWitt Clinton was the acknowledged leader in state politics. Joseph Ellicott, Resident-Agent of the Holland Land Company, was aware of the political power structure in 1803 when the question of nomination of officers for the newly created Genesee County arose.

Inasmuch as the appointment of county officers was essential to the organization of Genesee County, Ellicott felt impelled to return to Albany in 1803 to encourage the Council of Appointment to fill the new posts quickly and with men who would be friendly to the Company. "As the appointment of the officers is important to the respectability of the County," Ellicott explained to Busti, "I shall remain here until these appointments are made." [17] Ellicott's patience was rewarded when the 1803 Council of Appointment announced the first officers of Genesee County. This Republican-dominated Council appointed James W. Stevens as county clerk and Richard M. Stoddard as county sheriff. Joseph Ellicott knew each of these men and rejoiced at their appointments.

James W. Stevens, the first clerk appointed to the newly created Genesee County, had had a long and friendly association with Ellicott. At the start of the land sales in 1800, Stevens had joined the Company as office assistant to Ellicott and remained with it until he died forty years later. The two men got along well together. Ellicott respected the quiet efficiency and unflagging industry of his clerk, and admired the careful and methodical way in which Stevens kept an exact account of all facets of the business. In addition, Ellicott appreciated the sensible advice that Stevens offered him. He even admitted to Busti that his clerk also served him as a close advisor. In fact, when Ellicott went to Albany to lobby for the creation of Genesee County, he took Stevens with him as a special aide. If he could not have continued the trip, Stevens would have substituted for Ellicott. Furthermore, Ellicott enjoyed the companionship of his clerk. Stevens had graduated from Princeton College, had fine cultural taste, and, prior to coming to western New York, had contributed to a literary magazine in Philadelphia. In the lonely frontier life of the purchase, Stevens' healthy sense of humor and his keen observations, based on a hard core of incorruptible honesty, added to the pleasure of his company. Ellicott regarded Stevens as his "invaluable Friend." [18]

Many of Stevens' governmental duties as county clerk dovetailed with his tasks as Ellicott's office assistant. The law required that the county clerk record all deeds, mortgages, and wills; thus, he registered each land sale. As Company clerk, Stevens already kept a record of all deeds and mortgages on the purchase. So, to perform most of the duties of county clerk, he simply had to prepare an additional copy of many of the entries that he had already made in the Company books. In Stevens' appointment Ellicott therefore felt confident that the land records so vital to his business would be kept accurately at the county clerk's office. Moreover, Ellicott would know at all times any changes that occurred in deeds and mortgages elsewhere in western New York. The county clerk also had the duty of keeping the minutes of the meetings of the board of supervisors. This particularly interested Ellicott, for through Stevens, he would have a direct line to the board and its actions. The council reappointed Stevens to this office annually until 1810. While serving as county clerk, he continued his work as office assistant to Ellicott, giving invaluable aid to the Resident-Agent and to the Holland Land Company.

Like Stevens, Richard M. Stoddard, the new county sheriff, had worked for Joseph Ellicott. When Ellicott had headed the survey of the purchase between 1798 and 1800, Stoddard had served as one of his principal surveyors. He enjoyed working for Ellicott more than for another employer in the field, and the Resident-Agent, on his part, respected Stoddard for his character and competence. When LeRoy, Bayard, and McEvers, the Company's banking house in America, sought the Resident-Agent's help to survey their recently purchased lands, Ellicott employed Stoddard for this important task, acknowledging his "especial Trust and Confidence" in Stoddard's integrity and ability.[19] In addition to his gratitude for this favor, Stoddard also felt indebted to Ellicott because the latter had loaned him $400 in 1801. Later, Stoddard married the daughter of Dudley Saltonstall, Ellicott's legal advisor in Canandaigua. Thus, the new sheriff of Genesee County had friendly feelings and several concrete ties to Joseph Ellicott, who considered Stoddard to be another important political ally of the Holland Land Company. Certainly, it would prove valuable to Ellicott to have as a friend the man who was primarily responsible for carrying out court orders and preserving the peace of the territory.

Joseph Ellicott, himself, had had several opportunities to hold political office and assist Stevens and Stoddard in supporting Company policies. At first, he rejected them. His contract with the Company had stated clearly that he could not take another job which would in any way interfere with his work as Resident-Agent, unless his immediate superior approved such action. Specifically, the agreement that he signed in 1800 stated that Joseph Ellicott was not to "accept or retain any employment interfering in the remotest degree with the Duties of the said Agency without the same consent obtained in the same manner, and the said Agent-General for the Time shall be the judge of such interference." [20] When Judge Phelps wished to have Ellicott appointed one of the judges of Ontario County in 1801, the Resident-Agent refused. The following year, Ellicott declined the request of the Republicans of Ontario County who wanted him to seek the office of assemblyman.

Joseph Ellicott continued to reject all political offices until 1803, when the newly elected Genesee County Board of Supervisors offered him the position of county treasurer. In this instance, he felt that he could not refuse, for he saw the many opportunities that such an office would give him. It would reveal to him the budgetary operations of the county; it would bring him into regular contact with all the supervisors; and it would create occasions for him to increase his influence over them. Inasmuch as the board decided the amount of taxes, as well as the allocation of moneys for road construction, Ellicott realized the power that the office of county treasurer would give him.

Contrary to the explicit terms of his contract, Ellicott accepted the post of county treasurer without first obtaining Busti's approval. After he had agreed to take the office, however, he informed the Agent-General of his action, reviewing for him some of the reasons that had influenced his decision. Busti endorsed Ellicott's conduct in accepting the treasurer's office, and also offered him additional support in that position. He would permit Ellicott to continue as county treasurer so long as it did not take too much time from his duties as Resident-Agent: "I give you my full and complete absolution for the sin you have committed in accepting against the litteral construction of your engagement of the office of treasurer of the County. You may even continue to act in that Office if the duties of the charge do not considerably interfere with the time you have to devote to the Agency." [21]

Busti went a step further and instructed the banking firm of LeRoy, Bayard, and McEvers to pay to the new county treasurer nearly $5,000 in back taxes that the Company owed to the county. He then notified Ellicott of this action, candidly admitting that he had made this move to demonstrate to the other county officers that the Holland Land Company was willing to cooperate with Ellicott in his new official position.

Originally, Ellicott had intended to keep the office of county treasurer for a one-year term, but before the year had expired, he became convinced that, as Resident-Agent, he should continue to hold this post. As the largest taxpayer in the county, the Holland Land Company, he felt, should control the position of county treasurer. If he kept this office, he could inform the Company in detail how the board allocated its tax money, he could recommend to the supervisors the best ways in which to spend the revenue, and he could help to limit unnecessary expenditures. Summarizing the reasons for his desire to remain in office, he wrote Busti that the county treasurer's office

> ought to be held by the Company's Agent, especially as the major part of the money raised is immediately from the Company. It affords me an opportunity of being informed for what

objects this money is expended, and also to advise the supervisors what sums may be expedient to be raised for County purposes, and also in some measure to be a Check on their Prodigality, if they should be disposed to raise more money than the exigencies of the County might require as well as to inform the Agent-General annually of the true State of all Taxes raised and in what manner expended, which I presume by doing this in my last report was not unpleasing.[22]

On this matter, for the time being at least, Busti agreed with the reasoning of his Resident-Agent, and Ellicott therefore accepted the board's annual reappointment as county treasurer for the next six years.

Despite his outward expression of full support for Ellicott, Paul Busti retained some nagging apprehensions. By 1804 three matters had developed that worried the stable, conservative Agent-General. One had to do with the sale of land. In full agreement with the Company Directors, he believed the land should be sold quickly and in large blocks. As early as 1798, the Directors had tried without success to dispose of the land in the state of New York; the attempt was made once again in 1802 (that is, when Ellicott was Resident-Agent), as the Company was to do many times more in the future. But instead of large-block sales, the Company's land was being sold in small parcels on long-term credit, and both of these departures from the original policy were being made with Ellicott's full approval.

A second foreboding grew out of the scattered reports of Ellicott's mercurial behavior with customers, of conduct that was nearer to rude than blunt. To Busti, unfailing courtesy, especially in Company dealings, was a way of life. And the third was Ellicott's growing political involvement. Busti tried to face the situation pragmatically but could not overcome his deep anxiety that neither the Company nor its employees should ever become involved in politics. On the issues of land sales and Ellicott's manners, he lacked at this point sufficient evidence that was tangible enough to permit him to act. Also, he was aware that Ellicott had entered politics reluctantly and only in the best interests of the Company. In 1804, then, the Agent-General suppressed his misgivings and permitted his Resident-Agent to hold the post of county treasurer.

Although he served as county treasurer for a number of years, Ellicott felt that his obligations to the Company were too great to permit him to accept other political offices. As a result, he refused most of the other political positions that were offered to him. In 1803, the same year that he became treasurer, the Council of Appointment chose him a judge in Genesee County, but he declined the position. The following year, the Republicans urged him to try for the assembly. In 1805, his party encouraged him to run for a seat in the state senate, and later that same year, it sought his candidacy for Congress. Each time Ellicott rejected the honor. He did, however, accept his appointment as a presidential elector in 1804 because he saw no way of evading his duty. Besides, this office required only that he travel to Albany once to cast his ballot. For the rest, he preferred to devote himself almost exclusively to his task as Resident-Agent, for he considered that position more important than any other one and assured Busti: "I [neither] seek, nor wish for any greater honor than that of being one of the subordinate Agents to the Agent-General of the Holland Land Company, [that] being in my opinion more honorable than any office the Government can bestow." [23]

When the question arose of encouraging his brother, Benjamin, to hold political office, Joseph applied the same criterion that he used for himself: Benjamin could accept a political office to the extent that holding the position would benefit the Company. Such an opportunity arose in 1804, when the Council of Appointment chose Benjamin as a judge of Genesee County. Benjamin preferred to reject this appointment; Joseph, however, knew that a judge had the authority legally to recognize deeds and mortgages. With Benjamin serving in this office at Batavia, Joseph could eliminate the need to travel over those poor roads in quest for a judge. Therefore, Joseph persuaded Benjamin to accept the judgeship, and explained his logic to Busti: "I conceive it would tend to our convenience for him [Benjamin] to serve in that capacity, although it is not with his inclination, but have a Character of that description in the office for the purpose of taking the acknowledgement of Deeds and Mortgages Saves us much trouble in going some distance for that purpose." [24]

Being satisfied that key political positions in the organization of Genesee County were filled with men who were favorable to the Holland Land Company, Joseph Ellicott now proceeded to use such political strength to remedy a situation that was troubling the Company. For some time, Ellicott had objected to the inadequate representation that the town of Batavia had on the board of supervisors. The Holland Land Company owned about three-fourths of all the land in Genesee County, but their holdings were concentrated about one town, Batavia. The remaining one-fourth of the county lands were located in three towns—Northhampton, Southhampton, and Leister. Yet, in 1803 Genesee County had four supervisors, one from each of the four towns, who made up the county board of supervisors. Neither the area of the town nor the size of its population altered its representation on the county board. Ellicott considered this arrangement unfair, since the area of Batavia was far greater than any of the other three towns. To him, the ratio on the board of three supervisors to one did not adequately protect the interests of the Company.

To redress this inequality of representation, Ellicott suggested that the legislature should divide the town of Batavia into four smaller towns. According to his plans, the board would then number seven supervisors, four of whom would come from the area of the Company lands. This change, he felt, would "prevent the ¼ Part of the County from having too great an ascendency over the Part owned by the Dutch Company." [25] Ellicott, therefore, planned to instigate lobbying activities in Albany for such a reorganization of town representation. Busti endorsed Ellicott's plans completely, and again complimented him on the valuable role that he was playing in the organization of Genesee County.

Ellicott was not satisfied with mere praise from Busti; he insisted that the Agent-General also assist him by altering the Company's land sales program. Specifically, Ellicott recommended that Busti open the rest of the Company's land for sale, so that the settlers would spread out more evenly on the purchase. With the additional settlements that would result from such action, Ellicott would have a valid reason to petition the legislature to create new towns in Company areas. This, in turn, would increase the number of supervisors on the board, a majority of which might soon represent towns that were located in the Company's territory. Ellicott, realizing the advantages of such a change in board membership, contacted Busti and pointed out: "We should thereby at a much earlier period be enabled to subdivide the Company's Territory into such a Number of Corporate Towns as to have a Majority of Supervisors residing within the Territory of the Company to dictate where Monies raised by Taxes Should be expended, and for what purposes, as well as a Number of other important Objects, regarding the Policy of the County." [26] Busti approved of Ellicott's idea and increased the amount of land that the Resident-Agent offered for sale from the original 500,000 acres to over 3 million acres, an area which included all of the Company's lands west of the Genesee.

Joseph Ellicott's friends and business associates, cheered by Busti's cooperativeness, now drafted a petition that sought to divide the town of Batavia into four towns, and submitted it to the officials of Batavia. In this document, the petitioners specifically suggested that the legislature should "erect the Town of Batavia into four Separate towns." [27] Five men signed the petition: Alex Rea, Ebenezer Cary, Isaac Sutherland, Benjamin Ellicott, and James W. Stevens. On September 8, 1803, the town meeting took place and endorsed the idea of dividing Batavia; however, it changed the number of towns to be created from four to five. The town officers then forwarded this revised petition to the legislature for its official action.

Independent of the actions of the Batavia town meeting, Joseph Ellicott sent a petition to a state senator, Lemuel Chipman, urging the division of Batavia. This request was identical with the one that his five friends had originally submitted to the town: it advocated the division of Batavia into four separate towns. Chipman was confident that the legislature would approve Ellicott's petition and assured the Resident-Agent that "there can be no doubt that the result will be favorable." [28]

After studying the two petitions, the legislature on April 11, 1804, divided the town of Batavia into four separate towns. Effective February, 1805, the town of Batavia was to become the towns of Batavia, Willink, Erie, and Chautauqua. By this act, membership on the Genesee County Board of Supervisors was increased by three. Four of the seven board members now resided in the area of the Company lands and were in a position to support politically the policies of the Holland Land Company, if these supervisors could be made sympathetic to the Company's interests. The new law delighted Busti, of course, who recognized that Ellicott had strengthened his position. In a congratulatory note, he expressed his appreciation to Ellicott: "I shall only add that in affecting the devision of Batavia Town you have given a new convincing proof of your attention to the interest of the Company for it is evident that by servicing the majority of the County officers no vexation can be imposed upon you." [29]

Busti's comments concerning Ellicott's role in the division of the town of Batavia might well have been applied to nearly all of Ellicott's political activities; for the latter had indeed "given . . . convincing proof of attention . . . to the interest of the Company." First, Ellicott had played an important role in the creation and organization of Genesee County. With the help of David Ogden, he had influenced many members of the state legislature to divide Ontario County and to run the new boundaries along the line recommended by the Resident-

Agent. To hasten the organization of Genesee County, he had speeded the construction of the court house and jail and encouraged the officials to approve the building quickly. Second, he had persuaded the Council of Appointment to choose his friends and employees, James Stevens and Richard M. Stoddard as the first officers of Genesee County. Although Ellicott had shunned political office for himself, he had accepted the post of county treasurer because he had felt that such a position would help the Holland Land Company. Finally, to insure the Company's hegemony over the Genesee County Board of Supervisors, Ellicott had persuaded the legislature to divide the town of Batavia into four towns.

These were achievements that strengthened the Company's position west of the Genesee and pointed toward a solution of the multiple problems involved in the sale of Company land. These accomplishments, too, helped to solidify Ellicott's personal reputation in the affairs of western New York. Little wonder, then, that Paul Busti should grant him "complete absolution" for his participation in political life; for when politics brought dividends, Busti was only too ready to serve as cashier for forgiveness and compliments. Ellicott accepted his praise and pardon with graciousness and modesty, and calmly readied himself for his next task—the strengthening and expanding of his newly won political power.

IV. The Big Family

Once Joseph Ellicott had entered politics to solve the land problems of the Holland Land Company, it was almost inevitable that he would be dragged further into other aspects of political life. This is just what happened.

Specifically, there evolved three new areas of politics in which Ellicott felt that he was forced to participate: campaigning in state elections, establishing working arrangements with other political figures, and sharing responsibility in the distribution of political appointments. In considering the first area, he realized that state elections were important; he could expect political favors from the Council of Appointment only if he had helped to elect the legislators who chose this patronage-dispensing council. He understood, secondly, that he would have to deal harmoniously with other politicians who were bound to emerge on the purchase or, failing to gain their cooperation, would have to be ready to fight them. Finally, he knew that his position as Resident-Agent in western New York required loyal and responsible friends who would form a tightly knit political hierarchy obedient to him. To make this organization possible, he needed considerable personal influence in the apportionment of political offices. Thus, the problems of land sales steadily pushed Ellicott into his initial political mold which, in turn, pressured him into newer and broader spheres of political activity.

In the process of meeting his increasing political responsibilities, Ellicott faced his first problem in the state election of 1804. Until that date, Ellicott had had no reason to campaign actively for a particular candidate for governor. He had accepted the office of Resident-Agent in 1800, and felt that it was unnecessary to take part in the gubernatorial election of 1801. He had helped to organize Genesee County in 1803, however, so the election of state officials in 1804 was of particular importance to the Holland Land Company. If the voters chose a majority of Federalists to the state assembly, the followers of Alexander Hamilton would then control the Council of Appointment. The council, conscious of the importance of patronage, would in all probability select mostly Federalists to fill key offices in the recently created Genesee County. Aware of the serious consequences of a Federalist victory, the Republican-oriented Ellicott watched the developments in 1804 with considerable interest.

The election produced a serious battle within the Republican party rather than an interparty contest between the followers of Hamilton and those of Jefferson. The disunited Federalists declined to advance their own candidate for governor in 1804 because his chances for victory were slender; the annual election of 1803 had given the Democrats such a large majority that the Federalists decided to avoid the embarrassment of a certain and crushing defeat. When the Federalists defaulted in this gubernatorial election, the results were a foregone conclusion. The Republicans needed only to dictate who would occupy the governor's chair, for the campaigning and voting became formalities. This apparently minor matter of naming the new governor, however, erupted into an intra-party brawl as the Republicans disagreed among themselves regarding the choice of their candidate.

In the search for a gubernatorial candidate, the Republicans wavered between two kinds of contestants. On the one hand, there were advocates of the type of man who sought the office but lacked the popular support of the party. On the other hand, there was a demand for candidates whom the majority of the party would accept, but who declined the office. George Clinton and John Lansing belonged to the latter category. Clinton, the incumbent governor, had held that office for seven terms, six of which had been successive. Anxious to become vice-president of the United States, Clinton had accepted an offer to serve as a running mate with Jefferson in 1804 and therefore refused an eighth term as governor. The Republicans then asked Lansing to agree to be a candidate. After many years in state politics, he had climbed to the highest judicial office of the state —that of chancellor—and would be an attractive nominee. He accepted the call of his party reluctantly because the tenure of the chancellorship was virtually for life. Lansing withdrew his name shortly afterward, however, when he learned that some Republican legislators were opposed to him and had come out for Aaron Burr in a special caucus.

Aaron Burr was typical of the candidate who wanted the office, yet failed to have the confidence of the party. Small in stature but large in talent, Burr had successfully applied his great energy to two vocations: law and politics. As a lawyer, his agile mind, careful preparation of prudently selected cases, and shrewd court tactics had brought him earnings in excess of $10,000 a year, a large sum surpassed by few in those days. As a politician, Burr had made good progress, holding the offices of attorney general of New York, United States senator, and state assemblyman. He was now completing his term as vice-president of the United States but had no hopes for re-nomination to that office; his seemingly evasive tactics in 1801, when the House of Representatives was forced to choose between Jefferson and Burr, had lost him the backing of many Republicans. Despite this defection, enough of his Republican friends remained loyal to Burr to place his name in nomination for the office of governor.

The bulk of the Republicans, however, turned to the brother-in-law of the influential Livingston family, the amiable but lackluster Morgan Lewis. Although he was far from a first choice of the Republican party, the followers of Clinton and Livingston again joined forces against Burr; they chose Lewis as their candidate for governor and John Broome, member of the 1804 Council of Appointment, for lieutenant-governor. When the Lewis-Broome ticket was placed in nomination, the election of 1804 developed into a bitter battle between the supporters of Lewis and the followers of Burr.

Until now, Ellicott had watched the nomination of the gubernatorial candidates without taking sides. However, when Oliver Phelps accepted the invitation to run for the office of lieutenant-governor on the same ticket with Aaron Burr, Ellicott found himself increasingly involved in the election. Like Ellicott, Phelps was an ardent Jeffersonian, and the two men had supported each other on several occasions. One of the earliest frontiersmen in the western part of New York, Phelps understood political tactics, and had become the first judge of Ontario County soon after the legislature had created that county. In 1801, less than one year after Joseph Ellicott had come to the purchase as Resident-Agent, Phelps had offered to get him appointed as a judge of Ontario County. In return, Ellicott had given Phelps valuable support in 1802, when the latter had won election to Congress. Phelps always recognized the value of this help.

Not only were his personal relations with Phelps pulling him into that state election, but Ellicott also felt pressure from other people who urged that he play an active role in the election of 1804. For example, his older brother Andrew, who was living in Pennsylvania, warmly endorsed Burr's candidacy as an end to the "equalising and leveling mania." [1] Moreover, Andrew regarded his brother's position as so pivotal that Joseph could determine the actual victor. "In New York," Andrew continued, "it is supposed that if you take an active part in favor of Mr. Burr, his election will be certain." On the other hand, Jeremiah Munson, the surrogate of Genesee County, and Simeon DeWitt, the surveyor-general of New York State, both of them friends of Joseph Ellicott, wanted him to support Morgan Lewis.

Since Phelps and Burr were running as a team, Joseph Ellicott found himself in the dilemma caused by his desire to support Phelps and his unwillingness to back Burr. His antipathy to Burr, like his friendship for Phelps, antedated the 1804 election. Ellicott's dislike for Burr stemmed from the latter's checkered relations with the Holland Land Company. In 1796, Burr had contracted for 100,000 acres of land from the Company and, as evidence of his good faith, had agreed to pay a penalty of $20,000 if he defaulted in his payments. The boom in land sales collapsed by the end of 1796, and Burr was in trouble. Unable to pay the Dutch owners for the land, he was also threatened by a heavy penalty for defaulting.

Aaron Burr and the Holland Land Company were involved in a much more serious problem. Aliens, like the Dutch owners, could not legally own land in New York State. New York was not unique, for the only state in the union that permitted aliens to own property was Pennsylvania. The Dutchmen were aware of the legal restrictions but minimized its seriousness. Sophisticated businessmen, they were confident that the state legislature could be persuaded to rescind the law barring alien ownership, and if the lawmakers refused, the Dutch owners had great trust that the state would never resort to confiscation. Thus the Holland Land Company empowered American trustees to hold their lands in western New York.

Less confident than the Dutch owners was Theophile Cazenove, the first Agent-General of the Holland Land Company and predecessor of Paul Busti. Patiently and persistently, Cazenove had tried various methods to get the state legislature to rescind the limits on aliens owning land. His direct proposal was overwhelmingly defeated by the lawmakers in 1793. He then employed legal counselors to serve as lobbyists, but the legislature in 1794 again voted down Cazenove's proposal. By now, the Dutch bankers were becoming uneasy and instructed Cazenove to continue his efforts. The prestigious Alexander Hamilton was added to the staff of legal advisors. Despite their skillful stratagems, the Company lobbyists gained only a compromise from the legislature in 1796: "said lands," read the law, "after the expiration of seven years from the passing of this act . . . shall be forfeited to and vested in the people of this State." [2] Alien landowners were granted a seven-year tenure to keep their lands.

The act of 1796 was better than not having any law at all. But the

Holland Land Company still lacked adequate legal protection so essential in such a large real estate operation. At the end of seven years, according to the law, the unsold land could revert to the state. Looked at another way, the Company must survey and sell its 3.3 million acres in western New York within seven years. There was little likelihood that the Company could do this in so brief a period.

Still dissatisfied, Cazenove continued to fight for a law without any restrictions on alien ownership of land. At this time, Philip Schuyler, Hamilton's father-in-law, had offered to use his political influence with the legislature to support Cazenove's measure if the Holland Land Company would reciprocate by supplying money to the Western Inland Navigation Company. Schuyler was president of that company and needed funds to advance his plans for the construction of a canal. As a result of Schuyler's great efforts in Albany, the legislature, in 1797, extended its alien land tenure "to the term of twenty years" provided the Holland Land Company furnished the Western Inland Navigation Company with $250,000 either as a loan or in purchase of stock.[3] Cazenove and the Dutch owners, however, saw too many flaws in the arrangement and refused to agree to this loan.

Determined to make an all-out effort to mobilize support in the legislature to eliminate all restrictions on land tenure, Cazenove, at this juncture, asked help from Aaron Burr. A key member of the New York State Legislature in 1797, Burr agreed to help Cazenove. So well did Burr succeed that on April 2, 1798, the legislature passed the Alien Land Holding Act that permitted foreigners to own land in the State of New York "forever." [4] In the process of persuading the legislature to approve this law of 1798, Burr had distributed $10,500 of Holland Land Company money for "counsel fees." A sizable sum in those days, the $10,500 was parcelled out to several people. $3,000 was given to Josiah Ogden Hoffman, the attorney-general of the state, $1,000 went to Thomas Morris to reimburse him for fees he had paid, and $1,000 was accepted by a Mr. L—— who stubbornly refused to give a receipt or to reveal his name.[5] The remaining $5,500 went to Aaron Burr. However, Burr did not get this money outright but received it as a loan with the understanding that he would refund this sum within two years.

The previous good relations between Burr and Cazenove now began to sour. In 1798, when Burr did not pay his installment on the 100,000 acres which he had bought two years earlier, Cazenove pressed him for the money. Burr simply did not have the cash to pay, so in December, 1798, he offered to return the land and thus cancel the contract. Cazenove, however, insisted that Burr pay the $20,000 penalty clause. After considerable haggling, the two men agreed to rescind the contract of 1796. According to their agreement of May, 1799, Burr returned the 100,000 acres of land and paid a penalty by giving the Company an additional 20,000 acres of land that he already owned in another part of the purchase; Cazenove, in return, cancelled the $5,500 loan which had been part of the "counsel fees" for lobbying in 1798.[6] The transaction left a bitter taste in Cazenove's mouth because he felt that he had already compensated Burr very well for the latter's efforts to support the law of 1798.

Sharing Cazenove's distaste for Burr's conduct involving the contract of 1796, Joseph Ellicott enumerated his own reasons for opposing Oliver Phelps's running mate. Burr's "baseness of principle in relation to his conduct toward the Company," Ellicott admitted to Busti, was "a circumstance alone, were there no other sufficient to render him too obnoxious to us." [7] Moreover, Ellicott had a genuine fear that if Burr won the 1804 election, he would join the State of New York with those of New England in a secession movement. The Resident-Agent favored law and order; the secession of states from the federal union, he felt, would remove the strong central government so essential to the protection of large landowners with property in more than one state. Although this belief held by Ellicott was also a cardinal doctrine of the Federalists, he remained a Republican because of his basic Jeffersonian convictions. Finally, the Resident-Agent knew that his superior, Paul Busti, also strongly opposed Burr's candidacy. In making his choice, the Resident-Agent decided to sacrifice his friendship with Oliver Phelps for the welfare of the Company and to oppose the Burr-Phelps ticket. Ellicott was determined to stop Burr by using every means at his disposal.

Despite Busti's similar strong feelings against Aaron Burr, the Agent-General's characteristic caution took precedence over his personal preference for Morgan Lewis. Busti used the 1804 election to enunciate his general policy on the place of Company agents in politics. He believed that the agents should remain aloof from political elections; and, although Busti greatly opposed the election of Burr, he maintained that he could not exclude this election from his over-all principle of nonintervention. This position he clearly explained to Ellicott, instructing him as follows: "Notwithstanding my dislike that agents should meddle with the election (for in case of success no favor can be favored for the Company, and much harm in case of a failure) I am almost tempted in the case of B. [Burr] to deviate from my sistem. For the sake of consistency I confine my request to you not to come forward as a champion for 'B' in the struggle and neither to oppose publicly his nomination, even if from your private opinion you should be inclined to do so." [8] Busti concluded his instructions advocating caution and noninvolvement in political elections by reminding Ellicott: "The situation in which you are placed makes you so conspicuous, and with so much preponderance that it becomes necessary to you to act with as much circumspection as a prime minister of England."

For a time, Joseph Ellicott was as circumspect as a British prime minister and obeyed Busti's instructions. As the campaign became more bitter, however, Ellicott correspondingly grew more concerned about the effects of the election on his position as Resident-Agent for the Holland Land Company. The fight in 1804 had not only caused a rift in the statewide Republican party, but it also was affecting the unity of that party on Company land west of the Genesee. When state party discipline declined as a result of Burr's disregard of the gubernatorial choice of the regular Republican leadership, this schism was felt on a smaller scale in western New York. The split became accentuated when the influential brothers Augustus and Peter Porter threw their support behind Burr and Phelps.

Augustus and Peter Porter were active western New York businessmen whose political power had been steadily growing as a result of their ability and experience. Augustus, the elder of the two, had arrived at the frontier earlier than Peter, and for ten years had familiarized himself with the land by surveying activities. He surveyed East Bloomfield in 1789; in 1791 he marked boundaries for the Phelps and Gorham Purchase; and in successive years, he did the same kind of work for Robert Morris and Oliver Phelps. In 1798, Augustus continued his surveying, first for the Connecticut Land Company, and then for the Holland Land Company under Joseph Ellicott. Peter Porter, a graduate of Yale College, first came to New York's western frontier in 1793. Two years later, he started to practice law in the bustling village of Canandaigua. At this time, Peter preferred Republican principles and quickly involved himself in the political life of that party. The Republican-dominated Council of Appointment in 1797 rewarded him with the office of clerk of Ontario County. In addition to keeping this political sinecure, Peter won election to the state assembly in 1802, and his political star showed glowing potential.

The split between the Porter brothers and Joseph Ellicott over the gubernatorial election of 1804 was an unexpected one. Prior to this, the Porters and Ellicott had all supported Oliver Phelps in the congressional election of 1802. One year later, Augustus had sought Ellicott's backing for the assembly slate that he favored; and in 1804, Augustus had offered to endorse Joseph Ellicott for the assembly. Yet, in the 1804 gubernatorial campaign, the close friendship that the Porter brothers felt for Burr outweighed the strength of their attachment for Ellicott. Thus, in opposition to Ellicott's stand, Peter and Augustus came out in support of Aaron Burr's candidacy.

With the Porters' swinging to the side of Burr, Ellicott's fear of the consequences of a Burr victory grew to nightmare proportions as the election day neared. He even prophesied that, if Burr could increase his prestige by being elected governor of New York State, he might be tempted "to bring about a separation of the Union, which if ever effected cannot otherwise be than destructive to all the great Landholders that might fall in the Northern Section." [9] This thought so distressed the Resident-Agent that he decided to disregard Paul Busti's explicit instructions to remain neutral during the election campaign. He now openly announced and publicized his opposition to Burr's candidacy, justifying his actions to the Resident-Agent by stating: "This belief [that Burr was dangerously ambitious] produced such an effect upon my mind that it was impossible for me to avoid in some measure a little activity at the Election." [10]

The gubernatorial campaign of 1804 was sordid and one of the most savagely fought in the annals of the state's history. Not since the American Revolution had there been such coarse villification of candidates. As the election day drew nearer, irresponsible journalists and opportunistic politicians filled the air with lies, insinuations, innuendoes, and half-truths. Burr's curious conduct in Jefferson's 1801 election was dredged up and smeared, and his private life was exposed and maligned. Burr's followers countered with an especially effective broadside signed "Plain Truth," which enumerated in malicious detail the gross nepotism of the Clinton and Livingston families. [11] Party spirit infiltrated nonpolitical channels. Friends of long standing stopped talking, business partners wrangled, and commerce declined sharply.

In contrast to the turbulence of the New York campaign, the presidential election of 1804 was relatively quiet. The Republicans, predictably, renominated Thomas Jefferson, while the Federalists, without much enthusiasm, selected Charles C. Pinckney. Jefferson approved of George Clinton as candidate for vice-president, thus recognizing the importance of the New York vote. Clinton did what was expected.

He helped carry the state in 1804 the way that Burr had done four years earlier. Clinton's aid, however, proved less essential. The Federalists suffered a crushing defeat; Jefferson received 162 electoral votes whereas only 14 went to Pinckney. Thousands of Federalists, pleased with Jefferson's actions, had deserted to the Republicans. Even the most partial Federalists had to admit that, under the sage of Monticello, executive power had increased, the constitution had been given a broad interpretation, and the Bank of the United States, the federal debt, and the navy had been retained.

Jefferson's reelection pleased Ellicott, but the victory of Lewis over Burr relieved and delighted the Resident-Agent. Morgan Lewis won by the comfortable margin of nearly 9,000 out of a total of some 53,000 votes cast. The regular Republicans, who supported Lewis, also triumphed in the legislature. Whatever power Aaron Burr still wielded among the voters ended completely when he killed Alexander Hamilton in a duel on July 11, 1805.

Like the rest of the state, the majority of the voters west of the Genesee favored Lewis. As reported in the New York *Evening Post*, on June 9, 1804, western New Yorkers gave Lewis 197 votes to 123 for Burr. The election results in Batavia showed that the voters had overwhelmingly supported the regular Republican candidates. Lewis obtained 111 to Burr's 11 votes, while Broome received 115 for the office of lieutenant-governor to the 7 votes won by Phelps.[12] The Porters' opposition in this election had presented Ellicott with the first challenge to his position of power among the regular Republicans west of the Genesee. The election returns proved that, in this case, they did not have sufficient support of the rank and file voters to defeat the men whom Ellicott favored.

While Ellicott's influence in the 1804 election cannot be specifically weighed, the Resident-Agent, of course, interpreted the results as being highly favorable to him. The election convinced Ellicott that he had made a wise move when he disobeyed Busti's directive and openly opposed Burr. He cited the election results to his employer as proof that the voters of western New York had shown very little sympathy for Burr's philosophy. Furthermore, Ellicott felt that the election had strengthened the Company's position with the government elected to power.

Another consequence of the 1804 election was the separation of Peter Porter from his position as clerk of Ontario County. The Council of Appointment that selected the holder of this job had originally chosen Porter in 1797 as a reward for his services to the Republicans.

As a result of their victory in 1804, the regular Republicans now chose council members who opposed Burr and his cohorts. By the rules of the political game, Porter, who had supported the insurgent Burr, faced the loss of his clerkship. A friend of Ellicott's described Porter's mental state after Lewis' victory in the following manner: Porter "appears very sorry, and as sore, as he is sorry. He knows that he ought, and most probably will lose his office, which [has] so often warped his opinion, and [which he] has been very accommodating to save." [13] Notwithstanding Porter's regret, the Council of Appointment punished him for his political heresy by taking away his position.

The battle between Burr and Lewis had drawn Ellicott into a political area that was novel to him: participation in a state election. The election struggle of 1804 also revealed to him that several challenging political figures were emerging on the purchase, and that he would have to maneuver to retain his political strength. Ellicott, therefore, prepared to handle another major problem of political life—establishing satisfactory relations with other political leaders.

One of the rising political figures who sought additional power in western New York was Erastus Granger. He first appeared in Buffalo during the election campaign of 1804. Prior to this, Granger had lived in Connecticut, where he had vigorously supported Thomas Jefferson. Moreover, Granger had the good fortune to have as a cousin Gideon Granger, the postmaster-general in Jefferson's cabinet. Because of Erastus Granger's industry and his cousin's prominent political position, Jefferson appointed him superintendent of Indian affairs.

Joseph Ellicott's contact with Erastus Granger began during the series of conferences and discussions that were held over the disposition of Company land to the Tuscarora Indians. The Tuscaroras had fled from North Carolina in 1711 and had joined the Iroquois Confederacy a year later. Living on the territory of the Senecas, the Tuscaroras had not received land for their reservation in the 1797 Treaty of Big Tree. The Holland Land Company and the Senecas, therefore, each donated two miles square to the Tuscaroras. This grant was not sufficient, so the Tuscaroras sought more land. However, in 1803, when the Tuscaroras applied to purchase land from the Company, they had to obtain the advice and approval of the federal government before they could buy it. Henry Dearborn, secretary of war, had the duty of advising the Tuscaroras on the wisdom of such a purchase. In this case, the Secretary of War gave his opinion that the Company was asking too high a price for this projected piece of land.

Dearborn's action so disconcerted Busti that the Agent-General angrily responded to the Secretary of War. He did not realize, Busti heatedly told Dearborn, that the Secretary of War's advice to the Indians was based on his judgment whether the Company price was a just one. Busti maintained that the price of the land was justified and objected to Dearborn's decisive role in blocking the sale. But the Secretary of War clung to his position and insisted that it was his task to protect the Indians against their buying land at prices that he judged to be "considerably too high." [14]

Dearborn's position prevented the consummation of the land sale to the Tuscaroras so Busti sought help to complete the transaction. It was only natural that he should turn to Erastus Granger, who had just assumed the office of superintendent of Indian affairs. In February, 1804, Busti talked with Granger in Philadelphia in an effort to enlist his support; he, however, agreed with Dearborn's original opinon that the "prices and conditions appeared too high." [15] Busti persisted in his plans for this sale, and urged Ellicott to try to influence Granger to take action favorable to the Holland Land Company. Ellicott and Granger met in March to discuss the projected sale. Ellicott now learned that part of the trouble stemmed from Oliver Phelps, the 1804 candidate for lieutenant-governor and friend of Burr, whom Ellicott had opposed. Granger claimed that Phelps had suggested to Dearborn that the Company had asked too high a price for the land.

After considerable discussion, Ellicott succeeded in convincing Superintendent of Indian Affairs Granger that the price asked by the Holland Land Company was a fair one, and that Phelps's conduct was highly irregular. Granger therefore decided to support Ellicott; thus, with Granger's assistance, the Holland Land Company finally completed the sale. The Tuscaroras purchased 4,329 acres of land, paying the Company $13,722. The money came from a trust fund held by the United States as a result of a settlement of the Indian claims against North Carolina. The decisive role that Granger had played in that affair earned for him the gratitude of Ellicott and Busti.

After participating in the Tuscarora purchase, Granger sought to advance himself further. On September 3, 1804, he became the first postmaster of New Amsterdam (Buffalo) and held this office without interruption until 1818. He also accepted the position of financial agent in 1804 for some of the Seneca chiefs, a job which required Granger to receive the chiefs' annuities and to turn over the money to the Indian leaders. Since these annuities were paid by the Holland Land Company, Ellicott again came in contact with Granger and successfully developed working relationships that proved to be exceed-

ingly harmonious. Indeed, Ellicott was so pleased with Granger's cooperation that he demonstrated his gratitude by selling him three
choice lots in Buffalo at a low price.

In addition to his friendly relations with the politically important
Erastus Granger, Joseph Ellicott got along well with other western
New York politicians. Alexander Rea, for example, had come under
obligation to Ellicott soon after the latter became Resident-Agent. In
1801, Rea humbly solicited from Ellicott "any job he may have to
offer next season." [16] Two months later, Rea went to work for the
Resident-Agent. Rea added to his obligations to Ellicott by borrowing
money from him. Already $250 in debt to him, Rea, in 1804, asked
Ellicott for an additional loan of $80. The job and loan paid large
dividends to Ellicott, for Alex Rea soon rose in political stature. He
had progressed from assessor and commissioner of highways for the
town of Batavia, in 1803, to supervisor of the same town one year
later. The voters then elected Rea to the state assembly in 1804, and
reelected him to that office until 1808; in that year, the electorate sent
him to the state senate where he served two terms until 1817. While
a senator, the assembly elected him to the Council of Appointment
in 1809.

When Alex Rea acquired a position of considerable political
strength, he was quite ready to repay Ellicott for his earlier favors
to him. As soon as he gained the seat in the state assembly, Rea sought
Ellicott's advice on lawmaking matters. "I shall also be glad to have
your concile [*sic*]," he told the Resident-Agent, "on Legislative business." [17] Furthermore, Rea recognized Ellicott's paramount role in
the choosing of candidates for county position by informing him: "I
would be glad to have any nominations that may be forwarded as
soon as it was convenient. I presume they will mostly come through
your hands." On several occasions, Rea repeated this same type of
request to Ellicott: "I would wish you to make the nomination." Rea
even offered to do whatever Ellicott desired, assuring the Resident-
Agent: "Should you have any commands to Albany I will be happy
to serve you." [18]

Another western New York politician who cooperated with Joseph
Ellicott was Joseph Annin. A state senator from Aurelius, who served
in the upper house from 1803 through 1820, Annin, like Alex Rea,
willingly granted favors to Ellicott. Grateful for Ellicott's support in
the early stages of his career, Annin often waited for Ellicott to choose
the nominees for county posts, and offered to use his senatorial influence in the promotion of people whom the Resident-Agent wanted.

Thus, Ellicott had worked out arrangements with several politicians from western New York, and in the main these men cooperated with the Resident-Agent. Granger, Rea, and Annin supported Ellicott in many matters, their loyalty proving to be of considerable assistance in the operations of Holland Land Company policies.

Once he had established a cooperative climate with other politicians, Ellicott felt that he now needed the loyalty of family relations to assist him to direct his political affairs. For as the number of land sales increased, Ellicott's tasks as Resident-Agent rose proportionately, and he had correspondingly less time in which to care personally for his numerous obligations. Moreover, as the settlers spread out and populated the various parts of the vast purchase, he could not possibly maintain alone the close contact with local political figures so essential to an understanding of the residents' political thoughts. If Ellicott wished to fulfill adequately his duties as Resident-Agent and also to continue to attend to his political needs, he required the most trustworthy help. For this kind of support, Joseph Ellicott turned to his family.

Joseph depended heavily on the wise counsel and the constant support of his youngest brother, the tall, spare, good-natured Benjamin. Their association had been close and their interests identical. Together, they had spent numerous hours and walked many miles surveying new areas. Together, they had shared the hazards of the wilderness, the heat of the summer, and the frost of the winter. Side by side, the brothers had slept in heavily timbered land, on rocky soil, and near mosquito-infested lakes. Bachelors, they lived under one roof, risking their moneys together and sharing equally their fortunes. The intense and impatient Joseph needed the tact and grace of Benjamin in handling the settlers. Coming from diverse parts of the country, some of the pioneers of western New York confused individualism with anarchy. However, they respected Benjamin Ellicott as judge of Genesee County for his sweet reasonableness, his imposing size, and his relationship to the Resident-Agent of the Holland Land Company. The voters also elected Benjamin to two terms in Congress from 1817 to 1821.

The warm attachment that Joseph felt for his family led him to recruit from among relatives other lieutenants to share his political and economic responsibilities in western New York. He came to rely on his nephew, David Ellicott Evans. In 1803, David Evans, the son of Rachael Ellicott Evans (the twin sister of Benjamin Ellicott), had left his home in Maryland and had come to Batavia at the age of fifteen.

Starting as a clerk in his Uncle Joseph's office, he made rapid progress and was soon promoted to cashier and then to accounting clerk. As a result of his close associations with Ellicott, Evans learned the intricate details of the land business as well as the political and economic problems of western New York. Then, with his uncle's approval, Evans ran for the state senate in 1818. Elected as a senator, he promoted the best interests of his uncle and the Holland Land Company. Evans frequently sought Ellicott's guidance, beginning each request for advice by stating: "I would wish your advice on." [19] Evans continued in politics and won a seat in Congress in 1826, but resigned his post the following year when the Company appointed him to an important administrative position. For many critical years, Evans worked closely with Ellicott, who so greatly respected the ability of his nephew that he granted him power of attorney to transact all of his personal business.

While Ellicott watched with pride the steady advancement of his nephew David Evans, the Resident-Agent was also impressed by the work of William Peacock. Peacock had entered the Company's service in 1803, beginning as a clerk in the Batavia office under the exacting tutelage of the Resident-Agent. In 1804, Peacock, a skilled surveyor, laid out the street arrangement for much of the village of Buffalo, and then performed the same tasks for the county seats of Mayville and Ellicottville. Several years later, he also marked the boundaries of most of the towns of Chautauqua County. In 1807, William Peacock officially joined the Ellicott family when he married Joseph's niece, Ann Ellicott Evans. He continued to climb in the Company, and in 1810 Ellicott sent him to Mayville, the county seat of Chautauqua, where he became a subagent directly responsible to the Resident-Agent. He held this office until the Company sold the rest of its land in 1836. Peacock, like Evans, became involved in politics and, with Ellicott's permission, accepted the position of county treasurer from the Chautauqua County Board of Supervisors; he retained this post for ten years, until he resigned in 1821. Peacock also served as a county judge. In all his dealings with the Resident-Agent, Peacock worked hard for the Company and remained loyal to Joseph Ellicott.

David Goodwin also had married a daughter of one of Ellicott's sisters and had joined the Holland Land Company as a clerk in the Batavia office. In 1817, the Resident-Agent showed his confidence in Goodwin by appointing him subagent for the County of Cattaraugus.

Finally, although James W. Stevens bore no relationship to Joseph Ellicott by birth or marriage, Stevens had worked so closely with him as his office assistant in Batavia that Ellicott considered him as much an ally in the organization as he did Evans, Peacock, Goodwin, and his brother Benjamin. The association between the two men had begun in 1800 and continued until Ellicott died in 1826. During this period, he had learned to appreciate Stevens' efficiency, industry, honesty, and sound advice. Above all, Ellicott cherished Stevens' constant devotion to the Company and the family.

This inner family circle of Joseph and Benjamin Ellicott, David E. Evans, William Peacock, David Goodwin, and James W. Stevens soon became known as the Big Family. It was a tightly knit family group that held considerable economic and political power in western New York and, by working closely together, succeeded in increasing and consolidating its strength. At the head of the Big Family towered the dominating figure of Joseph Ellicott, part father, part instructor, part counselor—but always in command.

With the incorporation of family relations into a smoothly operating organization, Joseph Ellicott had added a major accomplishment that merged well with his other successes in the field of politics and politicians. It supplemented the effectiveness of the role that he had taken in the state election of 1804; it implemented his valuable work in establishing friendly ties with other politicians; and it strengthened considerably his position of power in western New York.

At all times, however, Joseph Ellicott clearly maintained that he had entered politics only as a means of increasing land sales, and not because of the attractiveness of political power. As Resident-Agent of the Holland Land Company, he never lost sight of the fact that it was his primary job to sell property, not to gain political laurels for the sake of personal prestige. He rubbed shoulders with political figures not because he envied them their occupational garments, but because he wished to demonstrate the strength and quality of his own. He would need all of the political respect that he could obtain if he were to overcome the three major problems still facing the Holland Land Company—the creation of new county seats, the lack of roads, and the high taxes that threatened to extinguish Company profits.

V. Roads and the Unhappy Taxpayer

The road situation in 1800 was serious. Locked between the long Atlantic coast and the meandering Mississippi River were incredible stores of natural resources. The anthracite coal beds of Pennsylvania and the iron ore of Alabama and Lake Superior were nearly untouched. Iron production was low, and large mining developments were unknown. Broad tracts of fertile land awaited planting and harvesting. The conversion of these almost untapped riches depended on one thing: accessibility. These resources could be transformed into goods only when they could be reached, used, and delivered to other parts of the country. Until the road conditions were improved, the nation's progress would be slow indeed.

Water travel was a mixed blessing. The major highway for such travel was the extensive Atlantic coastline. Here, hundreds of adequate harbors protected the small sailing vessels of that day. Water travel was also cheaper than going by land, but the element of fortune was strong. The traveler must locate a captain whose plans dovetailed with his own. Once found, the skipper frequently did not go directly to the traveler's destination. The weather, too, made the arrival date unpredictable. For example, in good weather the 150-mile boat ride from Albany to New York City took three days, but in bad weather a week and sometimes two were often needed for the same trip. Moreover, the return journey upstream on the Hudson, like any water travel against the current, remained a serious handicap. Not until 1807 did the steamship become profitable. That year, Fulton's *Clermont* made the 300-mile trip from New York City to Albany and back in sixty-two hours.

Whatever the shortcomings of water transportation, the United States was dependent upon it. The great bulk of the nation's products was floated down rivers and streams on crude rafts and flatboats. Few crops could bear the cost of travel over roads, and most farm produce that went to market was carried by road to either a seaport or a river town. There, the items were moved by boat to their final destination. Until 1800, about 90 percent of New York's trade used the waters of the Atlantic, the Hudson, and New York's bay. The splendid New York harbor was perfectly situated to accommodate the Atlantic, the coastal, and the inland trade, but for the early settlements inland, the rivers and their tributaries provided the only economical routes of trade.

In contrast, and certainly by twentieth-century standards, the roads in 1800 were unbelievably poor. They were little more than widened Indian trails that wound through the forest. Where dry, they had thick layers of powdered dust. When wet, the roads had numerous and deep mud holes. And where swampy, they were covered with logs laid side by side to form what were called "corduroy roads." Most streams were forded, for there were few bridges. In 1787, a toll bridge of more than 1,500 feet was constructed to span the Charles River at Boston, and in 1800, New Yorkers could cross Lake Cayuga on a mile-long bridge that connected Auburn and Geneva.

Until 1800, little had been done to improve the roads. The predominantly rural communities lacked the capital and the labor to spend on such a vast job. What money and energy they had were used first to clear the land, erect homes and barns, and build schools and court houses. Road care had a lower priority. Another factor that had hampered road construction stemmed from an old Anglo-Saxon tradition. Road-building was regarded as a community responsibility. The job was done by those residents who "worked off" rather than paid their highway taxes. They assembled when farm demands were low rather than when it was a good time to work on roads. Using rakes, hoes, and plows pulled by oxen or mules, they felled trees and pulled stumps. They meant well but were ignorant of the basics of good highway engineering.

A more important reason, perhaps, for the inadequate roads was the attitude of most farmers. They did not believe it worthwhile to spend the required time and money to construct good roads. Bad roads, they reasoned, were an inconvenience to which one learned to adjust. In the North, farmers used sleds in the winter to travel the frozen roads; in the South, they depended on mules to pull the "mud" boats through the mud to the river bank. In short, bad roads, like bad weather, were taken in stride rather than fought.

As the nation expanded, the road impasse was becoming critical. In most urgent need of repair were those highways over which large amounts of freight traveled into and out of main towns. Also in miserable condition were the roads going westward, where growing numbers of pioneers were moving and new settlements were being started. A campaign for improving the road situation had started in the 1790's. Pressing for better roads were two groups: the merchants and the land speculators. The merchants would benefit by the expanded area of business, while the land speculators would profit by the increased value of land.

The crusade for roads was applauded by many, yet was unsupported by almost the same number. Local governments on the town and county levels, by custom, built and maintained the roads. The local residents wanted the roads but not strongly enough to pay the cost required. Because road-building benefited so many outsiders, they reasoned, the local communities should not be saddled with the expenses. The state legislatures also voiced approval and likewise shied away from taking action. Lacking sufficient funds to provide an adequate network of hard-surfaced roads, the lawmakers, on sound political grounds, declined to favor certain communities. A way out of this dilemma was finally found: the state legislatures passed laws to allow private companies to construct roads.

In the 1790's, several private roads or turnpikes were built. "Turnpike" was the name applied to a road built by a private company whose profit depended on the tolls collected. One of the first and most well known was the Lancaster Turnpike. Chartered by the Pennsylvania legislature in 1792, the Lancaster toll road was to link Philadelphia to Lancaster. Within two years, the company met its commitment and constructed an admirable sixty-two-mile stone roadbed covered with gravel. The financial success of the Lancaster Turnpike encouraged emulation. Rhode Island chartered its first turnpike in 1794, followed by Connecticut a year later, Massachusetts in 1796, and New York in 1797. Due to financial troubles, no other turnpike was built in the middle states during the 1790's, and the problem of roads remained acute.

The group that was perhaps most affected by the road crisis were the large landowners. Robert Morris, one of the biggest of all land adventurers, had fallen upon hard times in 1796. His decline triggered the collapse of the real estate market and left the other large landlords in serious trouble. They had made their purchases in a rising market, and now the glamor had gone out of the land business; prices had fallen sharply. At the same time, the real estate owners had to pay taxes as a continuing expense. The market had changed in another way. Previously, sales for large tracts of 100,000 acres or more were not uncommon. By 1800, however, those mainly interested in buying land were pioneers willing to accept frontier hardships but unable to pay cash for even the small lots.

In New York, the road problem hurt all the large landholders whether speculators or resident-owners. In the East, for example, the

Van Rensselaer family clung to its million-acre estate which included present-day Albany, Rensselaer, and Columbia Counties. Unwilling to sell the land, the Van Rensselaers had difficulty collecting rents from tenants who lacked good roads over which they could carry their produce to market. In the North Country, Alexander Macomb and his associates owned the largest land tract ever sold by New York State. The Macomb Purchase included 3,636,000 acres and had been bought in 1791 at eight cents an acre. Despite the cheap price, the Macomb Purchase was a failure, due in large part to its inaccessibility.

In western New York, the Sir William Pulteney Association had purchased in 1791 an attractive area of one million acres between Seneca Lake and the Genesee River at twenty-six cents an acre. Charles Williamson, the agent in America for the Pulteney Association, was convinced that internal improvements were an indispensable first step toward profit. Before Williamson sold a single acre of land, he had laid out a road to connect the Pulteney lands with outposts of settlement in Pennsylvania. Beginning in 1791, he had started some roads each year with two thoughts in mind: to help the new settlers get to the Pulteney Purchase, and to assist the old ones carry their produce to market. Between 1791 and 1800, Williamson had spent about one million dollars on improvements and had received from land sales a little less than $150,000. How much of the one million dollars went into road-building is not clear, but the money so spent was a wise move. Less prudent were other investments: building a hotel and a theater, setting up a race track, and importing misled, disillusioned Germans as settlers. These helped bring about Williamson's removal in 1800. Replacing Williamson was Robert Troup, a thrifty-minded lawyer from New York. Troup drastically reduced spending on all kinds of improvements and concentrated on collecting what the settlers owed the Pulteney Association.

West of the Pulteney Purchase lay the holdings of the Holland Land Company with its 3.3 million acres. Joseph Ellicott was as keenly concerned with the road situation as the other dealers in real estate. Contrary to the lavish expenditures of Williamson, Ellicott preferred the Troup method of achieving his objectives with a minimum of expense. Joseph's plan was to develop economically a few major roads. With this in mind, he concentrated on building two routes running from the Genesee River to New Amsterdam (Buffalo). The first would lie between Big Tree (Geneseo) on the Genesee and a point on Lake Erie south of the Buffalo Creek Indian Reservation, and was known as the Middle Road. The second would extend from Batavia to New

Amsterdam and would parallel the projected Middle Road route. The Batavia–New Amsterdam thoroughfare, eventually called the Buffalo Road, would provide the Company and the settlers with several advantages: it would link the county seat at Batavia with New Amsterdam; it would bypass the Tonawanda Reservation; it would connect with the Genesee Road, which ran from Batavia to Connewagus; and it would enhance the value of the Company land through which it ran. Both roads were completed by 1810. Ellicott succeeded in keeping expenses low in both projects by hiring settlers to do the labor and then deducting their pay from the debts which they owed to the Holland Land Company. Thus, there was little outlay of Company cash involved, and payment of salaries was merely a matter of bookkeeping.[1]

The need for roads was so vital, however, that Joseph Ellicott was forced to build more than a few main highways. In 1801, the Holland Land Company started a road—called the Oak Orchard Road—from Batavia to a point on Lake Ontario, where Ellicott wanted a trading community. The Company also began work on a route to Big Tree— the Big Tree Road—which would join the road that Charles Williamson had built from Bath. By constructing the Big Tree Road, Ellicott hoped to induce some of the settlers to go farther north to the Company lands.

In addition to these activities, Ellicott also furnished an occasional monetary incentive to stimulate new construction. In 1808, the Resident-Agent subscribed $200 "towards opening the Chautauqua Portage Road." [2] The same year he offered to pay $10 per mile to anyone who would cut a road fourteen to sixteen feet wide from Canadaway (Fredonia) to Mayville. The following year, he volunteered the sum of $40 to improve the road that ran from Buffalo to Black Rock. And in 1810, the Holland Land Company paid the expenses involved in completing the road from Angelica to Mayville.

While Ellicott and the Holland Land Company were busy with their road construction, the turnpike movement was attracting considerable attention in New York. The legislature had already made liberal grants toward road-building. Public land had been set aside after 1789 to provide the necessary compensation, and lotteries had been held in 1797. But the limited results of these projects left the large landowners, the frontiersmen, and the river towns still dissatisfied. With the success of the Lancaster Turnpike, a "spirit of turnpiking" spread over the entire state. Petitions deluged the legislature, and eighty-eight turnpike and bridge companies received charters

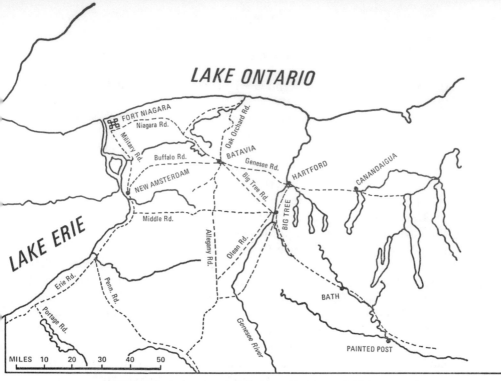

ROADS IN WESTERN NEW YORK — 1804

by 1807. By that year, too, twenty-eight turnpike companies had constructed some nine hundred miles of road, and twenty-one toll bridges had been erected.

When turnpikes were first built, Albany became a toll road capital. Because of its location near the junction of the Hudson and the Mohawk Rivers, Albany was the hub of commerce. Eight turnpikes radiated from the city like spokes on a wheel. Two of the more important highways that ran to the west were the Mohawk Route and the Great Western Turnpike. The Mohawk Route started as the Albany and Schenectady Turnpike. Chartered in 1797, begun three years later, and completed in 1805, the Albany and Schenectady Turnpike was one of the best-surfaced roads in the state. From Schenectady, the Mohawk Turnpike and Bridge Company completed a road to Utica; there, the Seneca Road Company built a highway to Canandaigua, the largest town in New York west of Utica. Moving parallel to the Mohawk Route was a strong rival, the Great Western Turnpike. The Great Western also started at Albany but then went through Cherry Valley, Ithaca, and Bath, and curved into Pennsylvania. Another link in the Great Western Turnpike chain turned at Cherry Valley, passed through Cazenovia, and terminated at Manlius, where it intersected the Mohawk Route.

The first efforts to construct turnpikes west of the Genesee occurred in 1805 when two companies sought charters from the legislature. Both roads were planned to go through the purchase. One company proposed building a northerly road from Canandaigua to Black Rock, two miles from Buffalo, while the other company wanted a more southerly turnpike from Bath to Lake Erie.

Uncertain of the attitude of the Holland Land Company toward the two turnpike projects, Ellicott's friends in the legislature sought his advice. Lemuel Chipman in the senate and Alexander Rea in the assembly, both anxious to serve the Holland Land Company, first asked Ellicott how they should vote on the proposed turnpike for the northern route.[3] Ellicott told them that he opposed the construction of this turnpike, because he believed that the Holland Land Company, as the largest landowner in western New York, would be expected by the public to assist the turnpike company by subscribing heavily to its stock. Since the turnpike cost far more to construct than the less ambitious roads which Ellicott was building, he opposed authorizing its construction. Furthermore, if the Holland Land Company did buy turnpike stock, Ellicott felt that there was no assurance that it would receive a sufficient dividend. As evidence for this point of view, he cited the case of the Utica-Canandaigua turnpike, which he maintained carried twenty times as much traffic as the planned northern route would, yet had not brought much profit to its investors.

Ellicott, however, recognized the public demand for turnpikes and agreed that "it would be next to Madness to endeavour to counteract public opinion."[4] He therefore reluctantly advised his allies in the legislature to cooperate in obtaining an act of incorporation for the northern turnpike, but only provided that the route passed through Buffalo and the Holland Land Company property. The legislature passed the bill for the northern route but, as Ellicott had anticipated, the turnpike company had difficulty in raising the funds necessary for the construction. When it finally turned to Ellicott for money, he pointed out that the Holland Land Company had already spent all that it could afford on road-building. As a token of cooperation, however, Ellicott did offer some of the Company's wild lands in exchange for stock in the turnpike company. He firmly refused, on the other hand, to invest any Company money. Without financial support from the Holland Land Company, the turnpike project for the northern route failed.

At the same time that the northern turnpike project was under discussion, Philip Church had taken the leadership for a southern turnpike that would extend from Bath to Lake Erie. Such a route would encourage settlers going over the Catskills to populate the southern tier, which in turn would benefit the large landholders in that part of the state. A southern turnpike interested Philip Church because his father owned 100,000 acres of land in Alleghany County. This planned road also caught the imagination of Robert Troup, land agent for the neighboring Pulteney Estate. Ellicott and Busti, however, refused to join Church and Troup in this project because they believed that this turnpike building was unnecessary—particularly since the Holland Land Company had almost no settlers living where the road would run. Church and Troup persevered, and in 1805 the legislature approved the construction of a turnpike over a southern route.

When the directors of the newly created company for the southern turnpike approached the Holland Land Company to invest money in this project, Ellicott and Busti faced a dilemma. Although they genuinely believed that the project would not benefit their Company for another fifty years, they feared the censure of the settlers if they refused to support it. Ellicott was convinced that the residents would interpret such nonsupport as overt hostility to road-building, and he told this to Busti: "It may & doubtless will be echoed by some envious Characters and probably by these very People [Church and Troup], that the Holland Company are not disposed to lend their Aid to public Improvements although they are the Proprietors of nearly 1/9 Part of the Whole State." [5] Ellicott and Busti therefore consented to give up some land on the purchase for shares in the turnpike company as a gesture of good will, but the movement for the Bath–Lake Erie turnpike died out when other support could not be obtained. Not until 1810 did the Holland Land Company start a narrow road—not a turnpike—from Angelica to Lake Erie. Work on the route was finally completed in 1814.

Despite Ellicott's road-building efforts, the highway that he had helped to construct between Batavia and Buffalo soon fell into disrepair because of insufficient maintenance work. Traveling conditions became so difficult that the residents on the purchase decided to take action. Some of the settlers of Niagara County held a meeting on December 3, 1811, and chose a committee to meet with a similarly constituted group from Genesee County. The residents of Genesee County appointed a committee of six; Company clerk James W. Stevens served as chairman, while Ellicott's brother Benjamin agreed to assist as a committee member. On December 12, the two committees met and petitioned the legislature to approve a lottery for $15,000 and to allocate this money for the improvement of the Batavia-Buffalo road. The Buffalo *Gazette,* the local newspaper, added its support to this plan by eloquently and energetically campaigning for the improvement of this highway. Responding to these appeals, the legislature voted "a grant of $5,000 for improving the Road from the Genesee River to Buffalo." [6]

Despite this and other efforts to keep up the roads, travelers in western New York, settlers on the purchase, and Resident-Agent Ellicott were still plagued by inadequate highways as late as 1812. The problem of poor roads nearly defied solution. In 1812, only 26,000 people lived on an area that spread over some 5,000 square miles of western New York. The resident landowners had complied with the road tax that required them to do a certain amount of work annually on the highway,[7] and Ellicott had helped the situation by donating Company money and land and by constructing some roads himself. However, he had depended too heavily on the creation of the new County of Genesee to stimulate road-building activity on the part of town governments in that area. The creation of Genesee County did increase road-building because the towns in the county no longer paid taxes to Ontario County and were now able to spend their money for improvements west of the Genesee. But the new county could not solve the road problem alone, and the amount of funds that the state government spent on highways in western New York was small compared to the need. In brief, the problem of roads in western New York was the same one that confronted the rest of the United States: too few people lived on too large an area at a time when they had too little money. And Ellicott could only hope that time and the nation's growth would bring about a solution.

At the same time that the problem of poor roads was troubling Joseph Ellicott, the question of taxation also presented him with serious difficulties. Taxes had reduced Ellicott's profits and, so far as he was concerned, also had threatened to destroy the Holland Land Company. The tax situation—even more than the problem of poor highways—had made him decide to enter politics and later to accept the post of Genesee County treasurer.

When Genesee County was organized in 1803, Resident-Agent Ellicott, as county treasurer, decided to make every effort to keep tax assessments at a low rate. Thus, as the time arrived for levying taxes to meet county and town expenses, Ellicott spent much time with the supervisors discussing the subject. The Holland Land Company profited from these conversations in 1803 because the town of Batavia, a part of the Holland Land Company territory, "paid the least taxes in the Dollar of any of the Towns in the County." Moreover, Ellicott maintained that the tax would have been lower than the previous year "had it not been for the circumstance of [Genesee County] being obliged to levy on the County the Sum of $1,600 for the purpose of paying its proportional part of the expense of erecting the Bridge over the Genesee River." [8]

Even the tax money that was paid by the Holland Land Company to the county was not completely lost, however, for Ellicott arranged to channel several tax appropriations of 1803 into projects that would benefit the Company. Some of the tax money, for example, was spent on roads and bridges located on the purchase, a fact which Ellicott promptly called to Busti's attention. Ellicott also reminded Busti of the less desirable situation which had existed in previous years, when Ontario County had spent no money for internal improvements on the purchase. Joseph Ellicott therefore concluded that the lower taxes levied by the newly constituted Genesee County and its willingness to spend some of the tax money for the benefit of the Holland Land Company proved "the manifest advantages that the Company has attained by separating their territory from the County of Ontario." [9]

The year 1804 was a crucial time for the directors of the Holland Land Company, and it was fortunate that Resident-Agent Ellicott and his associates were able to use their influence to lower the tax rate that year. The Dutch owners of the Company had by now reached their financial limits. Expenses from their American lands, especially those that they owned in Pennsylvania, had mounted steadily. In addition, the Dutch directors were being heavily taxed at home because of Napoleon's ambitions, and any profits in America were being drained off rapidly to Holland. The Company directors, therefore, informed Agent-General Busti that the purchase had to become self-sufficient. Fortunately, it was at this time that the county reduced taxes. In 1803, the Company had paid $4,548.64 in taxes; the next year, the total dropped to $3,399.10. The taxation in mills for each town in Genesee County revealed that in Batavia, where the Company lands lay, the tax rate was not so high as in the other three towns.

Ellicott's satisfaction over the tax rate suddenly changed to anger when the tax levy increased sharply in 1805. In that year, the taxes almost doubled as the tax rate rose from one mill to one mill and eighty-seven hundreds, and the total Company taxes climbed from $3,399.10 to $5,525.58. As a partial explanation of this tax jump, Ellicott told Busti that the creation of three additional towns on the pur-

chase in 1805 had increased the town expenditures, for the legislature
had divided the town of Batavia into the towns of Batavia, Chautauqua, Erie, and Willink. However the Resident-Agent indignantly refused to believe that the expenses of the new towns required "near
the amount that has been assessed." [10]

Angered by the rising tax rate, Joseph Ellicott fought the increase
with all the weapons at his command. He personally advised the board
of supervisors, the taxing officials of the county, against approving
such a tax increase, but the board ignored his counsel and acted "by
their own Discretion." [11] Although Ellicott, as county treasurer, had
previously exercised sufficient influence over the supervisors to keep
the tax rate low, the board now began to resent his unremitting pressure. Its members had come to believe that the Resident-Agent was
more concerned with profits for the Holland Land Company than with
the welfare of the settlers on the purchase. Thus, contrary to the county
treasurer's wishes, they boosted taxes.

Ellicott next challenged the board's legal right to nearly double
the taxes. To determine the board's authority, he consulted David
Ogden, the Company lawyer. Ogden's reply disappointed the Resident-Agent, for he informed Ellicott: "The Powers of the Board of
Supervisors in this State are great, and their Discretion almost unlimited." [12] Ellicott, in turn explained the situation to Busti: "In this
County, the several officers elected by the People appear not to be
governed by established Principles in the Discharge of their Duties,
but either their own erroneous Conceptions or by Information casually
or incorrectly obtained." [13]

Ellicott then tried another stratagem: he refused to pay his Company's taxes punctually. It had been the policy of the Genesee County
Board of Supervisors to accumulate bills throughout the year, and
then, at one meeting, to vote to pay all of its debts by passing a tax
levy large enough to cancel out these obligations. Previously, the
board could always count on the prompt payment of the Holland Land
Company to help it to settle its debts. But when Ellicott kept the Company from sending in its taxes on time, the board soon found itself
embarrassed by its inability to pay its own creditors. To encourage the
Company to pay its bills without delay, the board was forced to accede
to Ellicott's request that it carefully and regularly audit its accounts.
The Resident-Agent hoped that more efficient bookkeeping methods
would limit lavish and unwarranted expenditures and thus make
possible lower taxes. Ellicott considered that he had made a real gain
in winning this concession and proudly reported to Busti that in
the future, the Genesee County Board of Supervisors "will audit

the Accounts, make an estimate of Expenses, and Issue Orders on the Treasury in October the Time established by Law for that Purpose, instead of the Month of February as they have hitherto done." [14]

For a time, Ellicott's activities helped to keep taxes close to the 1805 figure. In 1807, for example, the Company paid $5,633.50, a small increase of $107.48 over its bill for 1805. This slight tax rise did not anger the Resident-Agent, for the additional money would benefit transportation facilities near his Company's property by bridge construction. The legislature had passed a law which ordered the counties of Ontario and Genesee to raise equally the sum of $4,000 or $2,000 for each county, for the building of a bridge across the Genesee River. To collect the additional $2,000 in revenue, Genesee County had boosted its taxes. Considering the fact that in 1806 the county had raised a total of $8,410.35 in taxes including those paid by the Company, while the following year the county collected $9,991.98, or an increase of $1,581.63, Ellicott felt no alarm at such a change. Had the legislature not ordered Genesee County to pay the $2,000 for the bridge, the total county taxes for 1807 would have decreased $419.37.

Despite all of Ellicott's efforts, the taxes rose after 1807 and increased steadily each year until 1812. The Holland Land Company paid $7,574.42 in taxes in 1808 and $8,717.21 the following year. In 1810, the Company remitted $9,314.74, and in 1811, this figure climbed to $12,142.44. After four years of steady increases, the Company taxes declined in 1812 to $11,975.15, a slight decrease of $169.29.

Unlike his attitude in 1805, when he had stormed at the board of supervisors for increasing taxes, Resident-Agent Ellicott resigned himself to these rising levies after 1808. He had hoped, of course, that the taxes would have decreased "in the same Ratio as the [Company] Lands were sold off"; [16] however, he soon recognized that he could no longer control the taxing policy of the county. In an effort to explain the situation to Agent-General Busti, he blamed the spiraling taxes on two major factors: first, the cost of government had increased with the creation of the Counties of Alleghany (1806), Niagara (1808), and Chautauqua (1811) and the organization of the newly formed towns in these counties; and second, the settlers, by their indifference, had permitted the boards to effect such tax increments. Ellicott also candidly admitted to Busti that he could not singlehandedly force the reduction of taxes. The Resident-Agent was convinced that the solution to the problem of taxation now lay in the hands of the settlers.

In addition to his explanation to Busti of the reasons for his in-

ability to reduce the levies of the Company, Ellicott tried to cheer up
the Agent-General by showing him where the Company was saving
money on taxes. He pointed out that while the settlers on the purchase
were obligated to meet the highway tax, the Holland Land Company
was free from this obligation. The highway tax compelled the residents
eligible for road service to work a minimum of two and a maximum
of thirty days in any one year, or to pay an equivalent in money; the
Holland Land Company, as a nonresident, was exempt from this tax.
An expert mathematician, Ellicott equated the highway tax for the year
1808 in dollars and concluded that the residents actually paid more
in taxes than did the Company.[17]

Fortunately, when the legislature designated Batavia as the county
seat of Genesee County, the long trek that Ellicott and the settlers
often had to make to Canandaigua was no longer necessary and the
problem was quickly solved. With Batavia the county seat, as well
as the location of the Resident-Agent's office, Ellicott could now
smoothly expedite Holland Land Company business that required the
official approval of county officials.

During all of his efforts to solve his problems, the Resident-Agent
had never lost sight of the basic purpose of these activities—to increase the sale of Company property. Ellicott had estimated that he
would dispose of 150,000 acres of land within the first two years that
he became Resident-Agent. The actual sales in 1801 and 1802, however, had totaled about 15,000 acres, or one-tenth of his calculations.
Partially because of his efforts, land sales grew a little in 1803 and
again in 1804. Although these increases still fell short of his goal,
Ellicott hoped that newly opened roads and internal improvements
would attract more purchases of land the following year. After four
lean business years, during which time he worked hard at road-building and alleviating tax pressure for the Holland Land Company, he
disposed of more land in 1805 than in any previous year. In 1806
business rose still more but land sales dropped off in 1807 and fell
even further the following year. The decrease in the 1808 business
Ellicott blamed on the Embargo Act, which was one of the results
of the commercial restrictions which England and France had established during the Napoleonic war. The sales slump ended, however, in
1809, when the American embargo was lifted, and business exceeded
that of any previous year. The next year, the sale of Holland Land
Company property outstripped even Ellicott's ambitious expectations
and he disposed of 300,000 acres of land, which was "more than double
that of any former Year."[18] Considering that he had sold less than

500,000 acres in the previous nine years combined, the total acreage that the settlers bought in small lots in 1810 was quite impressive. Delighted with the results, Ellicott attributed the great business upswing to the improved roads, the larger number of settlers, and the increasing purchasing power of the residents. Although land sales decreased in 1811, Ellicott confidently increased the land prices. In 1812, the income from land sales dropped below the previous year, a situation which Ellicott blamed on the war.

While the land sales increased from 1801 to 1812, the profits from the Company property in western New York can not be precisely determined. In the first few years, Ellicott remitted small sums of money to the Company, and after 1805 these amounts increased. In that year, however, the Dutch owners combined the finances of all the Company properties in New York and Pennsylvania to simplify the administration of its lands; this move ended the separate accountings of the various land holdings of the Company. As a result, Ellicott's finances were merged with those of other Company properties and were not listed as independent gains.

Notwithstanding the difficulty of estimating the profit and loss ratio of the Holland Land Company, it is clear that Joseph Ellicott had taken positive action during this period to meet the problems which hampered land sales. He had encouraged new counties and towns to build highways and bridges. By constructing roads himself and by exceeding his originally modest highway program, he had also set an example for local government to emulate. Furthermore, he had persuaded the board of supervisors to audit its finances efficiently and to allot some of its funds to internal improvements on the purchase. And, he no longer needed to make the long and inconvenient trip to Canandaigua for county business; Batavia was now the county seat of the Genesee area.

These were achievements which Ellicott felt contributed greatly to the increase of land sales and to the influx of additional residents. The settlers, however, came from a variety of places and brought with them customs and traditions that could easily create friction on the purchase. The increasing number of people living west of the Genesee created a new challenge for Joseph Ellicott—how to maintain his political position in western New York by successfully meeting the problems of an expanding population.

VI. Problems of an Expanding Population

During Ellicott's score of years service as Resident-Agent of the Holland Land Company, the population of the nation continued its phenomenal increase. The country's population nearly doubled, but the state and city of New York exceeded the national growth. Between 1800 and 1820, the state vaulted from third position to first, while New York City jumped from second place to first.

The rise of New York to the position of the nation's leading city came about through an alliance of nature's handicraft and man's industry. New York's port had many advantages. An ocean vessel, approaching New York, passed through an entrance some six miles wide. The ship then continued two miles by way of The Narrows, which sheltered the great port and kept it ice free; the last recorded freeze had occurred during the winter of 1779–80. The boat now anchored at a harbor that was navigable, deep, and 650 miles long. From New York, there was a serviceable water route to western markets by way of the Hudson and the Mohawk.

Capitalizing on their beautiful harbor, energetic New Yorkers introduced two features in 1817 that strengthened the city's leadership. In the first one, the state legislature passed a bill which ordered the auctioneers to accept the highest bids offered. Previously, the common practice was to offer goods at auction, but to withdraw them if the bids were unsatisfactory. Passed the same day as one that created the Erie Canal, this law helped make New York a favorite for buyers and sellers from all over the country. The second innovation was the announcement on October 24 of the first regular ocean liners that would sail on schedule to Liverpool. True to its promise, the Black Ball Line went into operation during the first week of 1818, and thereafter its ships ran on a set schedule from America to Europe. Heretofore, ocean travel had depended on the weather, the caprice of the captain, and the size of the load; now merchants could be assured of regular sailings. The trustworthy service attracted shippers, increased the city's trade, and helped keep New York the foremost urban center in the nation.

Dependable auctions and scheduled sailings attracted not only

94

businessmen and goods, but also immigrants. The population rose sharply in New York City, spilling over into the rest of the state. The census figures of 1800, 1810, and 1820 disclosed that, while the established cities in the East had sizable population increases, certain areas west of Albany showed marked gains, too.

Where the people built their homes in upstate New York was determined largely by geography. The Hudson Valley, for example, was naturally the first region to be settled. In the early economic development of the state, the cities below Albany were important. Settled in the seventeenth and eighteenth centuries, Newburgh, Pough-keepsie, Kingston, and Hudson tended to reach a population plateau by 1820, but resumed their growth a decade later. Between 1800 and 1820, Albany was second only to New York in population, trade, and wealth. In 1800, Albany's population was 5,289, then doubled to 10,762, and increased more slowly to 12,630 by 1820. To John Melish, the alert Scotch textile manufacturer who in 1811 was making his second trip to the United States, Albany was a progressive city. Melish noted that Albany had three banks, a city library, ten churches, and a the-ater. But Melish's keen eyes saw, too, the city's uneven streets, some of which were "spacious," while others were "rather narrow and irregular." This traveler, likewise, recorded that Albany had about 1,300 houses, most of them built of brick and many of them "elegant." [1]

Geography, too, influenced the settlements west of Albany. The Mohawk Valley, for those traveling from New York City to the Great Lakes, was in a sense an extension of the Hudson Valley. After 1800, the towns along the Mohawk Valley grew considerably.

However, measuring the expansion of new communities by statistics alone can be misleading. Originally, the population of many of these cities-to-be had been counted as part of other townships. After the villages split off from townships and emerged wtih independent char-ters, the growth of the new communities over the previous census report often gave the impression of phenomenal increase. A good case in point was Utica. Located on the south side of the Mohawk River and a hundred miles west of Albany, Utica in 1787 had three log huts. No mention of Utica had appeared either in the federal census of 1800 or 1810, because at the time it was part of the town of Whitestown. In 1817, Utica broke away from Whitestown, and the federal census of 1820 credited Utica with 2,972 people. An analysis of Utica's growth, based solely on the census, showed a population rise from seemingly no people in 1810 to nearly 3,000 in 1820. In reality, Utica had 200 people in 1801, and when John Melish visited that village ten years later, the population had risen to 2,000. With this background, the census figure of 1820 for Utica makes more sense.

Whatever the census evaluation, Utica was ideally situated. Located on the Seneca Turnpike, it appealed to stagecoach drivers who made Utica a center of road travel. The boat lines on the Mohawk also did a flourishing business there. By 1811, Utica had four hundred houses, six taverns, fifteen stores, two breweries, and three printing offices. Within thirty years, the city had come a long way.

As travelers journeyed west of Utica, they found the population sparser. Fifty miles beyond Utica and near the center of the state was Syracuse. At first a part of the Town of Salina, Syracuse was incorporated as a village in 1825, was chartered as a city in 1846, and did not appear in the federal census until 1850. In its early history, much of Syracuse was a dense forest area that lay under water most of the year. Only after the land was drained did it progress. The rest of the Town of Salina, however, prospered, with salt-making its big business. The water wells were eight to twelve feet deep, supplied between fifteen and twenty thousand gallons a day, and contained 16 to 25 ounces of salt per gallon of water. But Syracuse did not flourish. As late as 1825, the year that the Erie Canal was completed, the population of Syracuse numbered only a few hundred.

Some eighty miles west of Syracuse lay Canandaigua, the springboard into western New York. Far ahead of Syracuse and well in the lead of Utica, Canandaigua, between 1800 and 1820, had the largest population of any community west of Schenectady. The number of residents in Canandaigua had doubled from 1,153 to 2,387 during the first decade and by 1820 had redoubled to 4,680. A beacon in the wilds of western New York, Canandaigua charmed nearly all visitors, including the peripatetic John Melish. In his dry methodical style, Melish recorded that in 1811, Canandaigua had about 120 "handsome" houses, most of them of wood and painted white. In the center square were an attractive brick courthouse, a jail, and "an elegant academy." [2] He also chronicled that Canandaigua had six stores, six taverns, two tanning yards, two distilleries, six doctors, and six lawyers. Business oriented, Melish noted that land which had cost one dollar an acre twenty years ago now sold in some places for fifty times that sum.

While Canandaigua was flourishing, the neglected site of Rochester reposed some thirty miles to the northwest. In 1809, the Rochester site was pictured by a state legislator as "a Godforsaken place inhabited by muskrats, visited only by straggling trappers, through which neither man nor beast could gallop without fear of starvation or ague." [3] Astride both banks of the Genesee River, this site was isolated by thick forests and could be reached only by poor roads or perilous waterways. By 1812, Colonel Nathaniel Rochester had staked out the city that would bear his name. Two broad avenues intersected at right angles with quarter-lots offered for $50 each, and additional streets were located off the main thoroughfares.

After a lethargic start, Rochester won the battle to free itself from dependence on Canandaigua. The population of Rochester rose to 331 by 1816 and in the next two years tripled to 1,049. Its growth now became abnormal. Incorporated in 1817, Rochester, by 1821, had four flour mills and seven sawmills. By 1827, the population soared to 7,660, seven times greater than in 1818. Canandaigua, with 5,000 residents in 1827, was outnumbered by Rochester. Meantime, Rochester gained political and economic emancipation. In 1821, after a five-year battle, Monroe County was created from Ontario and Genesee Counties. The new county seat of Monroe was located at Rochester, thus reducing Canandaigua's political influence. And, in 1824, the Bank of Rochester was established, lessening still further Canandaigua's economic authority over Rochester.

Fifteen miles southwest of Rochester was the burgeoning village of Batavia. Unlike Rochester, Batavia's growth was steady, not spectacular. When Joseph Ellicott moved his headquarters to Batavia in 1802, the population totaled 56. It rose to 230 in 1803 and then increased about 100 a year until 1807. By 1810, the Village of Batavia had over 1,100 inhabitants, while the Town of Batavia numbered 3,660. During the next ten years, the Town of Batavia had declined to 2,597, but the explanation for the decrease was simple, since in 1812, the Town of Batavia had been subdivided into four smaller towns. Batavia in 1820 exceeded Rochester in population but was outnumbered by Canandaigua.

Batavia's key resident was Joseph Ellicott, and the loveliest home in the village belonged to the Resident-Agent. Ellicott's mansion was started in 1802, the year that he moved there. The east or right wing was completed first, and for a time Ellicott's office was located there. After several additions, the mansion was finally finished in 1818.[4]

On the wall of the Holland Land Office Museum in Batavia hang a copy of the architect's drawings and an old photograph of the Ellicott home. These two items reveal that the mansion was stately, symmetrical, spacious, and carefully designed. Located on West Main Street, the house was a three-story structure with two balanced wings and six tall pillars. Apparently, the first floor had ten rooms, the second story was similar to the first, and the third floor was a finished attic with five rooms. The grounds were extensive, formal, and functional. To the rear of the house were a pasture and a barn, and sections allocated for "early vegetables," "winter vegetables," and "fruit orchards." These were surrounded by large flower gardens and a lengthy hedge. In front of the house were huge trees, and near the walk was a fence.

The Ellicott home was furnished in fine taste. The eight-foot high musical clock, built by Joseph's father and willed to him by his mother, stood in the hall and fascinated visitors. Mementos at the Holland Land Office Museum, used in the Ellicott home, included pewter dishes, Sheffield candlesticks, candelabra with crystal teardrop prisms, and English china in dark flowing blue with matching coffee pot, sugar, creamer, soup tureen, large platter, and oversized coffee cup. All told, the Ellicott mansion in Batavia was one of the most handsome in all of western New York.

Many tourists came to Batavia. One of the more caustic was Timothy Dwight, president of Yale College, energetic traveler, and forthright recorder. When Dwight visited Batavia in 1804, he criticized the climate, and in a vein reminiscent of William Bradford's classic description of the Plymouth colony, wrote: "So many persons were ill of the diseases common to this region, that those who remained well, were scarcely able to nurse the sick." Dwight found fault also with the waters which "had stagnated in the road, were very loathsome, both in their appearance and smell." But the Yale President castigated the Holland Land Company, drawing a bleak picture of the owners. "Too wealthy to feel any necessity of selling their land," noted Dwight, "and knowing that they will of course increase in values, they proposed, as I am informed, conditions of purchase, which are not very alluring." [5] Seven years after Dwight's visit, John Melish came to Batavia and interviewed Joseph Ellicott. Without editorial comment, Melish explained in elementary terms the Company policy in the sale of its land. He recorded, too, that in 1811 the village had about fifty houses, four taverns, four stores, and a gristmill. By withholding opinion, the well-traveled Melish was seemingly less enchanted with Batavia than he had been with Canandaigua.

Neither Batavia nor Canandaigua was destined to become the Queen City of western New York; that title would go to Buffalo. Located three hundred miles west of Albany, Buffalo was at the eastern extremity of Lake Erie on the Niagara River. One day, Buffalo would outdistance Albany, Utica, Syracuse, and Rochester and would become the largest city in upstate New York.

Before the land that was to become Buffalo could be sold, how-ever, Ellicott had to settle two issues. The first involved the need to get control over the area on the eastern end of Lake Erie directly bordering Buffalo Creek. By the Treaty of Big Tree in 1797, the Sen-eca nation had kept a little less than 200,000 acres for Indian reserva-tions. These acres were scattered over western New York, and the exact boundaries were to be worked out later. The treaty, however, had specified that one portion of the reservation was to be located on Buffalo Creek. To complicate the matter further, New York State owned the Mile Strip, a one-mile-wide piece of land east of the Niagara River from Lake Erie clear to Lake Ontario. Seneca ownership of Buf-falo Creek shut out the Holland Land Company from access to that harbor, while the Mile Strip excluded the Dutch proprietors from ad-mittance to the Niagara River. It was important for the Company to gain entry to the mouth of Buffalo Creek and also to acquire enough land surrounding the harbor to establish a village. The situation was apparent even to the French tourist, Le Comte de Colbert Maulevrier, who was visiting western New York in 1798. Mr. Ellicott felt, Mau-levrier recorded in his journal, "that the Holland Land Company could one day gain a great advantage from this situation," if the Indians did not "include this place in the territory they have re-served." [6]

Keenly aware of the importance of Buffalo Creek, the foresighted Ellicott fought skillfully to keep it out of the Seneca reservation. He approached the one man whose help was indispensable, Captain Wil-liam Johnston. An Indian trader and interpreter, Johnston had married a Seneca woman and settled near the mouth of Buffalo Creek. His sensible intelligence, high influence with the Indians, and marriage to a Seneca had brought him a gift of two square miles of land at the very mouth of Buffalo Creek. The Seneca donation included a large part of the area which today is Buffalo; it was the very land which Ellicott needed. Although Johnston's title to the land was questionable, the Indians could, if they were so inclined, insist that Buffalo Creek be definitely included in their reservation.

The crisis called for quiet diplomacy. With complete Company support, Ellicott and Johnston, in 1799, worked out a private agree-ment. Johnston promised to surrender his claim to the two square miles of land and to use his influence with the Senecas to have these two square miles and the Buffalo Creek kept out of the reservation. In return, the Dutch proprietors deeded to Johnston 685½ acres in other parts where the village of Buffalo was to be. After long negotiations and with the dexterous support of Johnston, Ellicott achieved his purpose.

Once the ownership of land around Buffalo Creek had been settled, Ellicott was ready to handle the second issue. The Dutch proprietors had refused to permit the lands in and around Buffalo to be surveyed. With an eye to the law of supply and demand, they had hoped to enhance the value of the lands around Buffalo Creek as the nearby settlements grew. After repeated urgings by both Ellicott and Agent-General Busti, the Dutch directors relented, and in the early winter of 1802–1803, granted permission. Under the general direction of Joseph Ellicott, the survey was started by his nephew William Peacock in 1803. However, the Resident-Agent finished the task personally the following year.

Ellicott's plan for laying out the streets of Buffalo was similar to the one that he and his brothers Andrew and Benjamin had followed in 1791 when doing the same for Washington, D.C. The streets radiated from Buffalo Creek like bars from a hub. When it came to selecting names for the streets, Ellicott tried to honor the Dutch proprietors and the two Agent-Generals. The avenues were called Willink, Van Staphorst, Schimmelpenninck, Vollenhoven, and Stadnitski in deference to the Dutch owners; and Busti and Cazenovia out of respect for the present Agent-General and his predecessor. Some other streets were given names after Indian tribes: Chippawa, Delaware, Huron, Mohawk, and Seneca. The Indian names and those of the Agent-Generals have been retained, but those associated with the Dutch owners and even the very title of New Amsterdam have been replaced.[7]

Once the survey was completed, Buffalo grew with controlled rapidity. In 1804, when Timothy Dwight visited the village, he counted "about twenty indifferent houses." Dwight, a dogmatic Yankee Puritan, reported that the inhabitants were "a casual collection of adventurers" who had retained "but little sense of Government or Religion."[8] By 1810, Buffalo's population was 1,508 and increased to 2,095 by 1820. The growth might well have been greater were it not for Ellicott's policy of reserving some of the better lots. This practice was defensible in terms of future public buildings and better structures, but it was carried to extreme. By 1820, much of the vacant land still available in Buffalo had been set aside for the Company, for Ellicott, and for his relatives. Despite Ellicott's policies, Buffalo had doubled its 1820 population to more than 5,000 by 1825 and then increased its numbers to over 8,000 by 1830. By that year, only Albany of all upstate cities had a greater population than Buffalo. The Queen City had arrived.

During Ellicott's twenty years as Resident-Agent, the population growth of western New York was remarkable. When he had started to sell land in 1800, he described the territory of the Holland Land Company as "one huge Forest and extended Wilderness." [9] Indeed, at the time, there was only one county (Ontario) for western New York, and even though it included considerable territory east of the Genesee, its total population was little more than 15,000. As the number of land sales grew, however, the area changed from a "wilderness" to one of many small communities developed by an ever increasing number of settlers. By 1820, more than 100,000 people lived in western New York. Moreover, the percentage of increase of the population of western New York between 1810 and 1820 had soared 365 percent, while that of all of New York had grown 43 percent. (See Tables I and II, Appendix.)

The expanding population in western New York created two major problems that involved Resident-Agent Ellicott and the Holland Land Company. The first was the suffrage limitations that made it difficult to obtain a sufficient number of qualified voters to organize Genesee County properly. The second was the unwieldiness of Genesee County which necessitated the additional division of the territory. Both were problems that demanded immediate action.

From 1800 to 1820, the population of western New York rocketed to such an extent that it made almost mandatory the widening of suffrage rights to the inhabitants. In 1807, 2,267 western New Yorkers could vote; seven years later, the total number of electors tripled; but by 1821, only 14,007 men out of a population that exceeded 100,000 in western New York met the suffrage requirements.

The population surpassed the number of electors because the state constitution had set up restrictions limiting suffrage. The conservative Constitution of 1777 had required such high property qualifications for voting that comparatively few men could meet the requirements. Furthermore, the same constitution had placed electors into two voting groups: the men who owned land worth a minimum of one hundred pounds could cast their ballots for all offices, while those in the second category, who possessed land valued at twenty to one hundred pounds or who rented tenements of annual value of forty shillings, could vote for all offices except those of governor, lieutenant-governor, and state senators. To keep a more accurate record of the changes in the status of the electors, the Constitution of 1777 had provided also for a census every seven years. In western New York, these legal restrictions permitted only one-third of the qualified voters to ballot for the highest and most significant offices. (See Table III, Appendix.)

In addition to the suffrage limitations established by the Constitution of 1777, state laws required that all state and local officials be freeholders. Positions such as assessors, town clerks, overseers of the poor, commissioners of highways, and jurors could not be held by nonvoters. A settler could become a freeholder only if he owned an estate and could prove such ownership by showing a deed. The policy of the Holland Land Company, however, resulted in the granting of few deeds, the transfer of complete ownership being withheld until the resident had paid for the land in full. Instead, the Company granted the purchaser an "Article of Agreement," which merely explained the terms of the sale; title to the land remained with the Company. The Dutch owners justified this policy on the grounds that a state law of 1798 prevented alien landowners, such as themselves, from repossessing the land once the title had passed to the settler—even if he could not pay his debts.[10] To protect itself from defaulters, the Company used the technique of withholding deeds.

Joseph Ellicott was anxious to have the newly formed Genesee County organized as efficiently as possible, and he realized that the limited suffrage resulting from the withholding of deeds prevented the county from having a wider choice of personnel to fill key offices. He therefore sought permission from Agent-General Paul Busti to modify the rigid policy of the Holland Land Company in the granting of deeds. Shortly after the legislature had created Genesee County, Ellicott explained the problem to Busti. He pointed out that there were "not more than 30 Freeholders in the whole County . . . [and this was] not a sufficient number to perform the Duties of the grand juries." Furthermore, unless Busti promptly authorized the creation of additional freeholders, Ellicott informed him: "We shall not be able to organize the County by the time the Courthouse is erected."[11] After seeking the advice of David A. Ogden, the Company's counsel, Busti finally permitted Ellicott to grant deeds to those purchasers who had paid for one-fourth of the land.

The shortage of freeholders in Genesee County continued however, for even one-quarter of their debt was too high for some settlers to meet; and Resident-Agent Ellicott still found it "extremely difficult to Transact legally the County concerns."[12] In 1804, he sought permission from Busti to liberalize further the transfer of deeds by reducing the requirements from 25 to 10 percent of the purchase price.

A specific criminal case had impelled him to ask for the change. At this time, the Genesee County court had to handle a serious trial of manslaughter. This "very important case" required a sufficient number of competent and unbiased jurors, and Ellicott was, therefore, forced to exceed his authority by conveying deeds to the non-freeholding jurors who were otherwise qualified to judge the trial.[13] Despite Ellicott's pleas that the granting of deeds be broadened, the conservative Busti insisted that the Resident-Agent should continue to collect 25 percent of the purchase price before he parted with any land titles.

Ellicott persisted, however, in asking Busti to reduce the restrictions for transferring legal ownership to the land. An act passed by the legislature in 1805 provided the Resident-Agent with unexpected help. According to this law, alien companies, such as the Holland Land Company, could now repossess their "real estate" from settlers who could not meet their debts—even if titles to the lands had been given to the latter.[14] This change was made possible by introducing a new mortgage system: the settlers could receive the deeds to the land in exchange for a mortgage; but if they did not meet their payments, title would automatically revert to the land company. Ellicott, who welcomed the opportunity to grant additional deeds and increase the number of freeholders, now saw no risk in conveying deeds in return for mortgages and told Busti: "This Law renders it perfectly safe to grant Deeds for Lands, the payment to be secured by Bonds & Mortgages—I therefore beg leave to suggest whether it would not in most cases be to the advantage of the Company to grant Deeds & take Mortgages in lieu of the present mode of giving Articles of Agreement."[15] Despite Ellicott's suggestion, however, Busti refused to change his position and to transfer deeds on a mortgage basis.

Still convinced that his own policy was the correct one, Joseph Ellicott tried again to persuade the Agent-General to reduce the qualifications necessary for the transfer of deeds and thus extend suffrage rights. He pointed out to Busti that suffrage "among Americans . . . [was] considered as one of the most dear and invaluable Privileges." The power to vote, continued Ellicott, gave the residents "a voice in the choice of those who . . . [were] to make the Laws & the Execution of those Laws . . . [and] no settlement in any part of the United States can be considered respectable unless the People possess all those Rights & Privileges."[16] In 1807, when Resident-Agent Ellicott presented these views, only one-fifth of the potential voters on the purchase, or exactly 2,267 residents, had the legal qualifications to vote.

Continuing his explanations to Busti on the need for liberalizing deed transfers, Ellicott ominously predicted that "Anarchy" would result if the residents were denied the right to vote. The Resident-Agent did not use this argument merely to frighten Busti, for Ellicott genuinely feared that unless the settlers obtained legal suffrage right "Anarchy . . . will be the effect in such Settlements." In the 1807 election, Ellicott's fears of anarchy were realized when the trouble-laden question of suffrage restrictions produced physical violence. The majority of the settlers on the purchase by 1807 had come from Vermont and had brought with them their strong Republican convictions. The constitution of that state had none of the property qualifications for suffrage that were required by New York. Accustomed to vote, they went to the polls as though their articles of agreement were deeds and they were entitled to the ballot. In an effort to reduce the number of Republican votes in Genesee County, the Federalists in this election decided to place qualified challengers at the voting places to see that only the legally qualified residents balloted.

Unaware of the Federalists' intentions, the Vermonters came to town to cast their ballots. Many of them had traveled as far as twenty miles over almost impassible roads to reach the voting headquarters. After refreshing themselves at the local taverns, they made their way to the polls to give "their Suffrages to a favorite Candidate." When the Federalist checkers challenged their right and demanded deeds as evidence of their status as freeholders, the Vermonters ignored the niceties of law and order and used their fists to express their point of view. "The Consequences," Ellicott later reported to Busti, "was that more quarreling and Blows passed which occasioned bloody Noses and black Eyes than has been done . . . ever since the Commencement of the Sales on the Company's Lands." [17]

Fearing that the hard feelings engendered by the 1807 fist fight would spread to the rest of the purchase, Ellicott pleaded with Busti to modify the present 25 percent cash requirement for the transfer of deeds. The Resident-Agent proposed that Busti should convey titles to settlers who had bought a minimum of 240 acres of land, had improved ten to fifteen of these acres, and who resided on the property with their families. Ellicott suggested two safeguards to protect the Company against loss: one, the deed should not cover the entire property, but should include that part which the resident had improved; two, the settler should give the Company a mortgage on the undeeded land toward which he had made partial payment. Ellicott believed that this plan should be put into effect at once, for he realized that while the Vermont settlers had directed their wrath at the Federalists in 1807, eventually they might vent their rage on the Holland Land Company. Paul Busti, who had lived through the excesses of the French Revolution and knew of the great expropriation of land that had followed in France, understood this kind of reasoning. The brawl between the Vermonters and the Federalists had frightened the prudent Agent-General, and he finally acceded to Ellicott's wishes.

Although Ellicott had at last persuaded Busti to alter the manner of granting deeds, an unexpected complication arose in putting the plan into effect. Most of the settlers had cleared lands which were located in the middle of their properties, and the leveled portions were frequently oddly shaped. As a result, Ellicott found it difficult to measure the cleared lands on which to grant deeds. Realizing the complexity of the problem, he decided not to concentrate on exact measurements of land, but granted deeds without giving too much attention to the accuracy of the number of acres of cleared land involved.

The more liberal plan of transferring titles of ownership aided Ellicott and the settlers. This new program furnished additional incentives to the residents to cooperate with the Company, and many of them paid their debts on the mortgages more punctually than on the articles of agreement. What is more, they worked harder to get a deed under these easier terms because they now saw the possibility of becoming freeholders. Ellicott was satisfied, too, because county affairs could be run more efficiently. By enlarging the electorate, he made the county more respectable, removed a source of trouble, and helped to postpone the uprising against the Company for another decade. His fight for broader suffrage also strengthened his position with the democratic-minded settlers and consolidated his leadership of the Republican party in western New York.

In addition to producing the difficulty of deeds and suffrage, the expanding population also pointed up a second problem—the need for more counties. The motives behind the specific demands for the division of Genesee County varied with the individuals who would profit from the new boundaries. Since 1802, this county had been the only one west of the Genesee, and the county seat was located at Batavia. With settlements springing up in various parts of the five-thousand-square-mile territory and with travel so difficult, additional counties and county seats closer to the settlers would expedite county business. Dividing Genesee County would favor some settlers over others because it would enhance the value of the land nearest to the new county seat. The legislators themselves realized that the longer they delayed the creation of the new counties, the greater would become the dissensions among the growing population. In 1806, under the pressure of a mounting number of petitions, the lawmakers took action.

Philip Church was one of those who, in 1806, sent his petition to the legislature for the division of Genesee County. A grandson of General Philip Schuyler and a nephew of Alexander Hamilton, Church was serving as sales supervisor for his father's 100,000-acre tract that bordered the southeastern boundary of the purchase. He wanted a new county because he believed that it would stimulate his lagging land sales. Church, therefore, sought the help of his influential relatives in creating a county south of Batavia and north of the Pennsylvania line that would include the Church tract. He suggested specifically that the legislature should locate the county seat at Angelica, the heart of his property. Church introduced his petition as quietly as possible, as if he feared to arouse opposition. Such caution was unnecessary, however, for when Ellicott learned of Church's plans through private channels, he did not oppose the creation of this county. On April 7, 1806, the legislature approved the Church petition creating the county of Alleghany, and designated Angelica as the temporary county seat.

James Wadsworth, who owned much of the land around Geneseo and had been a candidate for the office of Resident-Agent of the Holland Land Company, also submitted a petition to the legislature for the creation of a new county. Wadsworth proposed that the legislature should organize a county by taking "a slice off the Western Part of the County of Ontario & [another piece from the] Eastern Part of the County of Genesee." Thus Geneseo would be located almost in the middle of the new governmental unit, and the Genesee River would "run nearly through the Center of the County."[18] Ellicott opposed the Wadsworth plan because it would have increased the value of Wadsworth's holdings rather than those of the Holland Land Company. However, the Resident-Agent had nothing to fear because the legislature did not act on Wadsworth's petition in 1806.

Like Church and Wadsworth, Joseph Ellicott wanted the legislature to divide Genesee County and accordingly sponsored a petition to that effect. He realized that it was "becoming more and more urgent" to achieve his goal quickly if he was "to prevent the new County of Genesee from being dismembered and subdivided in an improper manner."[19] Agreeing completely with Ellicott, Agent-General Busti gave him only the most general instructions for boundary changes, suggesting that he "endeavour to effect at the ensuing session of the

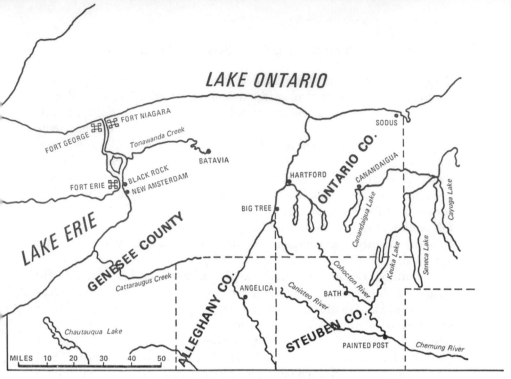

COUNTY ORGANIZATION — 1806

Legislature the Division of the County of Genesee into as many Counties as its geographical limits . . . [seemed] to point out as necessary." [20] Ellicott therefore petitioned the legislature in 1807 to divide Genesee County into four counties of almost equal size: Genesee, Niagara, Chautauqua, and Cattaraugus. Inasmuch as the boundaries of the proposed counties of Niagara, Chautauqua, and Cattaraugus covered "about three-fourths of the Company's whole Territory," Ellicott felt that such a division would improve further the administration and organization of Company property.[21]

Joseph Ellicott chose a poor year to hope for legislative action on his petition to divide Genesee County. Although the Clintonians and the followers of Livingston had worked hard to defeat Burr in the 1804 election, they had split shortly after their victory. DeWitt Clinton had precipitated this cleavage in 1805 when he had opposed a bank charter favored by the friends of Livingston and Governor Lewis. Joseph Ellicott had consistently sided with Clinton, and he paid the price for this loyalty when the Lewisites and Federalists combined to defeat his measure to divide Genesee County.

The Clintonians, however, made a clean sweep of the 1807 elections, when the voters chose Daniel Tompkins governor and gave the followers of Clinton control of the assembly. In addition, several candidates who were quite friendly to Ellicott also gained positions in the legislature. William Rumsey, for example, whom Ellicott had employed as a surveyor, won a seat in the assembly, and Alexander Rea was chosen to the senate. Pleased with the election results, Ellicott confided to Busti: "To be candid I am very happy with the Result, because I do know that the leading men of our Party are favourably disposed to the Holland Land Company." [22] The Resident-Agent now felt confident that when he resubmitted his petition for the division of Genesee County, the Clintonian-dominated legislature would give its approval.

Carefully, Ellicott prepared for the passage of his petition. He examined the wishes of the other parties interested in dividing Genesee County and made compromises. He bargained with Philip Church and agreed to support a proposal for an enlarged Alleghany County where the Church tract lay, if Church would swing behind the Ellicott petition. He consented to a modified plan for a county division that James Wadsworth desired and pledged his cooperation in its attainment in return for Wadsworth's help. Throughout all these maneuvers, however, the Resident-Agent never lost sight of his goal—to divide the county in a manner "most conducive to the Company's Interest." [23]

To make certain that his petition would receive favorable action in the legislature, Joseph Ellicott also introduced his friends in both houses on his plan of attack. He directed Senator Alexander Rea "to originate the Bill fo Dividing the County of Genesee in the Senate" for in that way he "would no Doubt continue to . . . [be named] as one of the Committee." "By that means," explained Ellicott, "the Business might be carried through without Delay." He assigned the task of guiding the bill through the assembly to his friend William Rumsey, who represented Genesee County. To coordinate the passage of his bill in both houses, Ellicott notified Rea: "Letters that I send to yourself . . . [should be] considered as directed to Col. Rumsey and yourself jointly." [24]

Ellicott was so concerned over the passage of his bill that he employed the services of David Thomas, a lobbyist. A strong Republican, Thomas had served four years in the state legislature and eight years in Congress. Shrewd and careful, he understood practical politics, knew many of the local political leaders, and had direct contact with DeWitt Clinton. Ellicott notified Rea of his plans to enlist the aid of Thomas and admitted that he would "compensate him for his Trouble

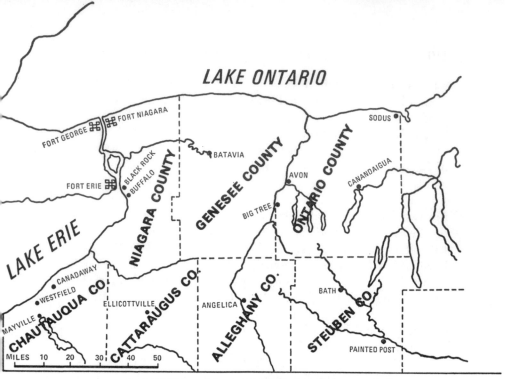

COUNTY ORGANIZATION — 1808

as far as it" concerned the "Business in which we were interested in the Issue." Moreover, explained Ellicott, if the bill ran into unexpected snags, Thomas would "be a proper character to amend or alter it as it ought to be done." [25]

Despite all of Ellicott's careful preparations, an unexpected difficulty arose. In his compromise with Philip Church, Ellicott had agreed that the legislature should take two parcels of land from Steuben County, east of the Genesee River, and add them to Alleghany County. Robert Troup, agent for the Pulteney Estate which adjoined the Holland Land Company, complained that such a move to enlarge Alleghany County would hurt the Pulteney interests and he opposed it. Ellicott needed Troup as an ally; yet, if he refused to support the addition to Alleghany County, he would lose the equally valuable support of Philip Church. Ellicott therefore found himself being pressured by two conflicting points of view.

Upset at Troup's opposition, Senator Rea suggested that Ellicott should abandon Church and accede to the wishes of the Pulteney agent. Rea maintained that Troup had more political influence than Church and that the loss of the latter's support would not be too serious. The Senator, however, respectfully awaited further orders from Ellicott, assuring the Resident-Agent that he could "delay any proceedings for some time from any party." [26]

Replying to Rea, Ellicott gave him and Rumsey further instructions. He told them that they were to continue to support the division of Genesee into four counties, and that he had no intention of reneging on his promises to Church. Recognizing, however, that without Troup's support it might be difficult to push through the bill, he suggested to the two legislators that they delay the fight for its passage until the time was more propitious. So many details needed to be ironed out, Ellicott explained, "between all Parties interested in the Event . . . [that] it had better be postponed to the next session of the Legislature, at which Time we shall be more generally prepared for such a measure." Along with these instructions to Rea and Rumsey, Ellicott optimistically enclosed a list of nominations for officers of Niagara County, so that it would be available when the legislature approved the partition of Genesee County.[27]

Shortly afterwards, Rea again tried to persuade Ellicott to forsake Church and his plan for enlarging Alleghany County, because he would alienate Troup by such a stand. He pointed out to the Resident-Agent that Troup had strong allies. George Hornell, for example, a Federalist representative in the legislature from Troup's district, supported the Pulteney agent. And Henry Townsend, Republican friend of DeWitt Clinton and a relative of the veteran State Senator John Taylor, warmly defended Troup and the existing boundaries of Steuben County. Even though Ellicott was "apprehensive" that his bill would not pass, he again ignored Rea's suggestion, stating that unless the legislature passed the bill in its present form, "it would be much better off that the General Arrangement had never been thought of." [28]

Ellicott's loyalty to Church and his firm advocacy of the passage of the bill finally brought him the reward that he sought, for on March 11, 1808, the legislature passed an act that completely incorporated his petition. The lawmakers divided Genesee County into the four counties of Genesee, Cattaraugus, Niagara, and Chautauqua and chose Buffalo and Mayville as the county seats for the latter two counties. The legislature directed the Counties of Cattaraugus and Chautauqua to act in conjunction with Niagara until each one had five hundred taxable inhabitants. The act of 1808 also enlarged Alleghany County and made Angelica its permanent county seat.

After the legislature divided Genesee County, the minor matter of fixing the sites of the courthouses and jails in the counties of Cattaraugus and Chautauqua had to be handled. For this task, Governor Tompkins appointed commissioners whom he told Ellicott were "recommended by Genl. Rea and Colonel Rumsey before they left Albany & I believe [were] the same you recommended." [29] After Tompkins had made the appointments, Ellicott informed Asa Ransom: "I took the liberty to mention yourself, Isaac Sutherland, and Jonas Williams for those Commissioners to the Governor, who has forwarded your Commission to me to be presented to you." [30] Dutifully, the commissioners proceeded to select the sites that Ellicott wanted.

Between 1805 and 1812, Joseph Ellicott had thus successfully handled his two major problems that had stemmed from the expanding population in western New York. He had increased the number of people who could legally vote by convincing Agent-General Busti to liberalize the Company policy of granting deeds. And he had facilitated the administration of Company land by convincing the legislature to adopt his plan for the division of Genesee County into four counties.

He had achieved his objectives by careful planning, political insight, and a willingness to persist in his demands. He had compromised when such action would not violate his basic principles; and he had remained firm on points that he had considered to be vital to his interests. He had demonstrated, in brief, that he possessed the ability and purpose necessary to maintain his effectiveness as a political leader in western New York. It was fortunate, indeed, that he had been able to settle the many problems that so far faced him in his position as Resident-Agent of the Holland Land Company—for the War of 1812 was about to break out and he would have to concentrate all of his strength to meet this new test.

VII. The War of 1812

By 1808, Joseph Ellicott could look with satisfaction at his accomplishments as Resident-Agent of the Holland Land Company. Largely through his efforts, the state legislature had divided the counties in western New York in a way that was favorable to his Company; Agent-General Busti had liberalized the granting of deeds so that more settlers could vote; a road-building program had been progressing without excessive expense; and Company taxes had not risen unreasonably. Moreover, Republican candidates who were friendly to Ellicott were being elected to the legislature, and the Holland Land Company's business had increased. The future indeed looked bright when suddenly, frightened by the threat of war with England, Congress passed the Embargo Act which produced new difficulties.

The Embargo Act came about after a score of frustrating years. A pawn in the drawn-out chess war between England and France, the United States desired isolation and independence. While Britain tightened its grip on the high seas, Napoleon extended his mastery over the European continent. When the struggle between the English shark and the French tiger became stalemated, both nations resorted to the more indirect warfare of blockade. Meantime, large numbers of British sailors had deserted to serve especially on American ships where salaries and treatment were better. The acute shortage of sailors imperiled Britain's control of the seas. England's warships now resorted increasingly to their old custom, dating back to 1793, of stopping American merchant vessels and removing any man whom they judged to be British.

The impressment of sailors was a long-festering irritant that came to a boil in 1807. On June 22 of that year, the British frigate *Leopard* subjected the United States naval vessel *Chesapeake* to a ten-minute bombardment and removed four sailors who happened to be escapees from the Royal Navy. The English, however, were flagrantly at fault and unwisely delayed reparations. In the United States, Americans were infuriated at the *Chesapeake* incident and demanded strong action. Resisting the national sentiment for war, President Jefferson adopted, instead, a plan of economic coercion. In December, 1807, he recommended and Congress approved the Embargo Act.

A bold experiment in foreign diplomacy, the Embargo Act was a drastic device. It forbade "all ships and vessels" within the "jurisdiction of the United States" from traveling "to any foreign port or place."[1] Special bonds were required for vessels engaged in coastal trade. The act virtually banned any trade between the United States and other nations. Jefferson was convinced that England and France needed American food so badly that a United States embargo of these supplies would compel the European nations to end their hostilities or respect American neutral rights.

To force such concessions from Europe required the fullest cooperation from the American people, and here Jefferson was disappointed. Opposition to the embargo ran deep, for the economic distress was genuine. The embargo brought the expected sharp drop in export and imports, but trade with Europe was not fully ended. American ships ran the blockade, because the high profits encouraged taking great risks, and the British Royal Navy willingly connived with the American blockade runners to defy the law.

The Embargo Act created two serious problems for Joseph Ellicott. The first was the drop in land sales that necessitated some action to redress this financial loss. The second was the threat to the political power of the Republican party in western New York caused by the opposition of many settlers to its embargo policy. Both problems challenged Ellicott in his positions as Resident-Agent and as political leader of western New York.

Joseph Ellicott "never was a strong advocate of the Embargo Measure,"[2] but he consented to give it a fair trial. An ardent Republican, Ellicott had great faith in the leadership of President Jefferson and endorsed the latter's beliefs that the United States should remain at peace and should avoid becoming embroiled in the Napoleonic struggle. Resident-Agent Ellicott realized that a war in the United States would sharply curtail migration to western New York and would seriously reduce his land sales. Although Ellicott did not fully agree that commercial restrictions were the correct tactics to effect the strategy of maintaining peace, he strongly opposed both the Federalists who wanted war against France, and the War Hawks who urged an open break with England. In the absence of a better solution to the threat of war, Ellicott accepted the Embargo Act.

With passage of the Embargo Act, Ellicott's land sales decreased. Because of the trade restrictions, Ellicott explained to Agent-General

Busti, "money has become an Article rarely to be seen." Business was so bad, Ellicott continued, that "our receipts the past year, out of the large Amount due, have been little more than barely sufficient to defray the incidental Expenses of the Administration, and pay the Taxes assessed upon the Lands placed under my superintendence." In fact, the Resident-Agent believed that the embargo had affected "our Receipts of Cash" more powerfully "than War itself." [3]

Although the commercial restrictions in 1807 and 1808 had hurt his land sales, an unexpected trade with Montreal compensated for Ellicott's loss in business. Before 1807, the Montreal traders had imported flour, produce, and potash from the American coastal cities, particularly New York. The embargo had suddenly cut off this trade. In searching for these commodities elsewhere, the Montreal merchants found that the western New Yorkers could furnish much of which the Canadians had previously purchased from New York City. Boats were now built to navigate Lake Ontario and the St. Lawrence River, and soon a thriving business developed between Montreal and western New York. From the purchase came flour, pork, whiskey, pot and pearlash enroute to Montreal. The residents west of the Genesee discovered, Ellicott informed Busti, that this market was "far more convenient and much less expensive to transport Produce to than that of New York." [4] The settlers learned, too, that certain of their exports brought them higher prices in the Montreal market than they had hitherto received elsewhere. Ellicott continued to explain that "had it not been for the Embargo Measure it [Montreal market] would not have been discovered at so early a period, probably by many years."

The illegal trade between western New York and Canada disturbed Ellicott in some ways, but he accepted this violation of the law because it counterbalanced the great drop in his land sales. The settlers used some of the profits from their illegal trade with Montreal to reduce their debts to the Holland Land Company. The property-minded Resident-Agent feared that the flouting of the embargo would lead to anarchy and cited the case of an informer who was tarred, feathered, and flogged for revealing smuggled goods to an officer of the law. However, Ellicott acquiesced in the embargo violations as the price he had to pay to improve his business. Thus, the problem of the drop in land sales caused by the Embargo Act was not met by any specific action on Ellicott's part. Rather, the newly organized Montreal market, an unforseen development, provided the necessary solution.

With the repeal of the embargo in 1809, Ellicott's business rose. The Non-Importation Act had replaced the Embargo Act and permitted Americans to trade with all nations except England and France. The numerous violations of the Non-Importation Act made the enforcement of this law almost impossible. Commerce revived, more money circulated, and Ellicott's receipts increased. In the same year, the so-called Erskine agreement also helped Ellicott's land sales; this Anglo-American arrangement provided that Britain would exclude American ships from its Orders in Council if the United States would end commercial restrictions against England and would forbid its vessels from trading with France. Ellicott reported to Busti that this rumored treaty, which never went beyond the discussion stage, had "such an Effect that money became more plenty . . . [as] evinced by our Receipts the present season, being nearly double the Amount they were last season this Period."[5] In 1810, when the Macon Bill Number 2 permitted unrestricted international trade, Ellicott's receipts exceeded his fondest expectations.

In addition to affecting land sales in western New York, the embargo acts sharpened a second problem—how to keep the Republican party in western New York in power. New York State was far from unanimous in its reactions to the Embargo Act. By conviction, the Federalists almost single-mindedly opposed the trade restrictions. The victory-starved Federalists also saw in the embargo a political issue which they hoped would bring them success at the polls. The shipping and mercantile interests suffered from the trade restrictions and denounced them. An English traveler who visited New York in 1808 described the paralyzing effects of the embargo on a harbor:

> The port indeed was full of shipping, but they were dismantled and laid up; their decks were cleared, their hatches fastened down, and scarcely a sailor was to be found on board. Not a box, bale, cask, barrel, or package was to be seen upon the wharves. Many of the counting-houses were shut up, or advertised to be let; and the few solitary merchants, clerks, porters, and laborers that were to be seen were walking about with their hands in their pockets. The coffee-houses were almost empty; the streets, near the water-side, were almost deserted; the grass had begun to grow upon the wharves.[6]

Moreover, the Republican leaders disagreed in their sentiment about the trade restrictions. At first, DeWitt Clinton was against the embargo, but Daniel Tompkins, in his first gubernatorial address to the legislature, clearly approved of the measure. As evidence of the depth of his conviction, Tompkins ordered out a detachment of militia to stop the illegal trade and later called on Jefferson to issue a proclamation that Oswego be placed in a state of active insurrection. The bulk of the Republican legislators supported Tompkins, and Clinton subsequently reversed his position and sustained the governor.

The western New Yorkers were as divided in their reactions to the Embargo Act of 1807 as the rest of the state. A great number of settlers felt friendly to England and opposed the commercial restrictions and possible war. Many of these residents had migrated from New England where the people sympathized with Great Britain. The drop in wheat prices hurt the settlers, but particularly upset those who could not easily get their produce to market. The settlers did not fear the Indians on their borders as did the frontiersmen in Ohio and further west, so this motive for opposing England, who was friendly to the western Indians, was slight. Then there were settlers who found that the Embargo Act benefited them because it opened a newly found market at Montreal. This group resented any efforts to curb its own illegal trade with Canada.

The political leaders of western New York reflected the great differences of opinion of the settlers over the Embargo Act. The Federalists on the purchase, like their party brethren elsewhere, almost unanimously opposed the act.. The Republicans, on the other hand, lacked such unanimity. Joseph Ellicott had acquiesced in the necessity of an embargo. Although he blamed the trade restrictions for the drop in land sales in 1808, he noted, too, that business increased the following year, that the Montreal market benefited western New York, and that the Company land sales around Lake Ontario had grown. While Ellicott fretted over the smuggling, he gained more from the embargo than he lost. For, as a result of their profits from illicit trading, the settlers were able to pay their debts to the Company, and this more than compensated for the drop in land sales.

Republican Peter B. Porter, who had reemerged from political darkness to become a congressman from the western congressional district, called loudly for war against Great Britain. The regular Republicans had punished him for supporting Burr in 1804 and had caused his political eclipse. Porter, however, regained his influence, for his friends in Ontario County had continued to support him. In 1806, the Ontario County Republicans had wanted Porter to run for Congress but "dared not nominate him without consulting . . . [Genesee] County." [7] Nothing came of their wishes, and two years later they repeated their suggestion to Ellicott. This time, Porter gained the Republican nomination, won the election, and was reelected in 1810.

Once in Congress, Porter became one of the War Hawks who sought an open break with England. A genuine and courageous patriot, Porter, like many Americans, felt bitter over England's conduct on the high seas and feared her close relationship with the Indians. Further-more, he wanted to add to his already sizeable land holdings and was not averse to expanding into Canada. He sought, too, a monopoly of the shipping trade for his company on the Great Lakes. He hoped to take over the business of the wealthy English firm of Robert Hamilton, which controlled the forwarding trade on the Canadian side. Porter and Ellicott thus held opposing views on the role of the United States in the Napoleonic war.

While in Congress, Porter's political influence grew steadily. A member of the Foreign Relations Committee, Porter received many requests for military appointments that ranged from lieutenant, cap-tain, major, to surgeon, and in this way, helped build up a following who were indebted to him.[8] In addition to granting favors to other people, Porter managed to advance his own interests. He introduced, for example, a resolution in Congress to move the customshouse from Buffalo to Black Rock. Porter owned much land around Black Rock, and also the Porter, Barton Company, which shipped goods on the Great Lakes, used that village as the base of its operations. Thus Peter Porter wanted to make Black Rock, not Buffalo, the key city in western New York. Congress dodged Porter's resolution and passed it along to Madison for a decision. Erastus Granger, who was collector of port at Buffalo, opposed Porter's proposal, but Madison compromised by or-dering that Black Rock have the port of entry from April 1 to Decem-ber 1, and Buffalo be used the rest of the year. Porter had really gained his objective because the Great Lakes had little traffic during the winter months.

The conflicting views of the people regarding the Embargo Act showed itself in the annual state elections east of the Genesee, but the western New Yorkers remained loyal to the Republicans. In the 1808 contest, that occurred four months after Congress had passed the trade restrictions, the Federalists gained seats in the assembly but the Re-publicans maintained their majority there. While the Federalists made inroads on their opponents east of the Genesee, the Republicans in western New York continued to return their candidates to office. Archibald Clarke and William Rumsey, both men friendly to Ellicott, won election to the assembly, and the Republicans also captured all four seats in the western senatorial district. Although Congress had rescinded the Embargo Act on March 1, 1809, it came too late to influence the April elections. In that year, the Federalists won control of the assembly for the first time in a decade. In western New York, however, Republicans Clarke and Rumsey were reelected to the assembly, and while Federalist candidates carried the western senatorial district, the Republican standard bearers ran ahead of their opponents in the counties of Genesee and Niagara.

The European war and the less stringent trade restrictions continued to sway the voters east of the Genesee, but the western New Yorkers remained loyal to the Republicans. The repeal of the Embargo Act aided the Republicans, and in the 1810 contest, they wrested control of the assembly from the Federalists and kept Governor Tompkins in office. On the purchase, Ellicott's friends won the assembly seats as Archibald Clarke of Niagara County and Chauncey Loomis from Genesee County emerged victorious. In the same year, Loomis married Rachel Evans, a niece of Ellicott, and thus drew closer to the Big Family. The voters also chose Republicans for the senatorial seats from the western district, and reelected Peter Porter to Congress. The election of 1811 went off quietly as the Republicans retained control of both houses of the legislature. The electors of western New York returned Clarke and Loomis to the assembly; the western senatorial district chose a Republican for the upper house.

The increased difficulties between England and the United States reflected themselves in the 1812 election. In that year, the Federalists won control of the assembly by a slight majority. The Republicans triumphed in western New York, however, as Jonas Williams and James Ganson won seats to the assembly and that party's candidates from the western senatorial district, including Archibald Clarke, were elected to the upper house. In that election, too, Buffalo was the only town in western New York that favored the Federalist candidates.

Thus while the voters of New York State fluctuated in their support of the Republicans between 1808 and the war, western New York, under the leadership of Joseph Ellicott, remained loyal to the party of Daniel Tompkins, DeWitt Clinton, and Thomas Jefferson. Even though the settlers on the purchase held various opinions of the Embargo Act, the "almost solid west" [9] gave their votes to Republican candidates. At the same time, the men who represented western New York in the legislature had the friendliest feelings for Resident-Agent Ellicott.

As the relations between the United States and England worsened, Ellicott became increasingly concerned over the defenses of western New York. He learned that the Governor of Canada had shipped rein-

forcements to the Niagara River area, yet the United States had made
no comparable effort to strengthen its undermanned Fort Niagara. The
contrast in the conduct of the two governments led Ellicott to raise the
question: "Is it not a little remarkable that while the British are
strengthening their Garrisons, that at this Time Fort Niagara on our
side of the River is garrisoned only by an Ensign and 8 men." [10] Uneasy at the inadequate protection of western New York with its vast
Company properties, he appealed to Governor Tompkins to improve
the defense west of the Genesee River. Tompkins shared Ellicott's concern, and in 1811 agreed to build a large arsenal at Batavia. The news
reduced Ellicott's fears and also delighted him. The erection and
maintenance of "the largest and most commodious Arsenal in the
Western District of this State," Ellicott explained to Busti, would result in greater spending and circulation of badly needed money.[11]

While Ellicott sought stronger defenses in Western New York to
prevent a conflict, Peter B. Porter and his fellow War Hawks in Congress wanted larger military forces to effect a war. Young men of great
ability, the War Hawks in Congress included Henry Clay and Richard
Johnson of Kentucky, Felix Grundy of Tennessee, and John C. Calhoun and Langdon Cheeves of South Carolina. Relentlessly, they
pressed for the annexation of Canada to the north and Florida to the
south. When Congress assembled in 1811, the War Hawks capitalized
on an opportunity to advance their ideas. The House of Representatives had chosen Clay as its speaker, and he proceeded to place War
Hawks on key committees. Porter, Calhoun, and Grundy, for example,
gained membership on the important Foreign Relations Committee
with Peter Porter as chairman. The War Hawks thus set the stage for
their desired war against England. Considering that he was serving
only his second term in Congress, Porter's rise had indeed been rapid.
Clay had facilitated his advance because of their common conviction
that hostilities against England were desirable.

Porter's position was further enhanced when Clay appointed him
chairman of a special committee of five. This group was to analyze
that part of Madison's annual message of November 5, 1811, related to
foreign affairs. On November 29, Porter's special committee submitted
a report to the Congress that hinted at war as a solution of America's
problems. The committee offered six resolutions that would strengthen
the armed forces by increasing the size of the regular army and by
arming merchant vessels.

In the congressional debate that followed this report, Porter and
Grundy spelled out the thoughts of this committee more clearly. Porter

favored a war against England and he said so openly: "It was the determination of the committee to recommend open and decided war—a war as vigorous and effective as the resources of the country and the relative situation of ourselves and our enemy would enable us to prosecute." The western New Yorker had also considered a way that the war would pay for itself. "By carrying on such a war at the public expense on land," continued Porter, "and by individual enterprise at sea, we should be able in a short time to remunerate ourselves ten-fold for all the spoliations she [England] had committed on our commerce."[12] Felix Grundy of Tennessee, who belonged to the same committee as Porter, admitted candidly that the War Hawks wanted a war with England primarily to conquer Canada and the Floridas.

In addition to the land rewards of Canada for the Northwest and the Floridas for the South, the War Hawks sought to goad the people into war by exploiting America's fears of the Indians and anger at the British impressment of its seamen. The inspired leadership of Tecumseh had united many of the Indian tribes and threatened to obstruct the white man's steady advance westward. The War Hawks contended that England supplied arms to Tecumseh's confederacy so that the Indians could restrict American expansion and also threaten the existing frontier settlements. In the South, hostile Seminole Indians, along with pirates and runaway Negroes, had infested the Spanish Floridas and had used that area as a retreat after their raids on the settlers to the north. The War Hawks accused England of allying herself with the Indians and denounced her for clinging to her practice of stopping and searching American ships and impressing their seamen. Insisting that only a war against Britain would solve all of these problems, they urged Congress to start hostilities at once, because the European war was already occupying the full efforts of both England and France.

The War Hawks timed their demands for war perfectly, for the American people had become increasingly impatient with the Jeffersonian methods to keep the United States neutral. Congress had passed and repealed the Embargo Act and had then done the same with the Non-Intercourse Act. Still feeling that the belligerent powers needed America's aid to win the war, Congress adopted the Macon Bill Number 2 in 1810. This law provided that the United States would cease trading with England if France repealed her decrees against American trade; or, if England rescinded her Orders in Council against American commerce, the United States would stop trading with France. Napoleon embarrassed Congress and the American people when he maneuvered the Macon Bill Number 2 to the benefit of France. The War

Hawks thus argued that the Jeffersonian ideas to use American trade as a weapon to maintain peace had failed.

Porter and his friends continued their unremitting efforts to bring the United States into war against Great Britain. In January, 1812, as a result of War Hawk efforts, Congress created an army of twenty-five thousand "to defend" the United States.[13] Porter, in April of the same year, introduced a bill in Congress that levied an embargo on British goods for sixty days, but the legislators defeated this measure. Finally, on June 3, John C. Calhoun, as a pro-war spokesman of the Foreign Relations Committee, recommended an immediate declaration of war against England. Both houses of Congress discussed the war motion in secret session. To the great satisfaction of the War Hawks, Congress declared on June 18, 1812, that a state of hostilities existed with England. Pleased with the war declaration, Peter Porter promptly resigned his office as congressman to join the actual fighting in western New York and to sell supplies to the army.

Joseph Ellicott had not believed that war would come and had opposed any suggestions for such a policy until its very declaration. Three months before Congress took the momentous step of June 18, 1812, Ellicott had firmly insisted: "I cannot believe that War will take place."[14] Furthermore, the Resident-Agent chided those people who warned against England and the Indians without sound evidence. Less than a month before the June 18 declaration, he confidently told Busti: "I do not feel the least alarmed on Account of any Scouting party from Canada, or any Irruption from that Province." Moreover, Ellicott did not consider his "situation so exposed as to place us in harms way," for he pointed out to Busti, "our vaults . . . [are] nearly as well guarded as those of the Bank of Utica."[15] Despite his opposition to war, Ellicott thought that a brief one could benefit the American people by broadening their knowledge of military science. However, he did not view tangling with Great Britain as an ideal learning situation.

While Ellicott opposed the War Hawks' desire for an open conflict with England, he had not applied pressure on Congressman Porter to alter his views. The Resident-Agent simply did not believe that Congress would approve such a risk-laden measure as a war against the mightiest maritime power in the world. Ellicott had therefore continued to concentrate his efforts on the state and local levels of government and had not interfered with Porter's conduct in federal matters.

The war brought two important problems to Ellicott. The first was how to win the war as quickly as possible so that people could feel secure in buying land and settling on the purchase. The second was how to keep the Republican party in control of western New York's politics. These two problems threatened Ellicott's position even more than the embargo had done.

The news of the June declaration caused great confusion and terror among the settlers on the purchase, and, uncertain of their future, the residents suspended their customary activities. They awaited an immediate invasion from Canada and also dreaded that the Seneca Indians in western New York might join Tecumseh's confederacy and the British. The Canadians, who feared an attack from the United States, did not make the prompt assault on the Niagara frontier that the western New Yorkers had expected. And the Senecas did not take sides. Erastus Granger, as superintendent of Indian affairs, had been working to keep the Indians neutral. Three weeks before the war started, Granger had met with Indian representatives of the Six Nations and had urged them to "take no part in the quarrels of the white people." Red Jacket, a prominent Seneca chief and a talented orator, counseled his brethren to accept Granger's advice, and "in the event of war between the white people, to sit still on their seats and take no part on either side." [16] The Indians in western New York followed Red Jacket's leadership. In fact, when the war came, they declared that the Mohawks, who lived in Canada, were no longer members of the Six Nations. The Senecas remained neutral until 1813 when several hundred of their warriors joined the American forces.

Joseph Ellicott acted to alleviate the fears of the settlers living on the purchase. Shortly after Congress declared war, he issued an appeal to the inhabitants of Alleghany County, assuring them that "There was not the smallest Danger to be apprehended from any Enemy whatever." Ellicott told the residents that he did not believe "any marauding parties will leave Canada & make Incursions on the United States side of the Lakes or Niagara River." Moreover, he prophesied optimistically, "the Number of Men we shall have on the Niagara in a few Days from this Period will not only be sufficient to afford all our Settlements the most complete Protection, but if Orders should be given, to be in a Situation to invade Canada." Although Ellicott had opposed the War Hawks' objective of taking Canada before the June declaration, he now predicted, "that in 8 Weeks or three months that that Part of the British Empire will be annexed to the United States." [17]

Despite Ellicott's assurances, shortly after the war started, a strange migratory process began on the purchase. "It was really surprising," Ellicott described to Busti, "to see Droves of Families passing through

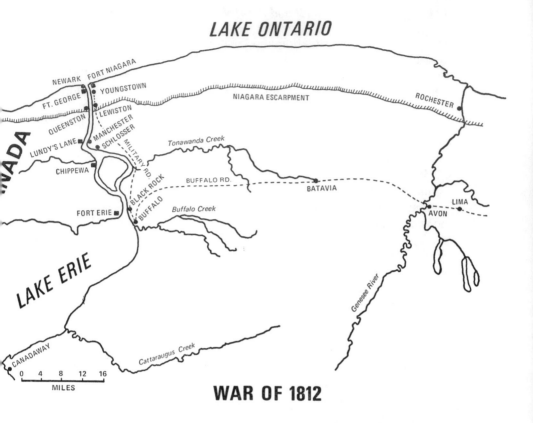

WAR OF 1812

this Village [Batavia] to the Eastward & at the same time nearly as many passing through this place to the Westward for establishing Settlements in Niagara, Chautauqua County & New Connecticut." Moreover, the Resident-Agent continued, "many of the Families that moved from their houses and Possessions, while they were seized with the first Panic of Fear have and are returning to their Farms." Ellicott thus concluded: "If the same Force should be kept along the Niagara River that is stationed there at present the People will return to their Dwellings, and pursue their various Avocations in like Manner as if War had not been proclaimed." [18] William Peacock, the subagent at Mayville, reported to Ellicott that many families had moved from that village to Buffalo, but for reasons other than a fear of the British. Peacock blamed the six week military despotism of John McMahan, the local commanding officer of the militia who, he explained, "had abused several of the militia in a shameful manner by beating them with his sword." [19]

When war did come, Ellicott, now fifty-one years old, quickly adjusted to the new situation and cooperated to the best of his ability. In addition to trying to calm the western New Yorkers by written appeals, he acted as liaison between Colonel Peter Porter and General Alexander Rea. Ellicott relayed a request, for example, from Porter to Rea that the latter should "order out immediately the last Draft that was made of the Militia." On his own authority, Ellicott added: "If you have not Orders to call out these Men you may proceed in that Business; because you will undoubtedly have in a few days." [20]

Ellicott also concerned himself with the appointment of the new commander of the Niagara frontier and consulted Peter Porter on this matter. The Resident-Agent wanted a strong leader assigned to that position, but Porter replied that no such appointment had yet been made. Strangely, Henry Dearborn, the senior major-general of the army, had failed to appoint a commanding officer of the forces in western New York. Governor Tompkins had selected General Stephen Van Rensselaer as commander-in-chief of the militia, and Dearborn finally got around to requesting the patroon in August to assume command of the Niagara frontier. Not pleased with the appointment, Ellicott shrewdly evaluated Van Rensselaer as a kindly man of limited ability who depended on guidance from other people. "I take him to be a good easy sort of man," he explained to Busti, "pretty much under the Guidance of others, without giving himself the Trouble to do the acting or thinking Part appertaining to such a Station as that of a commanding General; an amiable man in private Life, a station where he would always be highly respected if he had the fortitude to stand aloof from the homage paid to office." [21]

Although Joseph Ellicott did his best to help the war efforts, he was impatient and critical of the Madison administration and of the commanding officer, General Van Rensselaer. One month after the June declaration of war, the Resident-Agent complained to Busti of "the slow and tardy steps" of the administration and argued: "Had our Executive pursued War with Energy all Upper Canada [Ontario] might have been annexed to the United States in two weeks." He began to doubt whether Madison had "any serious Intention of annexing the Colonies [Canada] to the United States." [22] Ellicott ardently wished "that the Canadas were subdued," because, he later explained to Busti, it "would give us Peace at least in this Quarter, and rid our Minds of that Anxiety and Suspense that under present Circumstances we are burdened." He censured General Stephen Van Rensselaer for ordering out all men eligible for military duty in the northern part of Niagara County because that left few able-bodied males to harvest the fall grain. Furthermore, Ellicott insisted that Van Rensselaer could "have called out five Times the Number of Men" from the Counties of Ontario and Genesee because of their larger population.[23]

While no military action took place on the Niagara frontier immediately after the war started, General William Hull's invasion of Canada, begun July 12, 1812, led to disaster. During Hull's campaign, General Henry Dearborn, in command of all the American forces, and Sir George Prevost, the governor-general of Canada, agreed, in August, to an armistice on the Canadian frontier. Neither Hull nor his enemy learned of this compact before they had engaged each other in battle. General Isaac Brock, the able British commander, moved swiftly against the American trespassers, driving them back to the United States and forcing Hull to surrender Detroit.

When Madison ordered Dearborn to end the armistice and to open an offensive on the Niagara frontier, the situation in western New York would have discouraged all but the most dauntless of men. The well-meaning General Van Rensselaer had received orders from Dearborn to attack, but the patroon did not feel sanguine about success. Hull's defeat had alarmed the settlers on the purchase, and the news of the Indian massacre of the garrison at Fort Dearborn terrified them. In addition, the American troops lacked shoes, clamored for their overdue pay, suffered from sickness, and, as late as September, had not received the promised reinforcements in men or war material. Furthermore, when General Alexander Smyth finally arrived with the expected reinforcements, Van Rensselaer could not persuade him to cooperate. Smyth presented his own plan to cross into Canada above the Falls and refused to accept Van Rensselaer's already well-advanced strategy to invade below the Falls.

Despite the many handicaps, General Van Rensselaer obeyed Dearborn and proceeded with his own plan for the invasion of Canada and the seizure of Queenstown. The patroon selected the night of October 10, 1812, for the crossing, and on that date marched the men to their stations. No crossing was made because the boats lacked oars; the lieutenant in charge of the naval operations had caused this mishap by blunder or design. Two nights later, Van Rensselaer again assembled the troops for the invasion and this time a crossing was effected. A sentry, however, discovered the trespassers, sounded the alarm, and a British force assembled quickly to repel the Americans. Meantime, General Brock, who had moved his forces to Fort George after soundly beating Hull at Detroit, heard the exchange of shots at Queenstown, which was only a two-hour march away. Brock immediately assembled his men and hurried them to Queenstown. The Americans seized Queenstown Heights, and the British, in their first attack, failed to dislodge them. When Brock arrived with his forces, the second British attack literally pushed the Americans back into the river. The expected American reinforcements had not materialized, and the United States thus suffered its second humiliating defeat. The following day, Van Rensselaer asked to be relieved of his command,, and Dearborn gave Smyth the post that the patroon had held.

General Alexander Smyth tried his plan of attack, and failed ignominiously. He chose the night of November 27 for the invasion, issued a pompous address to the troops, and ordered that the crossing start. Suddenly, he recalled the already embarked troops because he felt that his plan would require a minimum of 3,000 men to succeed. Two days later, Smyth repeated the fiasco and the men were once more ordered out of the invasion crafts; without 3,000 troops, he refused to advance. Greatly angered, the troops got out of control, shot off their muskets, and directed much of their target practice at Smyth's tent. Peter Porter accused Smyth of "cowardice," and a harmless duel between the two men followed.[24] Greatly ridiculed, Smyth now requested a leave of absence which Dearborn quickly granted.

Bitter at the prolongation of the war, Joseph Ellicott blamed the poor generalship of Van Rensselaer and Smyth and the insubordination of the militia. Under Van Rensselaer, Ellicott explained, "the Army on this frontier . . . had more the Appearance of an armed Rabble than a military Band of heroes." Linking the patroon's conduct with politics, the Resident-Agent continued: "The loose Discipline in that Army and the great familiarity the General used both with private Soldiers and Citizens of every Grade induced myself and many others to believe that the General meant it more of an electioneering Campaign than that of actual hostilities, or an Intention to make the Conquest of the Canadas, and the result has proved the Correctness of our anticipated Opinions." Ellicott then laid his critical lash on Smyth, telling Busti: "General Smyth's Proclamations clearly evinced to my Mind that as a General he is a fool; and consequently unfit to command an Army." Refusing to censure Madison for appointing Smyth to that command, Ellicott added philosophically: "There is no knowing exactly what a Man is qualified by Nature to perform until he is tested by Experience."[25]

During the war, political elections continued to be held. After Van Rensselaer's defeat and prior to Smyth's ridiculous "invasion," the presidential election took place. Forced to choose between retaining James Madison or voting for their favorite son, DeWitt Clinton, the New York Republicans met in May and nominated the latter. Clinton accepted even though the regular national Republican caucus had already endorsed Madison. Joseph Ellicott did not deviate in his loyalty to Clinton, for he regarded the "Madisonian administration" as "truly a contemptible" one.[26] Under the able leadership of Martin Van Buren, the legislature chose presidential electors pledged to Clinton. The Federalists lacked a candidate from their party capable of defeating Madison so they supported DeWitt Clinton. In the final electoral tally, however, Madison gained 128 votes to 89 for his opponent. Although Clinton carried New York, New Jersey, Delaware, Maryland, and all the New England states except Vermont, he failed to capture a single electoral vote south of the Potomac.

In the first election for state and local offices since the war had started, western New York supported Republican candidates and played an almost decisive role in the gubernatorial results. In 1813, Daniel Tompkins defeated Stephen Van Rensselaer by some 3,600 votes, the smallest margin of his three terms. The western senatorial district gave the incumbent governor a plurality of nearly 3,300 votes and thus nearly decided the election. On the purchase, Van Rensselaer carried Buffalo and two towns in Chautauqua County where peace sentiment ran high, but the majority of the voters west of the Genesee favored Tompkins. Western New York also elected three Republican state senators from the western district to swell that party's majority in the upper house. Although the Federalists gained control of the assembly, the Republicans, led by Ellicott, reelected James Ganson and Jonas Williams from Genesee and Niagara Counties respectively. Thus, despite the war, the American military defeats on the Niagara frontier, and the political results in the rest of the state, Joseph Ellicott and the Republican party maintained their political dominance in western New York.

Buffalo's Cyrenus Chapin, the political leader of the Federalists, fought the war without support from his party. When the Federalists held a meeting in the fall of 1812 and violently condemned the war, Chapin strongly urged his party to assist the war measures but they refused. Militarily, he set them an example which they refused to follow as he fought the British on land and sea and organized a troop of mounted soldiers. Independently, he frequently led nuisance raids into Canada and annoyed the British a great deal. Chapin's colorful conduct during the war accentuated the differences within his party, and the Federalists in western New York grew weaker as the war advanced. The Federalists had supported DeWitt Clinton in the 1812 election, believing that he favored peace. Prior to the formal declaration of war, Clinton, like the Federalists, had opposed warfare against England. However, when war came, Clinton gave his full support to the side that favored the War of 1812.

In addition to political success, Joseph Ellicott was also able to report to Agent-General Busti that in the second year of war, 1813, prosperity had returned to western New York. In that year, the Company land sales increased and the Resident-Agent collected more money from the settlers on their debts. As early as February, Ellicott informed Paul Busti that the great influx of money in the past eight weeks had come from the sudden rise in the prices of wheat, rye, corn, oats, and hay. The war had brought many troops to western New York, and the government had paid cash for the supplies needed by these forces. The navy, too, had depots at Black Rock and Erie during the war, and these ports had stimulated trade a great deal. After Perry's naval victory on Lake Erie, land sales rose sharply.

Although the western New Yorkers prospered in 1813, the war on the Niagara frontier that year continued indecisively. American forces gained control of York (Toronto), the capital of upper Canada, in April, and before evacuating the village a month later, the United States troops got out of hand and burned the houses of the assembly. The United States captured Fort George in June, and one month later the British reciprocated by attacking Black Rock and destroying the barracks and a blockhouse there. At this time, Peter Porter, on his own authority, invited the Seneca Indians to join the United States in its war against Britain, and the Indians accepted. In September, Oliver Perry won a brilliant naval battle on Lake Erie to give the United States control of this important waterway. The British, however, continued to command Lake Ontario and thus balanced off their loss of Lake Erie. By November, 1813, nearly all of the British and American forces were concentrated around the St. Lawrence for the fighting there.

The economic prosperity of western New York had obscured for a time the growing military threat that culminated in the burning of Buffalo. To strengthen its forces around the St. Lawrence, the United States had withdrawn many troops from the Niagara frontier. General George McClure, who commanded Fort George, watched the number of his men dwindle to about 100 by December 10. On that date, not more than 225 regular soldiers guarded Fort Niagara, Black

Rock, and Buffalo and protected the inhabitants and military supplies in that area. When McClure learned of the approach of British troops against Fort George, he decided on December 10 to evacuate it. He then notified the residents of Newark that within two hours his men would burn the settlement. Newark, the capital of Ontario until 1796 and officially renamed Niagara two years later, had a population between five and six hundred, and the village lay about one mile north of Fort George. While the snow was falling and a wind was rising to a gale, the Americans burned eighty buildings and left some four hundred women and children homeless. In a letter to the Secretary of War, General McClure justified his action on the grounds that the enemy were "now completely shut out from any hopes or means of wintering in the vicinity of Fort George." [27] What makes the incineration and forced evacuation senseless is the fact that the General had left untouched barracks and tents for 1,500 men, and that only one of several magazines had been blown up.

Although Madison disavowed McClure's burning of Newark, the British repaid this wanton destruction. With the aid of Indians, the British proceeded to burn Youngstown, Lewiston, Manchester, Schlosser, and the surrounding farms. Fort Niagara, 900 yards from Newark, fell to the English on December 19 and remained in their possession to the end of the war. The British campaign of retribution reached a climax on December 30, 1813, when the invaders burned almost every building in Buffalo. Amos Hall, who had replaced McClure, gathered over 2,000 militia and Indians to oppose the British advance on Buffalo, but in vain. Many of the militia simply disappeared just before the battle started, and, after a few shots were exchanged, the rest of the American troops fled. Batavia became the rallying point where the remnants of the army retreated and where some of the refugees from the Niagara frontier halted. The Company office in Batavia was converted into a hospital for the American forces. The English thus avenged the burning of Newark.

The British invasion of western New York in the middle of winter caused great damage and severe hardship. Describing to Busti the panic and head-long flight of the settlers eastward, Ellicott reported· "The Alarm occasioned by the British and their Savages by the Descent they made upon our Shore, the Burning of every Building in the Village of Buffalo, and Massacre, not only of Men, but women and Children, filled the Inhabitants of the two Counties of Genesee & Niagara with terror, consternation, and dismay." Ellicott continued his narrative: "The Consequence has been that almost every family, who had the means of removing into this Country fled hither under the Impression that they would be more safe than to remain on the west side of Genesee River; as there was no force of any Description to prevent them from extending their predatory Warfare as far to the Eastward as they should see fit." The Resident-Agent tried to express his feelings of fear when he had fled from Batavia, admitting: "That same Terror I confess I felt to the Degree that I deemed it expedient to leave Batavia with our women and children and retreat to this Place [Lima] about 6 Miles East of Genesee River until the Alarm and Danger should be over." Ellicott planned to return to Batavia only after he had "learned that the Enemy has quitted our shore & that a force of drafted Militia . . . [was] stationed near the Niagara Frontier." [28]

In its petition to Albany in behalf of the refugees from the purchase, the Committee of Safety and Relief at Canandaigua described the extensive misery of these fugitives. "Niagara County and that part of Genesee which lies west of Batavia," the petition read, "are completely depopulated. All the settlements in a section of country forty miles square, and which contained more than twelve thousand souls, are effectually broken up." The petition elaborated: "Our roads are filled with people, many of whom have been reduced from a state of competency and good prospects to the last degree of want and sorrow. . . . The fugitives from Niagara County especially were dispersed under circumstances of so much terror that in some cases, mothers find themselves wandering with strange children, and children are seen accompanied by such as have no other sympathies with them than those of common sufferings." The residents of Canandaigua had worked hard to help the refugees and had "made large contributions for their relief in provisions, clothing, and money." [29] The task, however, exceeded the resources of that village, so the petition solicited the legislature to help.

Responding to this request, the legislature appropriated $50,000 toward the relief of those who had suffered from the British invasion of the counties of Niagara and Genesee. The act specified how the funds should be allocated: American citizens would get $40,000, the Tuscarora Indians $5,000, and the Canadians who had taken refuge in New York State the remaining $5,000. The legislature appointed Joseph Ellicott, William Wadsworth, and Graham Newell as commissioners and authorized them to distribute the $50,000. Anxious that the money be given away wisely and expeditiously, Ellicott promptly drew up careful plans for evaluating the war losses.

Shortly after the British burned Buffalo, Ellicott returned to Batavia and concerned himself with relief for those settlers who owed debts to the Company. At first, he suggested to Busti that the Holland Land Company lengthen the terms of the contracts and also suspend interest during the period that Ellicott had closed the Batavia office. After thinking through the complexities involved in executing these concessions, Ellicott recommended instead that the Company donate a sum of money outright as a simpler form of philanthropy. Thus, for the relief of the settlers on the purchase, the Company contributed $2,000 and Joseph Ellicott added $200 from his private purse.

During the third year of war, in 1814, the American army on the Niagara frontier succeeded in protecting western New York and also gained some victories before the war ended in December. General Jacob Brown took over the Niagara command in April and raised the morale of the army while General Winfield Scott drilled the men into a competent fighting unit. Peter Porter supplemented the regulars by raising a force of militia and Indians. Early in July, Brown's combined forces invaded Canada, won the battle of Chippewa, acquitted themselves well at the encounter of Lundy's Lane, and retired across the border in an orderly fashion. The British troops pursued Brown's army, attacked Fort Erie in August, but failed to capture it. His army weakened by the fighting, Brown asked General George Izard for help, and the latter, who outranked him, accepted the request and took command in September. After a weak sortie into Canada, Izard retreated into inactivity, his reputation tarnished. With Izard's failure, fighting ceased in western New York.

Following the war's progress closely, Joseph Ellicott believed that the British would reinvade western New York and try to seize the arsenal in Batavia. After the British attack on Lake Erie in August, he communicated his fears to General Izard, explaining: "It is my opinion that an enterprising party of the enemy of twenty-five or thirty men mounted on good horses by a coup de main might pass the Road from that Post [Fort Niagara] to this place in perfect Security, seize and take possession of the Arsenal before the people of the village would be apprised, and destroy the munitions of War and building." [30] To prevent such an attack, Ellicott offered to provide some Company land near the arsenal on which to build huts, if Izard would send more men to protect the arms stored there. Quickly accepting Ellicott's proposal, Izard promised: "In a few Days, I will send a Force which will be sufficient to protect the public stores and private property against the Depredations of the Enemy." [31]

Another year of fighting had also brought another state election, and the political results in 1814 pleased Ellicott and his Republican friends. The Federalists lost control of the assembly and had an even smaller minority in the senate. The pattern of Republican victories in western New York continued as Genesee and Niagara Counties elected Joseph McClure and Isaac Sutherland respectively to the assembly; both men were friends of Ellicott. The western senatorial district sent three Republicans to the upper house.

Resident-Agent Ellicott and the settlers in western New York were overjoyed when peace came because they had suffered a great deal in this war. The settlers west of the Genesee had endured as much, if not more, than any other group in the United States, for the land around Lake Ontario and Lake Erie had borne the brunt of the fighting. Money was scarce on the purchase in 1815, commerce had almost come to a standstill, and the settlement of new districts had practically ceased. Most of the residents were therefore in poorer condition than on the eve of the war.

It is difficult to gauge the effects of the Embargo Acts and the War of 1812 on the Holland Land Company in the Netherlands. One possible measure is to chart the stock quotations of the Company. The quarterly stock prices are listed in the Appendix of *The Holland Land Company*, a carefully researched book by Paul Evans, and the statistics used in these paragraphs are drawn from this source. In 1796, the stock had opened at a par of 100 and within one year fell some ten points. The decline accelerated so that the stock lost more than two-thirds of its value by 1800, closing at 28. The four-year fall was due in part to the collapse of the land market in the 1790's and also to the tardiness in getting a clear title from the Senecas, completing the Big Survey, and making actual cash sales.

From 1800 to 1807, the price rose slowly but steadily, reaching 38 and climbing to 41 by 1809. Meantime, Ellicott felt a sharp slump in land sales in 1807, when the embargo began, and this loss was somewhat offset by the subsequent illegal trade with Montreal. In 1809, the stock price took a steep drop, and by June 1810, it was 11–12, the lowest figure ever reached. One explanation is the Dutch fear that the United States would retaliate for the French seizure of American property. For Ellicott, though, the repeal of the Embargo Act in 1809 brought improved business. In 1811, the stock rebounded to 28 (there are no figures in 1812), fell back in 1813 to 20 where it stayed in 1814, and then spurted to 30 in 1815. The burning of Buffalo in December, 1813, caused a temporary dislocation, but then conditions improved, and Ellicott remitted mounting receipts by 1815. After 1815, the stock prices climbed steadily. If stock plotting is accepted, the Embargo Acts did not seriously affect the Company, for prices fell after the repeal. Nor did the war bring about any marked changes, for prices remained fairly constant, rallying in 1815. Basing the effects of the embargo and the war on stock prices alone, however, is not defensible because so many outside factors cause fluctuations in stock prices.

Despite the embargoes and the war, Joseph Ellicott had managed to maintain his position as Resident-Agent of the Holland Land Company and political leader of western New York. He had acquiesced in the embargo philosophy and then realistically accepted the illegal trade between western New York and Montreal when it brought prosperity to the settlers and to the Company. Although the embargo had at first hurt the residents on the purchase, they had remained loyal to the Republican party during the entire period of these commercial restrictions. Throughout the war, Ellicott had worked faithfully to bring the conflict to a speedy and successful close. Between 1808 and 1815, two other Republicans had increased their political influence. Erastus Granger, by keeping the Indians under control, had strengthened his position, but his authority centered mainly in the Buffalo area. Peter Porter's flamboyant role as a War Hawk in Congress and then as a military leader had made him better known throughout the United States, and by 1815, Albany and Washington saw vote-getting possibilities in his name. Porter, like Granger, posed no serious threat to Ellicott's political leadership west of the Genesee for the General's influence was not strong on the purchase.

The British had so ravaged the Niagara frontier that, at the close of the war, there was a serious decline in the morale of the western New Yorkers. Joseph Ellicott, however, remained optimistic about the future of that section of the state. He now turned his attention to the complex problem of banking. Bitterly controversial on the national level and a political football kicked about by the New York legislature, the issue of banking was to jeopardize seriously the position of Ellicott as Resident-Agent and as political leader.

VIII. The Bank of Niagara

When Joseph Ellicott had become Resident-Agent of the Holland Land Company in 1800, his task seemed easy to define and simple to delimit. He was to manage the Company lands in western New York, reside on the purchase, and make "regular and fair entries" of all sales.[1] In February of each year, he would submit a full report of land sold, money received, debts due, and lots still owned by the Company. For his services, he was to receive an annual salary of $1,500, a commission of 5 percent of all sales, and fringe benefits of free residence, an office, and two bonuses at his retirement. Over the years, some minor details had been added, but the agreement otherwise had remained the same.

Between 1800 and 1815, however, the peripheral aspects of his job had broadened considerably. During those years, Ellicott had been pushed into a number of tangential tasks. Road construction, higher taxes, wider suffrage, new counties and county seats, state and local politics, and the War of 1812—all of these had affected land sales and were, therefore, important to the Resident-Agent. Although these chores had not been included in his contract with the Company, he had been compelled to deal with them. Yet, it was his handling of these very problems that lifted Joseph Ellicott above the clerical level of recorder of sales, expenses, profits, and losses.

In the category of "related" tasks, there was another serious one that confronted Ellicott: the need for a bank in western New York. By 1816, the purchase, with a population approaching 100,000, had reached a level in its growth where some local controls over bank deposits and loans were essential. Until now, not a single community west of the Genesee had a bank. But banking, as Americans had learned from costly experience, was not a simple operation. It was an intricate business that called for confidence, integrity, good sense, and especially experience. In the 1780's, banking was a "novelty," wrote Thomas Willing, president of the Bank of North America, "a pathless wilderness, ground but little known to this side of the Atlantick."[2]

In contrast to America's inexperience, the Dutch had developed a high financial sophistication by a century of seasoning. As cited in the Introduction of this book, the Netherlands had fallen from their peak during the seventeenth century, but their banks still had sufficient stability and reserves to be recognized as late as 1796 as the Wall Street of western Europe. Dutch bankers had blended daring with caution. In the early years, they had favored taking risks, but as the years receded, circumspection outweighed speculation.

This conservative change reflected Holland's shifting position on the continent. During much of the eighteenth century, the Netherlands were in peril of being annexed by a powerful, expansion-minded neighbor, France. In self-protection, Holland reluctantly allied herself with France's enemy, England, and as a result became a British satellite. During the American Revolution, however, the Netherlands switched sides. Angered by the British seizure of Dutch ships on the high seas and encouraged by Russia to stand firm, the Netherlands embarked on the fourth Anglo-Dutch War (1780–84) and were beaten decisively.

But worse lay ahead. During the Napoleonic era, Holland experienced its first foreign occupation since the defeat of Spain in the seventeenth century. Between 1795 and 1810, the Netherlands became a dependency of France, then a Gallic province from 1810 to 1813. During the closing years of the Napoleonic period, she was at war against England who seized all the Dutch colonies. The period of Napoleon, then, was a catastrophe for the Dutch. The wars had broken her spirit, removed her colonial resources, and reduced her to hand-to-mouth poverty.

The nation that emerged from the Napoleonic wars with heightened international prestige and power was Great Britain. Coal, iron, and cotton had become more valuable than linen, spices, and herrings. The new machinery—for example, Watt's engine, the spinning jenny, and the power loom—profoundly restructured England from an agricultural society into the industrial workshop of the world. Her growing needs for food and raw materials, and her export of coal and manufacturing made England the largest trader in the world. With incomparable sea power and great wealth, commerce and industry elevated Great Britain into the richest nation in the world. By 1815, London had displaced Amsterdam as the Wall Street of western Europe.

For America, London had assumed this character somewhat earlier. Prior to the Revolution, the American colonies had been wholly dependent on the financial resources of England. It was during the American Revolution that banking in America had started. Because of the war, the new nation had been driven to create its own banking system. The Second Continental Congress granted a charter in 1781 to the Bank of North America. Proposed and supported by Robert Morris, the Bank of North America aided the war effort by purchasing supplies, paying the army, and loaning money to the shaky government. By modern standards, the Bank of North America was the first real bank in the United States, and for that matter in all North America. Located in Philadelphia, it prospered and expanded.

Rival cities noted the advantages of having a bank and followed the Philadelphia example. Led by Alexander Hamilton, the Bank of New York started business in 1784 and got a state charter in 1791. Less than one month after the Bank of New York had opened its doors, a group of Boston merchants organized the Massachusetts Bank. Some Baltimore businessmen, who had been trying for several years, finally received a charter from Maryland in 1790 and formed the Bank of Maryland. By 1790, eight years after the organization of the Bank of North America, the four leading cities of Philadelphia, New York, Boston, and Baltimore each had a bank. Of these four banks, the Bank of New York alone is still in business.

While Alexander Hamilton supported banks chartered by individual states, he was equally concerned with some financial arrangement to serve the needs of the federal government. It was Hamilton who had drawn up the constitution for the Bank of New York, and it was his plan to establish the First Bank of the United States that was approved by Congress in 1791. The First Bank of the United States did more than conduct commercial business. It aided the new national government in collecting taxes, storing federal funds, administering public finances, and granting loans to the Treasury. Despite an excellent record, the First Bank of the United States was doomed politically by the implacable opposition of the Jeffersonians; when the twenty-year bank charter expired in 1811, it was not renewed.

Meantime, the number of banks throughout the nation had increased sharply. There were 8 in 1790, 90 by 1811, and 246 in 1816. The large cities continued to seek banks as another instrument to forge ahead of their competitors. Banking had helped Philadelphia maintain its leadership over New York. The City of Brotherly Love had been the center of the national government throughout the American Revolution and also during the first ten years of the Washington and Adams administrations. With such political ties, it was not surprising that the Bank of North America was founded in Philadelphia and that the First Bank of the United States also had its main office there. During the 1790's, it was the undisputed banking center of the nation.

But New York City had assets that would help sweep it ahead of Philadelphia. New York's natural advantages could not be matched: it had a magnificent harbor, an ideal position at the mouth of the Hudson, and a convenient location near New England and the West. Moreover, it had the foremost business community in vitality and originality. Spurred by the Yankee invasion from New England, New York became the nation's biggest importer by 1796, its greatest exporter in 1797, and its most populous city by 1810.

Once New York had outstripped Philadelphia in commerce, it challenged that city's position as the financial center of the United States. The Bank of New York had flourished, paying stock dividends of 7 percent by 1791 and lending money to the federal government, to the State of New York, and to the city itself. The First Bank of the United States had established a branch office in New York City in 1791 and had cooperated with the Bank of New York; together, the two banks held a monopoly of the city's banking. New York's mercantile growth, however, brought a need for additional banks, but the two established ones opposed the creation of a third bank, and in the struggle the issue became political. Federalist-oriented directors controlled the two New York banks while the Republican-minded businessmen sought a third one. A delaying action for several years followed before a third bank, the Bank of Manhattan, came into existence.

The traditional story of the founding of the Bank of Manhattan has pictured Aaron Burr, its sponsor, as a cunning rascal who had resorted to Machiavellian tactics in outwitting the Federalist opposition. According to this conventional version, Burr had deliberately concealed his venal motives behind a reasonable-sounding bill. The measure sought to create the Manhattan Company, a corporation that would supply "the city of New-York with pure and wholesome water." [3] After only four days of rather perfunctory discussion in both houses of the legislature, the Manhattan Company received a charter on April 2, 1799. One month later, the Manhattan Company set up the Bank of Manhattan as a holding company, and in September of the same year, the bank opened for business. Burr's critics concluded that his request to charter the Manhattan Company was an immoral stratagem for the creation of the Bank of Manhattan.

More recent researchers have challenged this version and have tried to vindicate that aspect of Burr's life. Certain facts in the narrative have been generally accepted by all authorities. In its daily necessities and in the event of fire, New York City had a genuine and long-pressing need for a dependable water supply. The question was not the need but whether the water would be provided by a publicly or a privately operated company. The historians agreed also that Burr had proposed the creation of a privately operated company, the city council had supported his plan, and a charter was requested from and granted by the state legislature.

The nub of the controversy was Section Eight. Placed inconspicuously toward the end of Burr's proposal, it read: "That it shall and may be lawful for the said company to employ all such surplus capital as may belong or accrue to the said company in the purchase of public or other stock, or in any other monied transactions or operations not inconsistent with the constitution and laws of this state or of the United States, for the sole benefit of the said company." [4] A member of the assembly, Burr was queried by a senatorial committee about Section Eight. He admitted candidly that under the clause the Manhattan Company might start a bank, organize an East India Company, or do whatever the company deemed profitable. Although Burr's testimony was not known to the entire senate, this could not be blamed on him.

The debate has hinged on Burr's ulterior motive in seeking a charter for the Manhattan Company. Burr's censors claimed that the water works was a blind, to be dropped once the charter had been obtained. In reality, within one year after receiving the charter, the Manhattan Company had laid out a principal main of bored logs with lateral pipes and was distributing water to customers. It never earned as much money on water sales as the Bank of Manhattan profited from loans, but the Manhattan Company was a going concern that honored its obligations.

Burr's partisans have moved from defending him to attacking the Federalists. The Federalists, they said, had a majority in the city council and the state legislature. It was their job to scrutinize Burr's proposals more carefully before approving them. Moreover, the Federalists had singled out Burr as a scapegoat. To win the election of 1799, they had accused him of deceit, fraud, and misrepresentation in the creation of the Manhattan Bank. The tactic succeeded, and the Federalists defeated Burr and the Republican state ticket. Germane to this interpretation, the stigma against Burr stuck. Most historians, concluded Burr's defenders, have since accepted uncritically the Federalist version of Aaron Burr as the arch villain in the formation of the Bank of Manhattan.

In retrospect, neither the Federalists nor the Republicans had behaved with integrity. Key members of both parties had long records of seeking special privilege and private advantage. Blaming the opposing party for offenses they themselves had previously committed was like the proverbial pot calling the kettle black.

Burr can be faulted for his devious course. From the start, his primary goal had been to organize the Bank of Manhattan, not to create the Manhattan Company. His course appeared all the more devious because it flaunted the traditions of that period. Banks usually got their charters after considerable wrangling and the payment of graft. The Manhattan Company, however, was chartered with unseemly haste and apparently without the customary bribery. The charter also lacked certain safeguards normally imposed on banks. Most banks had a set number of years of operation before renewal was necessary; they had to submit periodic reports of their conditions to public officials; and, many of them paid a bonus to the state for getting the charter. But the Manhattan Company had a perpetual charter of almost uncontrolled latitude. In supporting Burr's conduct, the Republican party, too, shared some of the guilt. By 1800, Burr's main objective in getting the charter of the Manhattan Company had become all too clear. Yet Aaron Burr, instead of being chastised, was nominated by the Republicans for the vice-president of the United States.

The Federalists were not blameless. Ignorance of Burr's bill and especially of Section Eight was a weak excuse. More damaging was the fact that the Federalist majority in the legislature had voted for the chartering of the Manhattan Company. It was Alexander Hamilton who had originally helped to influence the city council to accept Burr's project, and John B. Church, Hamilton's brother-in-law, had accepted a directorship in the Manhattan Company. Although no evidence has yet been found that Hamilton knew about the plans for a bank, Church was named in the bill seeking the charter and probably had an inkling about Burr's objectives. In attacking Burr, the Federalists were guilty, too, of a calculated act of character assassination. Another factor in this indictment was the intransigence of the two Federalist-controlled banks against the creation of a third one. Whatever the conclusions, the Federalists and the Republicans came out with soiled hands in what one author aptly called, "The Strange Birth of the Manhattan Company."[5]

While New York was using dubious methods to strengthen its financial sinews, the area west of the Genesee was feeling the disadvantages of not having a bank of its own. Prior to 1812, using the post for the transmission of funds in western New York involved serious dangers. Company remittances included much paper money, which, when stuffed in bulky letters, attracted attention. As Agent-General Busti himself explained it, such packets excited "the covetousness of the many sharks lurking for prey in the post offices" between the Genesee and Philadelphia.[6] To lessen the dangers, he instructed Ellicott to send bills of larger denomination and, adding a penny-pinching thought, pointed out that lighter letters also saved money on "heavier postage." Despite the less conspicuous parcels, Ellicott worried over each shipment until he received confirmation that the money he had sent had arrived safely. What is more, he resorted to various devices to insure greater safety for his remittances. Ellicott tore the bank bills in half and shipped each separately; or, when he did not tear the bills, he frequently sent a description of the serial numbers of the bank notes that he had already mailed. By these methods, if any theft occurred, Paul Busti had the information necessary to advertise promptly the loss of the stolen bank notes.

All the trouble that Ellicott had over the safe shipment of remittances to Philadelphia added to his appreciation of modern banking facilities, yet did not blind him to their hazards. For one thing, as Resident-Agent he valued the conveniences of the banks' paper money, for remittances of gold and silver increased the bulk of the Company parcels. At the same time, he was suspicious of the soundness of the "bushels of banks" that had sprung up during 1812.[7] What he needed was a bank that was in strong financial condition, that would redeem paper money and transfer Company funds to other banks, and that was located near Batavia.

Meantime, to protect the Company money and its many legal papers, Ellicott had taken the additional precaution of erecting a fireproof building. Located on West Main Street in Batavia, the Holland Land Office was diagonal to Ellicott's own mansion, just across the road. As a safeguard against fire from nearby dwellings, the Land Office was set on a large lot 455 feet long and between 100 and 160 feet wide.

The stone building was a handsome structure. It had a broad porch which, supported by four stately pillars, ran the full width of the building. Inside was a nine-foot-wide hall from which radiated four square, identically sized rooms. Each one measured fifteen feet long, had ceilings twelve feet high, and was warmed by its own fireplace. The outside walls were one foot thick, and inside and adjacent to them were vaults sixteen inches wide. The vaults were fitted on the east and west wings of the building and were secured by half-inch thick, nine-foot tall metal doors, with hinges that were set in stone. A stairway led to the upstairs where there were four more rooms shaped similarly to those below. Under the main floor was a cellar type area with a room some thirty-six feet square.

From a wall in one of the main floor rooms hangs a bust-length portrait of Joseph Ellicott, painted by A. G. D. Tuthill about 1820. The picture reveals Ellicott dressed in the fashionable style of that day with linen ruffles on the front of his well-fitted black coat. It is an excellent likeness, for Ellicott at age sixty had wispy hair, a good-sized forehead, expressive and direct-looking eyes, and compressed lips. It is reproduced as the frontispiece for this volume.

The Resident-Agent was proud of the Land Office but defensive about its expense. The building, reported Ellicott with his characteristic passion for accuracy, cost $6,201.65. After the Land Office was occupied in 1815, there were other related expenditures. The low grounds adjacent to the building were filled, and a stone wall was needed to prevent further erosion of the bank of the creek nearby. This additional amount, explained Ellicott in almost apologetic detail, came to $2,751.17. The total spent for the project amounted to nearly $9,000, a sizeable sum in those days. All told, however, the Holland Land Office was functional, commodious, and a credit to Ellicott's security-conscious objectives. The Batavia Office had thus evolved in three stages: the log cabin on the corner of Thomas and West Main Street, first occupied in 1802; the east wing of Ellicott's mansion; and the fire-proof building that is today the Holland Land Office Museum.

Joseph Ellicott's quest for a bank continued, however, and this search seemed to end when the Ontario Bank in Canandaigua was established in 1813. He reported this event to Busti and added that the "knowing ones" felt that this bank should be a "profitable institution." [8] He was particularly pleased that the directors of the Ontario Bank agreed to arrange with the Union Bank in the city of New York to redeem paper money and assured him that they would transfer Company money to any bank in New York City which he designated. On the strength of these promises, Ellicott deposited the Company receipts in the Ontario Bank of Canandaigua. The Ontario Bank recognized Ellicott's importance, for three years later the directors of the bank elected his nephew, David E. Evans, a member of the board.

For a time this bank solved Ellicott's problems of deposit and discount, but the establishment of a branch of the Utica Bank in Canandaigua threatened the stability of the Ontario Bank. The Utica branch competed with the Ontario institution by discriminating against its bank notes, and made it extremely difficult for the Ontario Bank to discount the many notes that Ellicott deposited there. From the start, Chauncey Loomis had opposed the Utica branch as a "foreign Bank" and preferred that the local people create their own financial institution, if another be needed.[9] Ellicott, however, felt confident that the Ontario Bank was strong enough to withstand the competition of the Utica branch. In fact, he was convinced that the Ontario Bank was stronger than the city banks. To support his views, he cited the questionable policy of the city banks which accepted as collateral personal property and "the credit the shopkeepers may possess," and compared it with the Ontario Bank's sounder program which stressed freehold estates as security.[10]

The policy of the Utica branch in regard to the Ontario Bank notes accentuated Ellicott's wariness of the kind of notes that he himself would take in payment for the land. In truth, it was a problem to keep up with the latest reliable information as to which banks and currency were sound. Bank failures occurred frequently. In addition, the state legislatures granted numerous charters for the formation of new banks; thus, new institutions came into existence with insufficient backing and further complicated the situation. Ellicott recognized this and did not feel great pressure to accept all bank notes. His customers themselves did not "generally consider that the Company's agents [were obliged] to receive notes of any Banks" unless the banks in New York and Philadelphia accepted these same notes. Thus, Ellicott flatly refused to accept the notes of the "litter of Banks" that the Pennsylvania legislature had incorporated in the winter of 1813–14. Generally, he did not take notes from banks south of Pennsylvania. By the end of 1814, Ellicott recognized only the notes of banks in New York State and Philadelphia, and, on occasion, those banks of New Jersey. He violated this practice only when "a sale could not be effected without such accommodation to the purchaser." [11]

In addition to the uneven value of the various bank notes, the currency situation worsened when a shortage of specie occurred shortly after the War of 1812. The inhabitants of western New York, lacking sufficient American specie, were forced to use a bewildering variety of currency: six pence, shilling, Spanish dollar, copper cent, English crown and half crown, English guinea, Louis D' Or, and Napoleon. Traders, fortunately, accepted these foreign coins. Ellicott blamed the scarcity of hard money on two main factors: the recently chartered New York State banks had issued notes of questionable value that drove specie further out of circulation; and British merchants had flooded the United States with merchandise for which they accepted mainly specie in payment. Those living on the purchase who owned specie also aggravated the shortage by clinging to rather than circulating the specie. Toward the end of 1815, specie had nearly gone out of circulation.

With this almost total disappearance of specie, the settlers in western New York experienced economic hardships. To make matters worse, the cold summer of 1816, with frost and snow in June, greatly reduced the crops. What food provisions remained brought high prices because of their scarcity; pork sold at twenty-eight dollars a barrel, and flour retailed at fifteen dollars a barrel. To compensate for the high cost of living, both skilled and unskilled labor needed high wages, and this is turn discouraged the construction of buildings.

This economic recession, marked by the variety of paper currency and insufficient specie, precipitated demands for a bank in the Buffalo area. The advocates of such an institution hoped that trade would be stimulated by loans and better currency circulation. Before the sponsors of a bank in Buffalo asked the legislature for a charter, however, they consulted Ellicott.

Ellicott approved the establishment of a bank in Buffalo, for he believed that it was "much wanted" there. However, Ellicott specified the conditions that such a bank would have to meet before he would use his political influence in Albany to obtain a charter or give his support as a depositor. He objected mainly to "the principle of forfeiting the charter in case of nonpayment of specie, while all other Banks are at liberty at their discretion to refuse specie payments" on the ground that no new institution could survive with such a handicap. Ellicott wanted the charter of the bank at Buffalo to be similar basically to other bank charters and to have their freedom of choice in the exchange of specie and paper notes. Otherwise, Ellicott concluded with finality, "I shall never subscribe any of my funds to such a tramelled institution." He explained his ideas to Senator Chauncey Loomis and urged that the Senate "see this subject as I do and grant a charter upon the principle of other banks untramelled with specie until other banks pay specie." [12]

Although Ellicott seemingly altered his stand when he now insisted on a "non-specie" bank, he was merely taking a practical approach to an extremely complicated problem. It is true that he had complained for several years prior to this about inadequately backed paper notes and the "bushels of banks" that lacked sufficient security. Yet, as a capable businessman, he realized that since so many were "non-specie" banks, it would not be possible for a new specie bank at

Buffalo to survive against such competition. He was not reversing his original position; he merely wished to permit the new institution to survive its formative years, and hoped that it would later establish itself on a sound, hard-money basis. The decision on the character of the banks, nevertheless, depended on the legislature.

In 1816, the legislature voted to authorize a bank in Buffalo called the Bank of Niagara. The charter approved a capital of $500,000 and limited the period of operation to sixteen years; despite Ellicott's opposition, the legislature designated the Bank of Niagara as a specie institution. The many bank failures due to inadequate hard-money backing had persuaded the state legislature to insist on a specie bank for Buffalo.

Even though Ellicott had resisted a specie bank, once the legislature chartered the Bank of Niagara, he felt it desirable to support it. He agreed "to attend and superintend the subscription" of the Niagara Bank stock when it went on sale.[13] He urged Busti to invest a minimum of twenty thousand dollars of the Company's money in the shares of this bank and optimistically pointed out that a fifty thousand dollar investment would be safe. Such a bank, maintained Ellicott, would raise the value of the Buffalo land, as well as pay good dividends.

Even before the legislature authorized a charter, Ellicott had considered who some of the directors of the new bank might be. He made clear that neither he nor his nephew, David E. Evans, could accept the positions of directors; both of them simply had "no time to devote to that service." [14] Nevertheless Ellicott believed that two of the bank directors should come from Batavia and suggested the names of his friends, James Brisbane and Trumbull Cary. As additional members of the board, he preferred William Peacock to Zattu Cushing and hoped that Chauncey Loomis, too, would be chosen a director. In this way, the Big Family would have representation on the board of directors and share in whatever power the bank would eventually have.

Power in terms of what it could do was important to Ellicott. Before the Bank of Niagara was chartered, he had been at the core of the power structure of western New York. For fifteen years, he had dominated the political scene. His towering authority was succinctly stated by a settler who discussed the jail being built in Buffalo in 1810: "Mr. Ellicott's advice in all of these matters was the next thing to law." [15]

Joseph Ellicott could almost "play God" with the purchase. Because of the nearly unlimited confidence that Busti had in him, Ellicott as Resident-Agent had been making decisions that had affected the area, individual communities, and many, many people. In large measure, he had determined the location of counties, county seats, towns, and villages. The same could be said about his role in deciding where roads were built, bridges erected, and even courthouses and jails constructed. He, more than anyone else, had handled the multitudinous sales of Company lands to the settlers.

Land sales had given Ellicott a special authority. As Resident-Agent, he had set the price of lots and the down payment needed. This was more complicated than it appeared, for he had periodically changed the prices. In areas that had been heavily settled, the price of the remaining Company property increased; conversely, in places that had not been occupied, the figure was reduced. Because the down payment was a percentage of the total cost, the two figures were related.

The handling of down payments had also added to Ellicott's predominance. Originally, the Company had established a figure of 25 percent down. After making the down payment, the settler had not been required to remit more money during his first two years when he was so busy clearing the property. The balance was then to be amortized in six equal annual installments. The down payment of 25 percent had been too large, and under Ellicott's prodding it had been dropped to as low as 5 percent, depending on where the lot was located. The down payment, like the total cost, was flexible, and Ellicott had decided both figures for each settler. On the lookout for hard-working men who would prepare the land for cultivation, farm it, and pay their debts, Ellicott "adjusted" the down payments. In one instance, an early settler of Chautauqua County had left his watch at the land office until he could get the money to make the down payment.

The decision of what to do with delinquents added another dimension to Ellicott's controls. He had Busti's approval to resort to court action to collect debts and if necessary dispossess the defaulters. Beyond an occasional browbeating of a debtor, the Resident-Agent had rarely carried the matter into court or had sought eviction. The residents, however, were aware that Ellicott could use force if need be.

The power structure that Joseph Ellicott had so carefully built might be jeopardized by the creation of the Bank of Niagara. His experiences with different financial institutions had taught him the potential might that a bank could wield. In a bank's authority to make or deny a loan lay a powerful weapon to advance or retard certain people or particular interest groups. For fifteen years, the Holland Land Company had in a real sense served some of the functions of a bank in accepting down payments and holding mortgages on property. In this way, Ellicott had gained and retained his power. The Bank of Niagara could possibly become the new power structure and displace the Resident-Agent and the Holland Land Company.

By 1815, the economy west of the Genesee was changing, and the need for a bank could not be ignored. Agriculture had been the basic economy, but now commerce and trade were spreading from the big cities into the interior. In a mercantile system, credit was vital. Heretofore, the Holland Land Company had extended credit to the farmers, but it was not equipped to do so with businesses. The Bank of Niagara was chartered to serve the entire community, both farming and business. Aware yet apprehensive of the economic changes, Joseph Ellicott was determined to have a voice in the decisions made by the Buffalo bank.

Like Ellicott, the Porter brothers had their eyes on the stock as well as the directorships of the Bank of Niagara. Peter suggested to his brother Augustus that they and their business friends should buy enough stock in this bank to gain influence there. The Porters also thought in terms of specific people on the board. "I think on the whole," wrote Peter Porter to his brother, "That ourselves, Barton, Townsend, Bronson, Thompson & Sill ought to take so much as to give us a respectable influence, and if we do patronize it, we shall I presume get at least two [directorships]." [16]

The stockholders of the Bank of Niagara met in July, 1816, and elected thirteen directors: Augustus Porter, Ebenezer Norton, Isaac Kibbe, Chauncey Loomis, James Brisbane, Archibald S. Clarke, Jonas Williams, Benjamin Caryl, Jonas Harrison, Ebenezer Walden, John G. Camp, Samuel Russell, and Martin Prendergast. Ellicott managed to get four dependable friends on this board—Loomis, Brisbane, Clarke, and Harrison. The directors came not only from Buffalo but also from many places outside that village. By distributing the directorships geographically, the bank planned to serve western New York rather than Buffalo alone.

Two weeks after the stockholders elected the board, the Niagara Bank directors chose Isaac Kibbe to be president and Isaac Leake as cashier. Originally, Ellicott wanted Augustus Porter as president but then he switched his preference to Kibbe. Three years after the board elected Kibbe president, Ellicott revealed the reasons for his change: first, he was impressed that DeWitt Clinton had recommended Kibbe; second, he was encouraged by Kibbe's claims that he possessed some eighty thousand dollars, mainly in liquid capital; finally, he was in-

fluenced by Kibbe's assertion that if he moved to Buffalo, his wealthy
friends would settle there too. Ellicott thus admitted to Busti: "I used
my influence when the Niagara Bank went into operation to procure
him [Kibbe] to be elected president thereof." [17]

With the sale of Niagara stock and the election of the first officers,
the Bank of Niagara opened its doors in October, 1816, and experienced considerable success in its initial operations. Because of the
caliber of the men who supported the bank, many people were anxious
to buy stock and, as a result, shares sold for 10 percent above par.
Upon Ellicott's urgings, even the circumspect Busti purchased fifty
shares. Many Canadians also bought Niagara stock, and at Canada's
Fort Erie the commanding officer proposed to exchange British guineas
valued at ten thousand dollars for a like sum in notes of the Bank of
Niagara. The investors in this bank expected the Niagara notes to become the circulating media not only in western New York, but also in
the Michigan territory. In servicing such a large area, the bank would
circulate more money than it possessed in actual capital and, at the
same time, could give its stockholders large dividends. These hopes
seemed to be coming true, for in January, 1817, the directors declared
a 9 percent dividend.

For a time, Ellicott and the Bank of Niagara found each other
mutually helpful. Ellicott gave the prestige of his name in support
of the bank, thus attracting stockholders as well as depositors. He en-
trusted foreign notes and specie to the bank and accepted Niagara
notes in exchange. The bank, in turn, by loaning money to the farmers,
made it possible for the Company to collect its debts. Thus, Ellicott
confided to Busti, "had not this Bank been chartered I am impressed in
opinion that we should have found it difficult to have obtained sufficient Amount of circulating medium to have paid the Taxes of the
year." [18] Ellicott never forgot the banking inconveniences that he had
suffered during the first dozen years as Resident-Agent, and he appreciated the proximity of the Bank of Niagara.

While many signs pointed to a prosperous future for the Niagara
Bank, portents of trouble appeared early. Many of the bank loans of
the first three months had been made to farmers on the security of
their grain crops. When the summer of 1816 proved to be unusually
cold, the farmers had such a small harvest that they were unable to
meet their obligations. In addition to these poorly secured loans, the
directors disagreed on the credit relationships to be established with
the New York City banks. The board sought Ellicott's opinions on
this matter. He promptly advised the institution not to issue excessive

paper credit that would eventually find its way to the New York City banks on the ground that it might be impossible for the Bank of Niagara later to redeem this paper in specie. For a short time, the bank followed Ellicott's advice, but it soon ignored this sensible policy. As a result, the Niagara Bank permitted so many paper notes to circulate in New York City that when it was forced to redeem them in specie, it practically stripped itself of hard-money assets. Thus, the Bank of Niagara notes, rather than specie, became "almost the only medium [of exchange] in western New York." [19]

This condition and some of the operations of the Bank of Niagara disturbed Ellicott. He worried, for example, because the New York banks took Niagara notes only at a discount, and forced the Company to suffer a loss in this exchange. He was annoyed, too, that the bank did not maintain a stable credit arrangement in New York City as he had recommended. The Bank of Niagara, in short, had become a "nuisance" to Ellicott. Therefore, in March, 1817, he instructed Peacock not to accept Niagara notes unless they could be exchanged for those of an accredited bank. To protect the Holland Company, Ellicott also extracted the promise that the institution would handle the transfer of Company funds to other banks, when so needed.

In addition to Ellicott's reduced support, many other factors by the summer of 1818 weakened the Bank of Niagara. Business decreased in part because postwar immigration had dropped sharply, thus lessening the buying power in the western sector of the state. More important, most of the bank directors, including President Kibbe, had "drawn out large sums of money, [or] indorsed for others to a frightful amount." [20] Greatly concerned, Peacock continued in his report to Ellicott that "J. B. [James Brisbane] is in for 14 or 15 thousand, Camp for 8 or 10, Carryl for 15 or 20 and god knows how many others for the Like sums." Ellicott believed that some of the directors had deliberately discredited the bank so that the bank notes depreciated in value; in this way, these directors, as debtors, repaid their loans more easily by using Niagara notes as tender. The local newspaper, the *Niagara Journal,* weakened the people's confidence in the bank still more when it attacked the institution and especially singled out director Archibald S. Clarke, Ellicott's nominee, as a target.

Not only were many of the directors exploiting the bank, but the political aspects of the situation were equally disturbing. Since it was necessary for the state legislature to grant permission for the bank to begin its operations, those who sought the charter were compelled to bargain with key legislators. As a result, some of the legislators exchanged their votes for gifts of bank stock. DeWitt Clinton, one of the leaders of the Republican Party, Ellicott told Busti, borrowed three thousand dollars "the moment the Bank went into operation" and President Isaac Kibbe had quickly endorsed this loan. But the three thousand dollars did not satisfy Clinton and he increased this sum to forty-five hundred; again Kibbe underwrote Clinton's note. Requiring additional funds, Clinton now sought to enlarge the loan "considerably" more than forty-five hundred dollars, but at this point, Isaac Leake, the cashier, refused his request. The cashier explained that Kibbe, the sole endorser of Clinton's loans, had proven to be poor security himself; that Kibbe's story of his so-called eighty thousand dollar estate had all been a lie for "probably a more plausible man than Mr. Kibbe never existed." [21]

Leake's refusal to approve the additional loan to Clinton precipitated a bitter quarrel between the cashier and the president. Kibbe had approved many loans, even when the bank was hard pressed to sustain its credit. Many of these borrowers had made no repayments. When Leake protested, Kibbe glibly and deliberately provoked many of the depositors against the cashier. The directors became involved in this quarrel, for a majority of the board disagreed with Kibbe on the manner in which he was running the bank. At a full board meeting, and in the presence of Kibbe, the directors aired their grievances; then all but two of the board members voted to dismiss Kibbe as president. After the board removed him as president, Kibbe, his friends among the directors, and their associates openly declared war on the bank. They gathered Niagara notes, returned them to the bank and demanded immediate payment in specie. The institution withstood this deliberate run in July, 1818, as well as its continuation the following month.

In addition to the local pressures against the bank, the story gained currency that outside forces, too, sought the destruction of the Bank of Niagara. Some people accused William Kibbe, who was president of the Ontario Bank at Canandaigua and brother of Isaac, of using his bank's funds against the Niagara Bank "in a very secret manner." William Kibbe flatly denied these accusations and added that he had not "taken any part in the quarrel" between brother Isaac and cashier Leake. The Ontario Bank president blamed the Utica Bank and its branches for these attacks against the Bank of Niagara. As evidence of the good faith of the Ontario Bank, the directors of that institution planned to discuss a loan of some "four or five thousand dollars in specie" to the Niagara Bank in order to help that bank to redeem

Niagara paper. William Kibbe confided to Archibald S. Clarke, Ellicott's dependable friend, that Isaac "must withdraw" from the bank as a director because of the powerful opposition to him. At the same time, Kibbe offered his opinion that Isaac would leave Buffalo if he could sell his stock and property. Clarke agreed with this view and advised Ellicott that "we had better purchase" Isaac's stock and land if he would "give a pledge to cease hostilities to the bank." [22]

Faced by Isaac Kibbe's intransigent attitude, a divided board now beseeched Ellicott's aid in this desperate fight for the survival of the bank. In July, 1818, seven of the thirteen directors offered a directorship to Ellicott and explained their move "as a measure tending to raise the respectability and promote the welfare of the institution." [23] Later that same month, the board elected Ellicott president.

Ellicott accepted the presidency of the Bank of Niagara with misgivings, since his contract with the Company forbade him from holding other offices. Thus he had to explain promptly to Busti his reasons for accepting this appointment. He did this by pointing out that in the first place, the board elected him "without my knowledge"; further, "it was with some difficulty that I could prevail upon myself to accept" the office. When he agreed to become the president, he did so "with an understanding that I should be at liberty to resign after the next election of directors in November." Ellicott concluded his explanations to Busti by saying: "I want no office of any description; my ambition is fully gratified with that of agent of the Holland Company. I should not of [sic] accepted it, but I was told my name at the present time would be advantageous to the Institution." [24]

As president, Ellicott briefed himself on the condition of the Bank of Niagara by getting the subscription list. In so doing, he learned more accurately just how badly many of the directors had exploited the bank. Ellicott substantiated the story that several of the directors and subscribers had borrowed money from other banks and used these loans to buy stock in the Niagara Bank. Then, as stockholders, they had put up their Bank of Niagara stock as collateral to borrow large sums from the Niagara Bank; and, with the money they thus received, they repaid their original loans to the other banks. In some cases, the Bank of Niagara officials had loaned to such individuals larger sums than these stockholders had invested in the bank's stock. As a matter of fact, comparatively few people with real capital had purchased Niagara Bank stock.

To improve the conditions of the bank, Ellicott insisted that sound financial principles should guide its administration. He demanded a careful investigation of all requests for money before the bank granted them. He also insisted on the prompt collection of loans that the directors had already approved. This latter policy precipitated a bitter quarrel among the directors because several of them owed large sums to the bank that they could not repay. Heretofore, the bank's attorney, Ebenezer Norton, made the decisions on the collection of debts; and as a rule, he favored these directors heavily in debt. Ellicott determined to alter this so the president and not the attorney, would decide what debts to collect.

Archibald S. Clarke, as one of the bank directors, worked hard to put Ellicott's principles of sound banking into effect. At a directors' meeting, he moved to abolish the office of attorney and to give the president the power to collect debts. The board, however, refused to accede to this proposal despite the fact that unless the president were given the authority to collect these debts and put the institution on a sound footing, the bank's enemies could continue their harassing tactics. Clarke, therefore, insisted that the abolition of the attorney's office was "indispensable," "just," and would "gain many friends by it." Isaac Leake, the bank cashier, agreed completely with Clarke's motion to abolish the attorney's office.

Clarke felt that the bank now faced a serious crisis. It seemed to him that the stockholders would have to accept either the program of Isaac Kibbe and Ebenezer Norton or that of Clarke and Leake. Clarke argued that his group should either "compel" the Kibbe camp "to sell out" or Clarke and his associates should "get out of the business, with credit and reputation." [25] He even offered to buy out Ellicott's shares in the bank in an effort to have his group take over control of it.

Nothing came of Clarke's offer and the cleavage among the directors widened. Late in September, Camp and Peacock, two of the board members, "had a fisticuff." [26] The following month, the directors at their board meeting again refused to eliminate the office of the attorney.

In spite of the evidence of continued hostility, the Clarke camp began to feel optimistic about the situation. Clarke confided to Ellicott that "we shall soon have the institution in a good situation." There was reason for Clarke's optimism, for Attorney Norton, sensing the growing opposition to his position, now seemed ready to give up his post. Clarke, by the middle of October, felt so secure about the bank's status, that he informed Ellicott: "We have never been in so good credit & if we lose it, it is our own fault." [27] At the November bank election, "Kibbe & Co." did not make their appearance and all went off smoothly. As a result, the Clarke group gained positions in the organization that led it to believe that its members controlled the bank's operations.

Suddenly, the condition of the bank grew worse. The day after the apparently placid directors' election in November, the Kibbe group planted an advertisement in the Buffalo newspaper to discredit the Bank of Niagara stock. In this notice, a Kibbe follower offered the sale of Niagara Bank stock for 25 percent below par. When a purchaser appeared, however, the Kibbe representative hedged and agreed to sell the stock only "at a less rate than 1 percent and that in Specie." [28] Two days after this, the New York City banks, along with those at Auburn and Canandaigua, demanded specie payment for Niagara notes on hand. At the same time, Myron Holley, a canal commissioner, withdrew the deposits of the Canal fund. This last act Leake attributed to the machinations of Isaac Kibbe and Ebenezer Norton. In desperation, Leake sought Ellicott's assistance, and requested that he influence the Holland Company to deposit additional specie in the bank.

The maneuvers of the Kibbe group exasperated Ellicott to such a point that in December, 1818, he offered to withdraw completely from the Bank of Niagara. He made this proposal to Oliver Forward, a prominent citizen of Buffalo: Forward could buy all or a substantial part of Ellicott's 614 shares of Niagara Bank stock, but not fewer than 300 of these shares. If Forward accepted, Ellicott would give him the dividends which he had not withdrawn on this stock. Further, Ellicott would resign his bank directorship in Forward's favor. But Forward did not buy Ellicott's stock, so the latter continued to try to restore the bank to prosperity.

Ellicott used various techniques to heal the split among the directors. To an individual detractor of the bank, like Ebenezer Johnston, he wrote a letter asking him to stop attacking the Bank of Niagara and criticizing his action as president. Ellicott stated that he had "never done" Johnston "a single injury," and that he had it "abundantly" in his "power" to retaliate. "Let us therefore unite," he urged, "in preserving that institution & establishing its credit upon a solid basis." [29] Ellicott also tried to bolster the specie shortage in the bank by depositing there an additional thirteen hundred dollars in hard money.

In the over-all struggle between the two factions, Ellicott asserted that he took a straightforward course without being partial to either one side or the other. He demanded that those bank directors who had been discounting for themselves had to pay their debts or agree to permit "three of their opponents . . . into the Direction." [30] None of these directors resigned, however. In an effort to regain the confidence of the Buffalo depositors, Ellicott forced his brother Benjamin, William Peacock, and Jonas Williams to relinquish their board memberships in favor of respected Buffalo residents. Williams had been one of the original bank directors and Benjamin Ellicott and Peacock had accepted board positions after the bank had been in business. In their places, the directors elected Oliver Forward, Charles Townsend, and Samuel Wilkeson, all of Buffalo. By these moves, Ellicott hoped that he had reconciled the Buffalo depositors to the operations of the bank.

Still, opposition to the bank continued and demands now grew for the dismissal of Isaac Leake, the cashier. Forward, himself, encouraged Ellicott that the cashier be discharged. Even Peacock urged upon Ellicott this feeling that Leake's personal unpopularity was injuring the position of the Ellicott group, and agreed that "a removal of Leake will have to take place." But Peacock also observed that "nothing would satisfy Norton & Co. but the complete control of the Bank." [31] Directors Clarke, Brisbane, and Camp cited evidence that the opposition to Leake's continuation as cashier did not stem from the Kibbe-Norton group alone. These directors, normally loyal to Ellicott, claimed that they had heard board members Wilkeson and Forward declare at a board meeting that the plot to oust Leake originated with the cashiers of all the banks west of Utica, with the exception of the Bank of Geneva. Wilkeson and Forward, they reported, also stated at this meeting that this hostility would not cease so long as Leake was retained as cashier; but that if the directors of the Bank of Niagara would consent to displace him, "they [the cashiers] had the power to put an immediate stop to this annoyance and the injurious system should thereupon be discontinued." [32] But Ellicott, loyal to the cashier, refused to participate in his ousting.

At a stormy directors' meeting on January 30, 1819, the board argued violently about removing Leake. The debate brought out the conflicting ideas and deep emotions that had racked all the directors in the nearly two years of bank battle. Ellicott was torn between two extreme actions: to close the bank forever or to support its continued operation. "My feelings," he described to his nephew David E. Evans, "were in favor of winding up the concerns of the institution." "But," continued the practical-minded Ellicott, "in reflecting [I realized] that we had exchanged considerable Niagara paper with the friends of the Bank for other paper to enable us to sustain it, on which they might have suffered a loss." He, therefore, concluded: "Under all circumstances I was in favor of supporting it." The newly elected directors, Wilkeson and Forward, became "immensely alarmed" when they learned that most of the board planned to close the bank. They wanted the bank to remain open because they held much of the bank's paper money; if the institution did not redeem these notes, they might well have been "ruined." [33]

In an effort to place himself in the position of a nonpartisan observer and to relieve himself of the great personal strain, Ellicott first resigned as a director. Then, after considerable discussion, the board, to the great relief of Wilkeson and Forward, accepted Ellicott's advice and voted to keep the bank open. Ellicott had also made the recommendation that the directors continue to employ Leake; this, too, the board endorsed. "The truth was," Ellicott reminded the directors, "any other course would have been an improper one."

The Big Family felt relieved when Joseph Ellicott, head of the clan, resigned from the Bank of Niagara. Ellicott, himself, gave up a load that he had never enjoyed carrying. While his resignation may have reduced personal animosities among the directors, within six weeks after that hectic January 30 board meeting, the Bank of Niagara credit collapsed. Many of the banks east of Buffalo accelerated this fall when they returned so many Niagara Bank notes for payment that the institution soon had little specie left. The news of this shortage of hard money was reported in the *Columbian,* a New York City newspaper. With the publication of this item, the New York brokers refused Bank of Niagara paper at any discount. In March, 1819, the Holland Company followed suit and did not accept Niagara Bank paper for debts or land purchase. Ellicott notified Goodwin and Peacock, the Company agents for Cattaraugus and Chautauqua counties, to refuse that bank's notes until further notice. The Bank of Niagara thus paid the price for making too many loans on too little collateral, which in turn aggravated its serious shortage of specie.

Although the Bank of Niagara did not close its doors, the institution contributed little, if anything, to the economic progress of Buffalo from 1819 to 1825. Yet in its first two years of operation, the Niagara Bank had done much to revive the business economy that slumped so badly after the war. It had made possible for many of the residents in western New York to pay their debts to the businessmen as well as to the Holland Company. The bank loaned money to the farmers despite their poor crops, and these tillers of the soil used the cash to buy necessities. In this way, the bank currency circulated freely and helped many people. The settlers probably would not have been able to have paid their debts to the extent they had without the aid of the Bank of Niagara.

On the surface, the fight to control the Bank of Niagara stemmed from differences over banking methods, as well as from the conflict of personal ambitions. The board disagreed basically on various questions involving the handling of the bank's money: the amount and type of collateral needed for a loan; the promptness with which debtors must repay these sums; the minimum total of specie required to carry on business without frequent resort to emergency measures; and the ratio between available hard money and the quantity of bank notes issued. Some of the directors struggled to advance themselves so that they could gain control of the bank; such power would give these people access to credit so essential for their progress in a burgeoning village like Buffalo. When no one member of the board could get this control, the directors formed alliances with each other to facilitate their objectives.

The quarrel over the Niagara Bank was not limited to these disagreements but broadened into the realm of bank politics. By 1819, Ellicott was convinced that Governor DeWitt Clinton played a formidable though backstage role in this fight for the reins of the Bank of Niagara. Ellicott remembered that Clinton originally suggested to him that the directors elect Isaac Kibbe president, and that Kibbe honored increasingly larger loans to Clinton until Isaac Leake, the cashier, protested on the grounds that Kibbe lacked the necessary personal collateral to underwrite these sums for his friend. Clinton did not get his last additional request for a loan and this embittered him against the Bank of Niagara. Ellicott maintained that at this point the bank quarrel started. When the board forced Kibbe to resign, Clinton supported him and his faction in opposition to the Clarke group. Then, when the board elected Ellicott president, the Kibbe men fought him vigorously and Clinton continued to support Isaac Kibbe in this fight. Shortly after Ellicott resigned as president, David Evans reported from Albany that Kibbe "stood well with the Governor." Evans attributed Clinton's loyalty to Kibbe as being due to the Governor's great susceptibility to compliments. "The fact is," observed Evans, "Mr. Clinton is very fond of flattery—his hobby horse is a wish to be thought the greatest man in the State and any man that tells him so is sure to be taken into favor." [34]

Ellicott offered additional evidence that Clinton had betrayed him. Frederick B. Merrill, whom the Council of Appointment in 1816 had selected as clerk of Niagara County, had supported the Bank of

Niagara. Because of his aid, claimed Ellicott, the Clinton-controlled Council of Appointment in 1819 chose John E. Marshall in the place of Merrill. Ellicott accused Marshall of assisting in the artificial runs on the Niagara Bank. As further proof of Clinton's perfidy, Ellicott identified the *Columbian,* the New York City newspaper that had been first to carry the news "that the Niagara Bank was insolvent," as "Clinton's paper." "I am fully persuaded in my mind," concluded Ellicott, "that his Excellency through Kibbe his bosom friend gave sanction to the running of the Bank." [35]

The Governor's interference in the Bank of Niagara dispute greatly upset Ellicott. As leader of the Republicans in western New York since 1802, Ellicott had consistently supported DeWitt Clinton. Clinton's conduct thus disillusioned him and he dolefully told Busti: "confidence in him [Clinton] has I must confess considerably abated, and I begin to be of the opinion that our great politicians are not overburthened with old fashioned honest integrity." [36]

Clinton's behavior in the fight over the Bank of Niagara so disappointed Ellicott that, shortly after he resigned from the bank, he took a momentous step and broke with the Governor. The disagreement over the operations of the Bank of Niagara was the primary reason that Ellicott terminated his long and genuine allegiance to his friend. He now gave support to the bitter enemies of the Governor—Martin Van Buren and his Bucktail Party.

The irreparable split between Ellicott and Clinton had come, paradoxically, after their friendship had reached its highest point. For many years, the two men had worked harmoniously as political allies. They had had an unshakable faith in the future of the state in general and of western New York in particular. Even after the British had ravaged the Niagara frontier, Joseph Ellicott and DeWitt Clinton had remained optimistic about that section of the state.

When Clinton had started to talk about building a canal linking Albany and Lake Erie, Ellicott, who could visualize its great value to the purchase, had readied himself in support of this rehabilitating project. It was their joint efforts to get the canal built that had brought them more closely together. During the canal project and before the split over the Bank of Niagara, their association had ripened from friendliness into a close friendship. The lives of both men were to intertwine again as they now turned their great energies and keen minds to devising an all-water route from Albany to Buffalo.

IX. The Grand Canal

Transportation continued to be a serious problem. Despite all the money and energy already spent on turnpikes and government-built roads, most of the highways into the interior of the nation were deplorable. Only a drastic move could significantly improve the situation.

It was in the power of New York, more than in any other state, to make such a dramatic change. New York had two natural advantages: a gap through the Appalachians and a series of almost adjacent waterways. The magnificent Hudson stretched from New York City to Albany, and westward were the Mohawk River, Wood Creek, Oneida Lake, and the Oneida, Oswego, and Seneca Rivers. These could provide the basis for an uninterrupted system of inland navigation from the Atlantic to Lake Ontario. By eliminating the rocks and sandbars, widening and deepening the rivers, and constructing short canals with locks across the portages, the state would have a navigable thruway. A short canal around Niagara Falls could then connect Lake Ontario with Lake Erie. If such a project were completed, New York City would have ready access to the Great Lakes and into the very heart of the continent. Nature had already done most of the work, so man could finish the job.

Much of this projected route had been used for over a century. The Hudson was an economical waterway from New York City to Albany. From there, fur traders had carried Indian goods sixteen miles overland to the Mohawk River at Schenectady. Then, they had paddled their canoes up the Mohawk River, Oneida Lake, and Oswego River and into Lake Ontario, with only one sizable portage of three to five miles at what is today Rome. This passage had not been fully utilized because of the Indian wars and the American Revolution. Nevertheless, New York held a precious natural resource that was an invaluable key to unlock the enormous potential of the areas around the Great Lakes and the Mississippi River.

The formula for this transportation revolution was to combine river improvements and short canals. The prescription was simple and reasonable yet took many years to put together. Before the American Revolution, the canal project had been discussed in hazy fashion. After the nation had gained its independence, New York's war debts had discouraged additional loans for internal improvements. In the 1790's, the assumption of state debts by the federal government had rekindled an interest in the canal. However, it was the growing settlements in western New York that pushed the canal topic to the fore. The population increase had been explosive. In 1790, the area west of Seneca Lake was sparsely settled numbering 1,075, with the land west of the Genesee having only 51 people. Within a decade, the number living in Ontario County had climbed to 15,052; that county in 1800 was the only one in western New York. By 1810, the population west of the Genesee had mushroomed to 23,416 and more than quadrupled to 108,981 ten years later. (See Tables I and II, Appendix.)

A start toward implementing the formula of river improvements and short canals had been made in 1792. That year, the state legislature had granted charters to the Northern Inland Lock Navigation Company and to the Western Inland Lock Navigation Company. The former was to connect Hudsons river with Lake Champlain by a continuous water route, while the latter was to provide unbroken water travel from Albany "to be extended to lake Ontario and to the Seneca lake." [1] The Northern Company failed after a short existence. The Western Company was more durable. Beginning work in 1793, it constructed nine locks and completed three canals at Little Falls, Wolf Rift in German Flats, and at Rome. On these limited improvements, the Western Inland Lock Navigation Company collected tolls for about twenty-five years until relinquishing the charter and selling its property to the state. Technical ignorance, labor shortage, and financial limitations contributed to the downfall of the Western Company. One author concluded that the Western Company was a "premature experiment" but at least the formula was being tried. [2]

The concept now was of an all-water route directly from the Atlantic Ocean clear to Lake Erie. Credit for this brilliant idea goes perhaps to Gouverneur Morris, the witty aristocrat who had served the nation during and after the Revolution. In 1800, Morris had journeyed through the interior of New York, and observing the changes in the Mohawk Valley brought on by the Western Inland Lock Navigation Company, predicted that ships would one day "sail from London through Hudson's River into Lake Erie." [3]

The Morris idea was carried one step further by Jesse Hawley. A little-known merchant in Geneva, New York, Hawley and a partner had been sending flour to the New York market. He was frequently annoyed by the difficulties of shipping cargo on the Mohawk. When the water level dropped during the summer months, it increased the carrying fees. One day, while looking at a map of New York, he suddenly got the notion that water from Lake Erie could be carried from Buffalo to the Mohawk. His friends considered this view visionary, but Hawley clung to the idea. In 1806, he went bankrupt, and as a debtor spent twenty months in jail. It was during this period of incarceration that Jesse Hawley started to write a series of fourteen essays explaining the feasibility of constructing such a canal. Signed "Hercules," the articles appeared in the Genesee *Messenger* in 1807 and 1808 and made Hawley, as one authority neatly described, "the first publicist for the Erie Canal." [4]

Jesse Hawley's plan called for a Genesee Canal two hundred miles long. One hundred feet wide and ten feet deep, the canal would carry the almost inexhaustible supply of Lake Erie water down the Mohawk to Utica. His proposed canal started near the mouth of the Niagara River, continued along the Niagara Escarpment, and fell 410 feet as it moved eastward, flowing into Mud Creek, Seneca River, finally entering the Mohawk. Hawley also assumed that the great accretion of water would make easy navigation possible to Schenectady. When the portage to Albany was eliminated by a canal, he concluded, the water would flow freely from Buffalo to Albany and into the Hudson to New York City. Prophetically, Hawley proposed a route that was almost the same one later followed by the Erie Canal.

Hawley's essays received limited circulation, were read with skepticism, yet had sufficiently concrete suggestions for further action. Interest in the canal grew as the settlers increased in number, produced larger crops, and found the problem of getting the goods to a market increasingly acute. The entire state, but particularly the western sector, was suffering from growing pains. As the discussion about the canal mounted, the question of the best route began to be debated. The choice lay between a canal to Lake Ontario or one to Lake Erie. Joshua Forman, a member of the state assembly from Onondaga County, was very much aware of the transportation needs of his constituents in central New York. In 1808, he introduced a resolution that called for a survey of the most direct route for a canal between the Hudson and Lake Erie. A wary legislature approved the Forman motion but voted only $600 for the survey.

Hawley's essays and Forman's resolution culminated in the indispensable report of the surveyor. Simeon De Witt, the surveyor-general, was instructed to make an accurate survey of the "rivers, streams, and waters . . . between the Hudson River and Lake Erie" and "such other routes as he may deem proper."[5] For the first time, the citizens would get more factual information about the suitability and location of a canal. The survey, therefore, became vital to the prospects of an all-water route from the Hudson to Lake Erie.

As a shareholder of the Western Inland Lock Navigation Company, De Witt had personally preferred the more conventional route to Lake Ontario, but he loyally obeyed the legislative directive. As part of his fact finding, he sent a letter to Joseph Ellicott, whose opinion as Resident-Agent of the Holland Land Company would command respect. De Witt's communication began with a sarcastic allusion to the meager sum of $600 voted for the survey, recognized that some people favored a canal running clear to Lake Erie, and asked Ellicott's opinion. Knowing that the Resident-Agent had already made surveys in western New York, De Witt requested any other information about "the feasibility of such a canal."[6]

Although Ellicott had not been convinced earlier that the canal would be built, he could see many gains if it were. He had always believed that improving transportation facilities would probably increase land sales. A canal would not only provide a substitute for the roads that were necessary to market goods, but most pleasant prospect of all, it would not cost the Holland Land Company an excessive amount of money.

Previously, Ellicott had favored building roads, but when he saw that his program increased the Company's taxes, he decided to use his influence to limit additional road construction. Yet, by 1808, the poor quality of western New York roads convinced him that some other means of transportation would have to be found to assist the farmers in marketing their produce. For, if this could not be done, the farmers' ability to earn sufficient funds to pay their debts to the Company would be seriously limited. What is more, without satisfactory transportation facilities, potential customers might be discouraged from buying land. Joseph Ellicott decided to act. When an opportunity arose early in 1808 for him to take part in the planning of a canal, he eagerly accepted.

Before responding to De Witt, Ellicott discussed the idea of a canal with Agent-General Busti. He praised the project and stressed the points that a waterway could be built at small expense and that it would greatly increase the value of Company lands. On the crucial question of how the canal might affect the value of the land, Ellicott assured Busti: "We might fairly estimate the Holland Company's Property here at $1,000,000 higher" provided, added the ever-circumspect Resident-Agent, "the Canal should be made sufficiently large to admit the Boats . . . capable of carrying twenty to thirty tons Burthen." The Resident-Agent also informed his superior that he wanted a direct all-water route rather than one which "might round the Niagara to Lake Ontario and from thence to Oneida Lakes." [7]

After informing Busti of his position on this matter, Ellicott answered DeWitt's request in a detailed ten-page letter. First, he carefully examined three possible routes: one swinging around Niagara Falls; a second moving down the Niagara River from Lake Erie to Lake Ontario; and a third connecting the Genesee River with Lake Erie. Then, he eliminated the first two possibilities and supported the third route. With typical efficiency, he approximated the water depths and the lock requirements, estimated the cost of excavation per mile, and even included a map for the western sector. Finally, as proof of his confidence in the practicability of the project, he offered to invest $2,500 in a company organized to build the proposed waterway to Lake Erie. Ellicott's recommendations revealed his vast and accurate knowledge of western New York and strengthened the hopes for a canal west of the Genesee. His final selection of the Erie route predictably coincided with the best interests of the Holland Company, for the canal would pass through the purchase.

In addition to charging De Witt with the selection of a route, the resolution of 1808 had specified that he should assume the responsibility of having a survey made of the proposed waterway. De Witt appointed James Geddes to make the necessary surveys. This was a critical juncture in the debate over the Ontario and Erie routes, and the Geddes report proved decisive. Geddes spent the summer of 1808 surveying the areas between the Mohawk and Lake Ontario and along the Niagara River. By then, he had spent the $600 appropriation but his curiosity drove him on. Using his own funds, Geddes turned east in December to study what was considered the greatest obstacle to an interior route: the land between the Genesee and Mud Creek (Palmyra). Until then, it had been assumed that this area had high ground with no source of water. Geddes, however, made what proved to be an important discovery. The Genesee was way above the high land. The canal water could thus be carried across the Irondequoit Valley to Mud Creek over a series of natural ridges. Geddes' findings cost the state an extra $73, but his disclosures were crucial. Making his report to De Witt in 1809, Geddes concluded that both routes were possible. Although he tried to be impartial, his report favored the Erie over the Ontario route, thus brightening further the likelihood of an Erie route.

Impressed by the possibilities inherent in a canal, the state legislature took a more forceful position. In 1810, both houses unanimously passed a resolution to survey two routes from the Hudson to Lake Erie. One would be the interior passage, and the other would run to Lake Ontario and around Niagara Falls to Lake Erie. The resolution also called for a recommendation of the most eligible route. The work of surveying and recommending would be done by a board of commissioners. The legislature then passed another resolution appointing a seven-man board of commissioners and appropriated $3,000 for their expense.

Aware that the prospects of the project might depend heavily on the board of commissioners, the lawmakers selected the men carefully. Political balance, public esteem, and competence were the primary criteria. Four men were Federalists: Gouverneur Morris, the wealthy patrician who in 1800 had suggested an all-water route from the Hudson to Lake Erie; Stephen Van Rensselaer, the large and influential landlord; William North, heir to part of the Von Steuben estate; and Thomas Eddy, insurance broker and successful businessman. Three commissioners were Republicans: DeWitt Clinton, talented naturalist, nephew of the seven-time governor of New York State, former mayor of New York City, and a strong political leader in the Senate who became interested in the canal at this time; Simeon De Witt, surveyor-general and land speculator; and Peter B. Porter, congressman, business entrepreneur, and land expansionist. Financially secure, the commissioners knew each other well, having dealt with one another in politics, land speculation, and business.

The legislative action was a milestone in economics, too. Until then, private enterprise had been encouraged to build canals. However, the failure of the Western Inland Lock Navigation Company, the mounting demands for better roads especially in western New York, and the favorable Geddes report were pushing the state into a new posture. The 1810 resolutions recognized two new trends. First, the canal movement, in two years, had grown from an object of scorn to a project of worth. And second, as a political issue, it was attracting votes in central and western New York. The high quality of the seven-man commission showed how seriously the legislature was approaching the subject. For many reasons, then, the resolutions of 1810 indicated that the government was making a serious shift. The traditional dependence on privately chartered companies for canal improvements was giving ground to the more novel arrangement of the state constructing the canal itself.

The canal commissioners took their jobs seriously. Morris and Van

Rensselaer, carrying with them Hawley's essays, Ellicott's letter and map to De Witt, and the Geddes report, examined the route from Albany directly to Buffalo. The other commissioners restudied the advantages of the Ontario route. James Geddes and Benjamin Wright worked as surveyors and laid out the line of the canals. In March, 1811, the commissioners made their first report. On the question of which route was the better, they favored the Erie over the Ontario passage. The recommendation was a victory for Ellicott, the Holland Land Company, and western New York; it was the first time that an official body had favored the interior route for a canal to Lake Erie. On the issue of who should be the builder, the commissioners took a firm stand that the canal should be constructed by public authority. They rejected the building by private enterprise because of insufficient capital, the danger of speculation, and the great national interest at stake.

Without taking sides about which route to use, the legislature accepted the commissioners' report and in April, 1811, passed the first canal law. Under this act, the old commissioners were reappointed, Robert Fulton and Robert Livingston were added to the canal board, and $15,000 was voted for their use. To push the project along, the act authorized the canal board to do several specific things: seek aid from Congress and other state legislatures; negotiate with the Western Inland Lock Navigation Company for the surrender of its rights; learn the terms on which loans could be made; and accept the land donations through which the canal would pass.

One month after the act of 1811 was passed, five of the nine commissioners met in New York and apportioned the assignments. Clinton and Livingston were to contact Congress and other states for assistance. Clinton and Fulton were to get in touch with the Western Inland Lock Navigation Company. Meantime, Morris and North were to determine the best terms for loans. Eddy and Fulton were to search for an engineer. And De Witt and Van Rensselaer were to encourage proprietors to cede land where the proposed canal would flow.

The commissioners moved swiftly to complete their assignments. Clinton and Morris went to Washington for federal aid, but constitutional scruples, jealousy among states, and the possibility of war blighted their hopes. Other states were not interested in helping, either. New York was thus left to its own resources. Clinton and Fulton found that the Western Inland Lock Navigation Company was willing to sell, but the final liquidation was delayed until the properties were appraised and purchased in 1820. Morris and North reported that Europe had a money scarcity but were confident that a loan of $5 million could be obtained at 6 percent interest for a period of ten to fifteen years. Eddy and Fulton wrote to England and selected an engineer. To get land cessions, De Witt and Van Rensselaer applied pressure particularly on the largest landowner that would profit from a canal, the Holland Land Company.

Businessmen to the core, Paul Busti and Joseph Ellicott were unromantic, careful, and above all opportunistic during the fluctuating fortunes of the canal project in its formative years. Busti doubted until the very eve of construction that the canal would ever be built, a skeptical view held by many prominent men. Ellicott realized fully the potentialities of the canal. More hopeful than Busti about the canal prospects, he shared with his superior a determination to act only in a way that would benefit the Company. The Agent-General and the Resident-Agent shifted their positions to the degree that the Company interests were affected. When it seemed that the canal would follow the interior route desired by Ellicott, they were zealous supporters. But talk of choosing the Ontario route quickly cooled their ardor.

Even before the legislature had appointed the canal board in 1810, Agent-General Busti, in an effort to encourage the construction of a canal, had offered to donate Company lands to the state. Proceeds from the sales of such lands could be used to finance the proposed waterway. Although Busti had previously opposed canal construction and advocated opening a few main roads, he reversed himself after Ellicott went on record as favoring the project. Thus, he endorsed his Resident-Agent's stand by offering "every other Lot adjoining each side of the said Canal in its passage through the Holland Company's Lands." [8] Each lot contained 160 acres, so the total Company grant would amount to 18,000 acres.

In the early part of 1812, the canal commission rejected Busti's offer, feeling that the special conditions that were attached to it prevented final acceptance. These conditions specified that the canal would have to extend from Lake Erie to the Seneca River; it would have to accommodate boats with twenty-ton loads; the federal or state government would have to build the canal; and the Company would not be responsible for the release of the land until construction of the canal had actually started.

The canal commission felt that Busti's proposals needed clarification. The land should be donated at once, insisted the commissioners, and, certainly, prior to the initial construction. The Company, on the other hand, could not release the lots until the commissioners had laid out the route; for to do so might mean sacrificing immediate opportunities to sell this land to private purchasers. Faced with this difficulty, the commissioners countered Busti's offer by requesting a definite block of land that would "at once be located." [9] Busti, a trifle uncertain of his next step, suggested that the Company might offer half a township, which was three miles square, in the neighborhood of the canal.

When Thomas Eddy, the distinguished philanthropist, canal commissioner, and friend of Ellicott, urged him to support a larger land donation,[10] the Resident-Agent decided to table Busti's offer of half a township and suggested, instead, a larger land grant. Eddy had given this advice because he believed that such generosity on the part of the Company would help to offset the criticism that the canal would mainly benefit the large landowners. Moreover, he reminded Ellicott, the land grant would also help to finance the canal construction. The new block of land which Ellicott proposed to donate to the state, therefore, covered an area of over 100,000 acres, in contrast to the half a township of 11,500 acres which Busti had suggested. With a practical man's consideration of the importance of the dollar sign and of public relations, Ellicott pointed out to Busti that such a donation would serve the Company in several ways: a larger grant would establish better rapport between the Company and the public; it would rid their organization of poor land that was not likely to be sold for some time; and it would comply with the commission's request for a grant that "could at once be located." He explained further that the Company might later receive compensation for Busti's half a township adjoining the canal, a substantial sum that it would stand to lose if an outright grant of this property were prematurely made to the state.

Busti studied this plan with all the caution of a man accustomed to the delicate balances of land values, and then, convinced of its merit, he endorsed the land grant that Ellicott had recommended. Thus, the Company offered to donate 100,632 acres of almost unsalable land in the mountainous region that Ellicott suggested. The donation stipulated that the state would have to pay taxes on this land, and return the land to the Company if it did not build the canal within fifteen years. The canal commission accepted this offer on November 27, 1813.

While the Company and the canal board ironed out their differences over the land donation that was to assist in financing the canal, Ellicott faced the equally troublesome problems involved in the selection of the canal route in western New York. He wanted a waterway that passed through the Company lands, for in this way the Company would profit from the project. Peter B. Porter, however, favored a canal route that facilitated trade on the Great Lakes, and sought a passage by way of Lake Ontario. The Ontario route would aid the Great Lakes shipping firm of Porter, Barton and Company at Black Rock, for the canal would run from Albany to Lake Ontario. The Porter, Barton Company had a twenty-year contract with the State of New York that gave the Company a trade monopoly on the Niagara River and over the Portage Road. Thus, the Ontario route would remove the need for a canal through the purchase and insure the trade position of Porter's Company.

Ellicott adamantly opposed Porter's route. In the ensuing clash, Porter had the good fortune to be one of the canal commissioners: this initial advantage was offset, however, when the board authorized Ellicott to make the recommendation of a route. The commission chose Ellicott because he probably had more information about the topography of western New York than anyone else. Prior to his appointment as Resident-Agent, he had spent two years tramping through the woods of western New York when he prepared the original survey of the purchase. In his position as consultant, Ellicott demonstrated that he was as effective a Company publicist as he was an advisor; for he persuaded the board to select a route favorable to his Company. In 1811, the canal board reported to the state legislature that it favored a canal route directly to Buffalo, in preference to Oswego on Lake Ontario. Ellicott had won his point.

In 1812, the canal commissioners made their second report to the legislature. They urged the immediate construction of a canal and pleaded for the necessary legislative action. Both houses approved an act in June of 1812 that allowed the commissioners to continue their surveys and to borrow up to $5 million from Europe on the credit of the state.

No sooner had this authorization been granted than the opponents of the canal project spoke up vehemently and from different quarters. The inhabitants of eastern New York felt jealous of western New York; residents around Lake Ontario demanded that the canal route go to Oswego; and several leaders of the southern counties that bordered Pennsylvania saw no personal gains from the canal and resented paying additional taxes to help western New York. Politically, Tammany Hall opposed the canal because its enemy, DeWitt Clinton, favored it. In 1814 these opponents united and, using the war as an excuse, persuaded the legislature to rescind the authority of the commission to borrow the money from Europe. The canal project had reached the nadir of its fortunes.

While the war delayed further progress in the building of the canal, at the same time it accentuated the need for such a waterway. It dramatically revealed the necessity for better transportation. Only with the greatest difficulty did the army transport cannon, and poor facilities slowed this movement to a snail's pace. Indeed, when the government, in 1814, moved to protect the western frontier from another British invasion, it had to spend large sums of money just to carry arms and ammunition to the frontier. A cannon worth $400 at Washington cost $2,000 to transport to Lake Erie. Thus the war proved that bad roads imperiled a sound American defense of the Canadian frontier, and the canal project gained additional converts. Unfortunately, the proponents of the canal lacked the leadership necessary to organize their efforts.

At this point in the canal's progress, DeWitt Clinton came forward and used his prestige to stimulate interest in the project. A canal commissioner since 1810, he had trained himself to be an expert on the subject. He had traveled extensively over the suggested canal route in 1810 and knew the topography well; he had also added to his knowledge of the subject by considerable reading. With the end of the war, he united the unorganized proponents of the canal. He did this by writing and distributing his famous "Memorial" of December, 1815, a brochure that convincingly demonstrated the advantages of such a waterway. A committee sent copies of the "Memorial" throughout the state. As a result, many responsible citizens signed petitions in support of the canal. Numerous mass meetings were held in the area between Albany and Buffalo, and speakers agitated in its favor. The newspapers added their encouragement and aided by informing the public of the issues involved. When the legislature received Clinton's "Memorial" in March, 1816, over one hundred thousand people had petitioned the lawmakers to build the canal.

Clinton's "Memorial" had specifically supported an interior route, so Ellicott gave his support. In January, 1816, he organized a mass meeting in Batavia that sent a petition to the legislature favoring a canal. Those present at this meeting appointed a committee to continue working for the waterway. The committee consisted of Joseph and Benjamin Ellicott; James Stevens, the Company's clerk; David Evans, Ellicott's nephew; and Ellicott's friends William Rumsey, James Brisbane, and Richard Smith. Ellicott urged William Peacock, his nephew by marriage and subagent of Chautauqua County, to call for a mass meeting in Mayville favoring the canal. He encouraged Jonas Harrison, collector of customs for the District of Niagara, to add his influence at a meeting that Buffalo had planned. He sent a map with plans for the canal to Senator Chauncey Loomis, a nephew by marriage, and told Loomis that he hoped the legislature would pass a bill to build the waterway. A week later, Ellicott informed Loomis that he had sent William Rumsey to Albany to lobby for the canal.

Despite the clamor and pressure for a canal, the state legislature passed a bill that instructed the commissioners merely to study the canal project further. Governor Tompkins, in his annual message of that year, mentioned the canal in one paragraph but did not urge the legislature to appropriate the needed funds for construction. In March, 1816, the commission recommended as it had in 1812 that the state begin to build the canal. Later that month, Rutzen Van Rensselaer introduced a bill that provided for the immediate construction of the Erie and Champlain Canals. In April, the house resolved itself into a committee of the whole, discussed the bill, and, after making a few changes, passed it. Martin Van Buren in the senate sucessfully amended the bill so that the commissioners could not begin immediate construction. After considerable haggling, both houses accepted the senate bill on the last day of the session. The act in its final form ordered the commissioners to make additional surveys to examine further the costs involved, and to study ways in which the state could issue the necessary bonds. Thus the legislature had again postponed the actual construction of the canal. The 1816 legislature also decided to appoint a new group of canal commissioners and to reduce the number of commissioners to five.

When Ellicott learned that the legislature planned to alter the canal board membership, he acted quickly to influence the lawmakers in their selection of a commissioner from western New York. He wanted James W. Stevens to replace Peter B. Porter as a commissioner because Porter had supported the Oswego route instead of the Buffalo one. Porter's mercantile interests clashed with Ellicott's desires to attract farmer-settlers. Further, Stevens, as the Company clerk, had served Ellicott with undeviating loyalty. Ellicott urged Archibald McIntyre, the state comptroller, to use his influence to get Stevens appointed. Ellicott also instructed Chauncey Loomis to use his senatorial prestige to obtain Stevens' appointment. To Loomis, Ellicott admitted that the real reason for preferring Stevens to Porter stemmed from the fact that the Company could control Stevens.

Ellicott did succeed in obtaining a canal commisssioner sympathetic to the company. It was not Stevens, however; by a strange tug of destiny, he found *himself* appointed one of the five canal commissioners. The appointment surprised Ellicott for he "had not the most distant expectation of being named as a commissioner." [12] In addition to Ellicott, the legislature chose as canal commissioners DeWitt Clinton, Myron Holley, Samuel Young, and Stephen Van Rensselaer.

As the canal evolved, so did its name. Originally the canal opponents had dubbed it Clinton's Ditch, a term of ridicule tinged with malice. As engineers constructed sections of the artificial waterway, the common man adopted the title of Big Ditch. By the time the builders had completed the entire project, the people identified it as the Grand Western Canal or more briefly the Grand Canal. And, with the passage of years when feeders were added to this man-made channel, they finally settled on the somewhat one-sided title of either the Old Erie or the Erie Canal.

Ellicott and DeWitt Clinton worked closely and harmoniously at this time. When Clinton asked Ellicott for suggestions for the waterway, Ellicott offered two practical ideas: the legislature should appoint a small group of commissioners to prepare a sample route that would include bridges, docks, and excavations; and the legislature should not employ foreigners because Americans knew better the business management techniques in this country. Ellicott also suggested various methods to raise money for the canal. Altruistically, he included a tax on bachelors despite the fact that he was unmarried; but he excluded any tax on landowners.

Clinton was impressed with Ellicott's proposals and confided in him. He blamed Tompkins for the split in the Republican party, and accused him of "shrinking from responsibility" in the canal project. He felt that Ellicott's suggestions regarding the canal "will I have no doubts be adopted either on this or future occasion." [13] And the lobbying of Colonel Rumsey, whom Ellicott had sent to Albany, he found "active and useful." [14]

Meanwhile the work of surveying the canal route went forward. Clinton examined the eastern sector and found "its practicability beyond all manner of doubt." [15] The commissioners next had to lay out a route from the Genesee River to Buffalo Creek. Ellicott knew the great importance of this route to the Company and appreciated its role in the over-all canal battle. He had won the first round in 1812 when he had persuaded the commissioners to recommend a direct route to Buffalo and Lake Erie, rather than to Oswego and Lake Ontario. Now he wanted to locate this canal route so that it ran through as much of the Company land as possible. This latest survey required that a detailed examination of the route be made, in contrast to the broad view resulting from the 1812 recommendation. With this in mind, Ellicott offered to organize a party "to trace a line for the canal from Lake Erie" to the Genesee River.[16] He was fully aware that he could thus serve both the state and the Company.

The canal commissioners accepted Ellicott's offer and in July, 1816, ordered him to lay out a route from the Genesee River to Buffalo Creek. Ellicott gave much time, thought, and energy to the examination of this sector of the waterway; fortunately, he found a satisfactory route that ran through the Genesee and Niagara Counties. He carefully investigated the reported "insurmountable obstacles" to his suggested waterway;[17] and, in order to assist him in his task, he organized a party to go over this route thoroughly. To execute this job, he assigned William Peacock as the engineer; then he appointed his nephew, Andrew A. Ellicott, as the surveyor. Ellicott maintained that only Peacock had "sufficient scientific skill in this part of the country capable of accomplishing it with necessary accuracy." To Busti, he admitted that he selected Peacock, too, because he "would be doing that which in the end would be equally profitable to the Company."[18]

The commissioners had two routes in the west from which to choose: a northern and a southern route. To complicate matters, the commission had already employed an engineer to lay out the northern route. Ellicott favored the southern route, so he tested his ideas scientifically. He stationed Peacock at Tonawanda Creek for an entire week to gauge the amount of water that flowed. Deliberately, Ellicott chose the driest time of the year to determine whether the Creek had enough water to fill a lock. Peacock's findings convinced Ellicott that Tonawanda Creek could promise enough water "to fill a lock 75 feet in length, 16 in breadth and 12 feet in depth in less than four minutes and 50 seconds which in 24 hours would admit the passage through the locks at each end of the summit canal respectively to the number of 148 boats."[19] Ellicott estimated that the cost of the southern route would be some $300,000 less than that of the northern. Thus, he found no barriers to his suggested route.

Six months after the commisssioners had instructed Ellicott to lay out the western sector, he presented a detailed report for such a route to the commission. In this account, he minutely traced the exact route, approximated the amount of earth that needed to be excavated, and gave estimated costs for the various sections of the route. The commissioners now submitted Ellicott's recommendations to the legislature. This delighted Ellicott because his proposed route went through more of the purchase than any other waterway and thus coincided with the best interests of the Company. He confided to Busti that the Company stood to gain some $1.2 million if the legislature adopted his route.[20]

Not only had Ellicott been compelled to work hard to get a western route that favored the Company, but he needed constantly to combat Busti's skepticism. Although Busti favored a canal and knew its advantages for the Company, he doubted that the state would ever construct it. Even after Busti approved the land donation for a canal, he badgered Ellicott with questions and comments that revealed his disbelief that a canal would be completed: he complained that the commissioners offered "vague plans" that left "ample room to doubts"; he requested that Ellicott elaborate on ways in which the canal would increase the value of Company land as distant as fifty miles away from its site;[21] he found fault with the route the commissioners had recommended in 1812, a route that Ellicott had suggested to the commissioners; and he hedged his offer of land with conditions stipulating the return of the land if the project failed. "I have so little expectation of the Canal ever being undertaken," he said, "that I have been tempted to reduce the number of years of its beginning to 10, but I rather submit to put a longer lien on the land, than incur the reproach of illiberality."[22] Even after Ellicott had chosen the route for the commissioners in 1816, Busti continued to doubt that the legislature or any groups would ever construct the canal, stating that "the magnitude of the undertaking of the Canal is so great that it is impossible for me to believe that the work will ever be perfected."[23] As late as 1817, Busti wrote gloomily: "I cannot divest myself of my old opinion that if ever begun it will in no age be completed. I am very much afraid that in case the work was begun and not completed in your quarters its imperfection would greatly depreciate every farm lot cut up by the dry canal."[24]

Notwithstanding Busti's pessimism, the act of 1816 provided for the survey of a canal route, and the question of a land donation promptly reappeared. The Company's offer of a grant of land in 1812 had become void in 1814, for in that year the legislature had cancelled the authority of the commission to borrow $5 million from Europe to construct the canal. For some time Busti refrained from making another definite land offer, growing increasingly skeptical about the building of such a waterway. At last, on February 22, 1817, Busti renewed his proposal of 1812 for the donation of approximately 100,000 acres of land in the southern part of the purchase; he also included the stipulations concerning taxes, the time limit for the canal completion, and the return of the land if the project were not completed. The same day that Busti offered the land grant to the state, true to form, he confided to Ellicott his pessimistic feeling that the government would never build the canal: "But the more I consider the nature of the undertaking and compare it with the temper of our State & general government the more I grow incredulous of its ever be[ing] perfected if begun." [25]

While Busti was trying to decide whether to renew his land offer of 1812, Ellicott sought federal aid for this project because he felt uncertain that the state legislature would finance the canal. To Congressmen Micah Brooks and Archibald S. Clarke, he presented many reasons for congressional assistance. A completed canal would serve as "the key to the commerce of a vast portion" of the United States and Canada.[26] A state-built canal would give sovereignty over the waterway to the state, which might selfishly exercise its power to the detriment of other states. The canal would affect millions of people in the west and thus require federal control. Congressman Brooks agreed with Ellicott's points, but he observed that Congress needed to study the problem further since other states also had projects to improve transportation. Clarke, long loyal to Ellicott, agreed with the Resident-Agent and tried to obtain the backing of several members of the Committee on Internal Improvements. In support of federal aid for internal improvements, both houses of Congress passed the so-called Bonus Bill in 1817 to distribute the dividends of stock owned by the national government in the Second Bank of the United States. The government would pro-rate the money among the states and, in this way, New York would get some $90,000 a year. However, Madison vetoed this bill and, in so doing, destroyed Ellicott's hopes of federal aid for the canal project.

Ellicott's concern about the financing ended in 1817 when the legislature made a decision that at long last started the construction of the canal. In February of that year, the canal board, in accordance with the instructions of the act of 1816, submitted its report to the legislature. It stated that the commissioners had surveyed the route, had estimated the total expenses of the Grand Canal at approximately $5 million and had examined ways in which the state could finance the construction. The proposed canal would connect Albany with Lake Erie and had these statistical dimensions: 353 miles long, 40 feet wide at the surface, 28 feet wide at the base, and 4 feet deep; the 77 locks could accomodate boats of 100 tons. Again the commissioners urged the state to construct the canal, but no one could tell in advance what the legislature would do about the commission's report. Governor

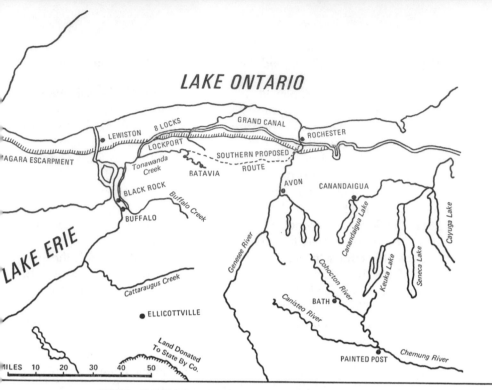

THE GRAND CANAL, 1825

Tompkins, in his speech to the legislature, had said nothing about the canal and Ellicott felt that the legislature would interpret Tompkins' silence as opposition to the project. In support of the canal, the Joint Committee on Canals in the legislature recommended that construction begin, albeit on one section of the entire route. Both houses debated the recommendation fiercely.

The tide began to turn in favor of the canal as the key counties along the Hudson River saw the possibilities of profit for themselves. After much debate, the assembly, on April 10, passed a bill that followed closely the commissioners' recommendations. When Senator Martin Van Buren endorsed the bill, the majority in the upper house followed the lead of the "little magician." The bill became law on April 15. The legislature reappointed the canal commissioners and thus cleared the way for immediate construction to begin.

The day after the legislature approved the construction of the canal, Clinton sent a complimentary letter to Ellicott, stating: "I cannot leave this place without congratulating you upon the success of the Canal bill. It has become a law by large majorities in both houses and after much opposition." [27] In this way, Clinton acknowledged how effectively Ellicott had worked on the canal project.

Ellicott had indeed played an important role in the selection of the canal route of the western sector. As early as 1808, he had favored a canal from the Genesee River direct to Buffalo Creek. He had helped to persuade the commissioners in 1812 to recommend to the legislature that the canal run directly to Lake Erie, rather than to Lake Ontario. He had convinced Busti to donate a larger piece of land to encourage canal construction. As a canal commissioner, he had urged a more southern route that passed through much of the Company lands. In 1817, the legislature vindicated his efforts by adopting the commission's recommendations to start canal construction.

Ellicott's efforts to build a canal paid dividends, for with the passage of the 1817 law, land sales in western New York increased. In response to the growing number of sales in the northern part of the purchase, Ellicott raised the price of all Company lands in that area by more than one dollar and fifty cents an acre.[28] He was achieving his goal of profit.

The Company profits continued to grow when the commissioners ordered that digging be started at once and pushed the construction work vigorously. On July 4, 1817, the contractor turned the first shovelful of dirt at Rome, and by the end of that year, the labor gangs had dug some fifteen miles of the canal channel. The following year the progress exceeded Clinton's "most sanguine expectations." [29] In 1819, a thousand men working in the marshes near Syracuse were felled by malarial fevers, but the canal building progressed, and in October of that year the workers had completed ninety-six miles of the canal project. In that year, too, the first boats navigated the completed section of the canal and Clinton found his dreams becoming a reality. Tammany Hall, jealous of the popularity that Clinton was gaining from the success of the canal, tried in 1819 to limit further construction westward to the Seneca River. The legislature defeated this move. From this point on, the building continued to completion.

The commissioners had given generously of their time to drive construction forward, but a "severe contusion" on commissioner Ellicott's right leg in 1818 forced him to resign from the board.[30] Although his injury was a real one, resulting from an accident while sleighing, some of his previous complaints revealed an illness more psychosomatic than organic, for he suffered from melancholy and had all the symptoms of hypochondria. In addition to his poor health, Ellicott felt that his "indispensable duties" limited the time he could spend as commissioner. As Resident-Agent, he was extremely busy meeting potential buyers, selling land, writing statements of land sales,

recording receipts, keeping numerous accounts up to date and attend-
ing to the many duties associated with his job. His annual reports
consumed much of his spare time. Further, Ellicott had his own handsome estate to supervise. Thus it was that when Ellicott thought that
his relative inactivity as a commissioner added to the burdens of the
other four members of the board, he offered his resignation to Clinton.

Busti regretted Ellicott's resignation. The opponents of the canal
were campaigning vigorously to stop the waterway westward at the
Seneca River, and Busti realized that the canal would have to continue to Buffalo, if the Company were to gain from its construction.
Moreover, he wanted a route in the west that passed through as much
of the Company land as possible. He knew the degree to which Ellicott
had influenced the commissioners in their original choice of a canal
directly to Buffalo rather than to Oswego, and he appreciated Ellicott's work in trying to determine the selection of a more southerly
route in the western sector. With all this in mind, he urged Ellicott
to accept some canal appointment that took less time than that of a
commissioner, but which still provided him with an opportunity to
affect the choice of the western route.

Paul Busti's concern was not without foundation for there remained
the knotty problem of which of the two routes the commissioners
should select for the western sector. One route ran on the south side
of the Niagara Escarpment, a mountain ridge that extended from
Lewiston to Rochester. Ellicott favored this route because it would
pass through some forty miles of the Company's land. The other route
ran on the north side of the Niagara Escarpment. At first, the commissioners supported the southern route. It would shorten the canal
by several miles and would correspondingly reduce the cost of construction. Furthermore, the Holland Land Company had donated
over 100,000 acres of land and the commissioners felt obligated to
please the Company. The southern route, however, had serious draw-
backs. The summit rose to seventy-five feet above the surface of Lake
Erie. The canal would thus lose the waters of that lake as a virtually
inexhaustible feeder. Moreover, the canal engineers were not convinced that the immediate creeks near the southern route could furnish
sufficient water to replace the expected canal leakages and to compensate for the losses from the use of many locks.

While the commissioners debated which route to choose, James
Geddes, a canal engineer, located a depression in the Niagara Escarpment. He found a break north of the Tonawanda Creek through which
the canal might proceed without too much cutting of the ridge. The

canal commissioners, therefore, abandoned the southern route, and, in 1820, adopted the route north of the escarpment.

Although the selection of the northern route deeply disappointed Ellicott, this setback did not end his influence or interest in the project. He understood how vitally the canal affected land sales and profit. Thus, when DeWitt Clinton asked him to recommend a suitable person "to examine Buffalo Creek and to report the plan of a safe and commodious harbor at that place for vessels navigating Lake Erie, together with an estimate of the probable expense," Ellicott accepted the Governor's request.[31] He saw that this report would probably decide the location of the western terminus of the canal. If Buffalo Creek had "a safe and commodious harbor," what better place could the board choose as the terminus—particularly since the lands washed by the creek were part of the Holland Land Company? Ellicott therefore submitted the name of William Peacock to Clinton as an excellent man for the position, for he felt that Peacock would favor the Company interest. Clinton promptly endorsed Ellicott's recommendation and appointed Peacock to the position.

The assignment of Peacock to the task of examining Buffalo Creek as a possible harbor on Lake Erie intensified the long-smoldering fight between Black Rock and Buffalo. Today, Black Rock is incorporated into the city of Buffalo, but during the early nineteenth century, the two were independent villages and bitter commercial rivals. The village got its name from a large black rock, one hundred feet broad, that jutted into the river. Located about three miles down the Niagara River, Black Rock had the only safe harbor at the eastern end of Lake Erie north of Dunkirk, fifty miles away. It was a natural port, sheltered from the lake winds by the rocky Bird Island and the larger Squaw Island.

The Porter Brothers had seen as clearly as had Ellicott that Peacock's report could well decide the location of the canal terminus. Starting in 1806, when the legislature had permitted the sale of lands in the vicinity of Black Rock,[32] Augustus and Peter B. Porter had accumulated sizable holdings in that area. They had joined with Benjamin Barton and Barton's uncle, Joseph Annin, in buying some lots along the Niagara River from Fort Niagara to Black Rock and in leasing the landing places at Black Rock and Lewiston.

Barton and the Porters had formed the firm of Porter, Barton and Company which grew into a substantial carrying business. As builders and owners of vessels sailing on Lakes Erie and Ontario, the Company supplied the military posts along the Great Lakes at Fort Niagara,

Wayne, Chicago, and Michilimackinac with meat, bread, flour, liquor, and especially salt; Black Rock was a great salt exchange. The firm also handled nearly all the business of the American fur companies as well as that of large Indian traders. With its monopoly of transportation along this much-used route, Porter, Barton and Company controlled the portage business using the Niagara River. So much was involved that the Porter Brothers understandably wanted the canal commissioners to choose Black Rock, not Buffalo, as the terminal point.

The Porters marshaled their forces for the coming fight against the agents of the Holland Land Company. Black Rock, they pointed out, already had a good harbor that seemed superior to that of Buffalo; and the canal would have to run at least three additional miles if the commissioners extended it beyond Black Rock to Buffalo. Porter, Barton and Company held strongly to its position because it had its store and warehouses at Black Rock, and also owned considerable land in the area. Earlier, Peter Porter had tried to influence Governor Tompkins in the selection of a canal route directly to Oswego and Lake Ontario. Clinton claimed that Porter had "infused his opinions into Tompkins who is profoundly ignorant of the subject, whose opinion [is] not worthy of respect but whose opposition is heretofore indirect."[33] In vain, Clinton had tried to persuade Porter to favor the Lake Erie route.

The Holland Land Company and Ellicott were equally determined that Buffalo should be the terminal point. The Company had much land to sell in and around that village; and Ellicott, himself, at one time reportedly owned one-third of Buffalo. If the canal terminated there, land sales and profits would rocket. Although only three miles separated Black Rock from Buffalo, the termination point of the canal would decide which of the two villages would become the "Queen City."

Peacock's report in 1819 explored the possibilities of a harbor at Buffalo and concluded in favor of Buffalo over Black Rock. Before forwarding his report to Clinton, he submitted it to Ellicott for his employer's approval. In the report, Peacock recognized that in the summer "vast quantities of sand and gravel" clogged the entrance to the Buffalo harbor. To solve this problem, Peacock recommended "the construction of a Stone Pier." He implemented this recommendation with various plans whereby the engineers could erect the pier. Peacock explained how the forces of nature aided Buffalo, for when ice broke up in the spring, the great discharge of water cut a clearance through the clogged gravel, and this passage formed a channel some twelve feet deep. Furthermore, the lake current flowed one-half mile an hour, added pressure to the spring flow, and eliminated the gravel and sand handicap. Peacock therefore concluded his report by advising that the commissioners select Buffalo for the harbor and the western terminus of the canal. As he put it: "Buffalo from its local situation is apparently the key which opens to the People of the State of New York a most stupendous path of navigation and of commerce extending the distance of more than 2,000 miles." [34]

Independent of Peacock's report and Ellicott's efforts, some of the more aggressive residents of Buffalo had petitioned the legislature for a donation of money to build a harbor. Ellicott felt that "the ever restless Buffalonians" had behaved impatiently in not permitting the legislature sufficient time to analyze Peacock's report concerning harbor facilities.[35] He was afraid that the blatant approach and agressiveness of this group might alienate the legislature's sympathetic attitude. He hoped that the legislature would therefore ignore the petition, for he felt that pushing it might endanger the entire harbor project. Senator Evans, Ellicott's nephew, agreed with his uncle's position but remained calm, for he thought that the bill had slight chance of passage.

Contrary to their expectations, on April 7, 1819, the legislature acceded to the demands of the Buffalo residents and passed an act for the construction of a harbor at Buffalo. The legislature, however, instead of making an outright grant, instructed the Comptroller to "lend . . . the sum of twelve thousand dollars" to all or any of the people of Buffalo; the debtors were to repay the loan in ten years.[36] Thus the legislature permitted them to form a special company to construct a harbor at Buffalo. In the event that the commissioners chose Black Rock as the canal terminus, the law allowed the corporation to charge a fee for every vessel that used the newly constructed Buffalo harbor. Ellicott strongly opposed this aspect of the act.

Ellicott's opposition to the petition for a Buffalo harbor brought him into conflict with the more influential Buffalo residents. Their resentment changed to bitterness when, in 1820, it appeared that the canal commissioners had decided on Black Rock as the terminus. Angrily, Oliver Forward, Samuel Wilkeson, George Coit, and Charles Townsend—all from Buffalo—turned to Busti for financial aid, explaining to him their grievances against Ellicott. They charged Ellicott with misrepresentation, claiming that he obtained high prices for lots in Buffalo on his promise that a harbor would soon be built. They blamed him for the reported loss of the canal terminus to Black Rock, and asserted that, by offering in 1818 a paltry $3,500 toward the Buffalo harbor construction, he had forced the residents to petition the legislature for an outright grant of money. When the legislature offered them a loan, instead of a grant, they had been forced to saddle themselves with debt to obtain sufficient funds to build the harbor.

Despite the gloomy outlook, Buffalo residents still hoped that the commissioners would choose Buffalo as the canal terminus. If Buffalo were selected, they felt that the commissioners would then "authorize the loan to be converted into part of the Canal fund." In an effort to impress the commission, they therefore proposed to make the Buffalo site more attractive by building a pier similar to the one that Peacock had recommended in the 1819 report. From the Holland Land Company they sought an appropriation for building this pier. If the appropriation did not materialize, and if the legislature refused to cancel their debts, they wanted the Holland Company to share "an equitable proportion of the loss." [37]

Busti refused to share the possible losses if the legislature refused to cancel Buffalo's debts. Busti explained that he always followed the rule of aiding public works programs, provided that the legislature, and not a private company such as theirs, undertook such a venture. Had the government undertaken the project, Busti would have raised the capital. As the situation was, he did not have sufficient confidence that a private company would succeed.

Despite Busti's refusal and Ellicott's noncooperation, Buffalo residents built a harbor which, in turn, influenced the commission to choose Buffalo as the terminus. Construction of the harbor started in May, 1821, and the following year Buffalo extended the pier. Progress on the Buffalo harbor weakened Black Rock's claim to selection as the canal terminus. Finally, in 1822 the commissioners decided in favor of Buffalo as the western terminus. Black Rock refused to accept this decision and continued desperately to try to reverse the commission's verdict. The bitter wrangling between the two villages continued. The newspapers of each village assaulted those of the other with vigor and venom; the *Niagara Journal* and the *Niagara Patriot* favored Buffalo, while the *Black Rock Beacon* supported Black Rock.[38] Like their newspapers, the citizens of both villages persisted to the very end in the fierce battle. Peter Porter commanded the Black Rock forces and Samuel Wilkeson led the Buffalo group. The commission, however, stuck firmly to its decision of 1822 that the canal would end at Buffalo. On August 9, 1823, six of the older Buffalo residents dug the first shovelful of earth that made Buffalo the canal terminus. Buffalo had won.

While Buffalo residents claimed credit for getting the canal terminus at their village, Ellicott deserved recognition for his part in the canal project in the west. Since 1808, he had played an important role in planning and building the western sector of the canal. In the selection of a canal route, his recommendations had received a careful hearing; engineering, and not political considerations, had decided the issue. The differences between Ellicott and the Buffalo group over the canal terminus rested mainly on tactics, rather than on objectives. Both desired and worked towards the identical end of making Buffalo the terminus; but in the process of applying their tactics, each occasionally lost sight of the common goal. These differences developed into the bitterness that many Buffalo residents harbored against Joseph Ellicott.

Despite his important role in the building of the Grand Canal, the antagonism against Ellicott continued. His many years as Resident-Agent and political boss of western New York had left an expected residue of opposition. His enemies gradually increased and now they coalesced. In demands that became increasingly strident, they clamored for the removal of Ellicott. The Resident-Agent's long-time friend and associate, Paul Busti, had now to make a decision fateful in the life of Joseph Ellicott.

X. *"Give in Your Demission Yourself"*

Between 1800 and 1820, the United States was taking shape. Physically, the area of the country had more than doubled. The fortuitous purchase of Louisiana had pushed the frontier westward to the Rockies, and the nibbling conquest of the Floridas had rounded out the territorial limits of the Southeast. Almost in step with the territorial expansion was the population boost from 5.3 million in 1800 to 9.6 million twenty years later. Within these two decades, seven new states had entered the union. From the Northwest Territory had been carved Ohio (1803), Indiana (1816), and Illinois (1819). Formed from the nucleus of French settlements was Louisiana (1812). In the deep South between Louisiana and Georgia were created the states of Mississippi (1817) and Alabama (1819). And whittled from Massachusetts was Maine (1820).

The nation was also taking institutional shape. Politically, the Jeffersonians had demonstrated the feasibility of a two-party system. They had taken over the reins of government pacifically and proved erroneous the Federalist prognosis of revolution, dissolution, and anarchy.

The evolving economic structure was a compromise: part Hamiltonian and part Jeffersonian. Portions of Hamilton's dream were coming to reality. Trade was growing, cities were rising, and manufacturing was increasing. Except for the embargo restrictions on trade, commerce had flourished. The War of 1812 had persuaded a Jeffersonian-dominated Congress to adopt much of Hamilton's program. An internal tax law was passed, and the national debt in 1815 surpassed by far that which the Republicans had inherited in 1801. Shortly after the war ended, a pattern of tariff increases to protect manufacturing was begun, and a charter was granted for a second Bank of the United States.

As Hamilton's business community was evolving, Jefferson's agriculturally based society was expanding. During the first two decades of the nineteenth century, the number of farmers and the acres under cultivation increased sharply. Agriculture was the economic backbone of the nation. In the South, the cotton culture was riveting itself both on the whites and the Negroes. After the 1790's, cotton production exceeded tobacco and became the agricultural staple of the country.

At the same time, an important process of settlement was taking deep root west of the Appalachians. Leading the procession were Indian traders, hunters, and trappers. Close behind them were the pioneers who created the conditions of settlements. The pioneers cleared the ground, planted crops, and while waiting for the harvest shot wild birds and animals for food. They were generally squatters with little or no money and after a few years moved farther west. Then came the steady farmers. These men had a clear title to the land, systematically cleared out the trees and boulders, and settled permanently on their piece of property

In 1800, the area between the Genesee and Lake Erie could well be considered a part of the west. When the Senecas had relinquished ownership of most of western New York at the Treaty of Big Tree in 1797, the land was a wilderness. But already the procession was started of Indian traders, hunters, pioneers, and settlers. This cycle of settlement was as characteristic of western New York as elsewhere on the trans-Appalachians.

The Indian traders were a diverse lot. Captain William Johnston, for example, had originally been with the British Indian Department and then had settled near the mouth of Buffalo Creek, where he was a trader and an interpreter. This was the same Johnston who had married a Seneca woman, had obtained two square miles of land at Buffalo Creek, and then in 1799 had swapped it to the Holland Land Company for land in another section of Buffalo. Silas Hopkins, another Indian trader, had bought furs at Lewiston as early as 1788. At Buffalo Creek, Cornelius Winne had erected one of the earliest buildings where he traded with the Senecas. Winne, according to a contemporary Deacon Hinds Chamberlin, ran a lively business: "He had rum, whiskey, Indian knives, trinkets, &c. His house was full of Indians; they looked at us with a good deal of curiosity. We had but a poor night's rest; the Indians were in and out all night, getting liquor." [1]

The fur traders were easier to isolate and identify than the hunters, pioneers, and settlers. Until the first crop was harvested, many of the pioneers and settlers had hunted wild life for their very survival. Furthermore, a number of pioneers moved to Ohio and then returned to western New York.

By 1820, the wilderness that was western New York was giving way to settled areas. Ontario, the only county in 1800, had been subdivided into six counties by 1820, and each one had new county seats, towns, and villages. Rochester, Batavia, and Buffalo were budding cities. The scars caused by the War of 1812 were healing. While the economy remained predominantly rural, shipping continued on the Great Lakes, communities traded with each other, and Buffalo had an independent though floundering bank. Roads were being constructed, and the canal was beginning to snake its way into western New York.

During these two decades, the population of western New York had risen from less than 15,000 to over 100,000. Yankees from New England alone accounted for much of this increase. Timothy Dwight, the peripatetic president of Yale who traveled through New York in 1810, estimated that three-fifths to two-thirds of the population came from New England. Ten years later, the proud Dwight wrote modestly that the state of New York was becoming "a colony of New-England." [2]

Dwight's claims notwithstanding, the Yankees from Connecticut and Vermont made a lasting impression on New York. They brought with them their town-meeting type of decision making, generally siding with the democratic forces as opposed to the landed aristocracy. Not long after clearing their lands, they erected the typical white, bare, and square churches topped by steeples reaching toward the heavens. Accustomed to tax-supported schools open to all children and disillusioned with the more backward system of New York's education, they started private academies. At first, the Yankees irritated, annoyed, and angered the Yorkers. Gradually, the New Englanders were accepted and became leaders in politics, economics, and social life.

Just as the Yorkers had been forced to adjust to the Yankees, so Joseph Ellicott could not remain immune to the inevitable changes sweeping western New York. When he broke with DeWitt Clinton in 1819 over the operations of the Bank of Niagara, Ellicott had taken the first step that was to lead to the ultimate crumbling of his great power in western New York. The fall of Ellicott was not the result of any single historical event but stemmed from several causes. Agent-General Busti, whose approval Ellicott needed to keep his position, had become deeply disturbed over three major controversies that came to a boiling point almost simultaneously after the war.

The first dispute revolved about the personality clash between the increasingly melancholic Ellicott and the more stable Busti. For many years, Ellicott's mercurial temperament and abrasive disposition had been noticed. John Brannan, who applied for a job at the Batavia office in 1823, recalled the situation almost two decades earlier. Starting in 1804, Brannan had worked as Ellicott's bookkeeper for three years. The Resident-Agent already showed "a very unhappy temper" and was even then "occasionally extremely abusive and insulting to every person about him." [3] Brannan's observations were corroborated by Busti's close associate and Company agent, H. J. Huidekoper. In 1809, Huidekoper had visited Lancaster, New York, and learned that Ellicott was "very unpopular" and "the unfittest man to intrigue" in that village.[4]

Since 1817, Ellicott had become more and more despondent, and as these periods of moodiness lengthened, his uncivil treatment of Company customers intensified. Before, he had always spoken his mind directly; however, in the period following the war he frequently treated visitors in a rude and blunt manner. Philip Church, who owned a large tract in Alleghany County, confided to Busti that Ellicott was "wholly wanting" in either "civility" or "politeness." [5] Although ill health may well have been responsible for reducing his fitness to deal with people, his disagreeable conduct was bound to add to the dissatisfaction that Paul Busti already felt for him.

Joseph Ellicott's unstable personality fanned still higher the flame of discontent that now raged in western New York. In the early years of his agency, he had managed to keep calm publicly in the face of the charges leveled against him. Fifty-five years old in 1815, he had held the demanding post of Resident-Agent for fifteen trying years. As Ellicott aged, however, he lost some of his ability to slough off adverse criticism. When the Buffalo *Gazette* of September 12, 1815, carried a story signed by "Cattaragus" which blamed the Holland Company and its agents for the poor conditions of the roads and bridges, Ellicott showed his petulence by promptly canceling his subscription to that newspaper.

Until 1815, Busti had minimized Ellicott's peculiarities because the settlers on the purchase had endorsed his Resident-Agent's excellent leadership. The settlers, on their part, supported Ellicott because his objectives, until the end of the war, had generally been beneficial to them. After the war, however, when Ellicott's handling of the Company's policies brought him into conflict with the residents of western New York, Busti became more critical of Ellicott's personal weaknesses.

The War of 1812 had engendered in western New York, as it had in other parts of the country, nationalistic sentiments. Nationalism was a mythical feeling that bound together people who had certain characteristics in common. As a nation, for example, Americans lived within geographical limits that separated them from other countries. They approved a political organization with an elected head, rather than a hereditary monarch. They had fought in wars together and interpreted the American Revolution and the War of 1812 as single-handed victories by the innocent over the aggressor. They spoke a common language, English, using idiomatic and colloquial variations. They worshipped one God, and the great bulk of Americans were Protestants. They depended on each other in earning a living, for most of the trade was internal. More items can be added to this list of national characteristics. The point is that Americans felt united by certain nationalistic ties that set them apart from other nations.

Over the years, this mystical feeling of togetherness had been cemented. The words *liberty* and *freedom* took on a connotation that Americans regarded as uniquely their own. Slogans became shibboleths. Phrases like "Give me liberty or give me death," "All men are created equal," "We have met the enemy and they are ours," or "Our country, right or wrong" were uttered as reverential blessings. The flag known as the Stars and Stripes emerged as a venerated symbol to be saluted, protected, and if need be died for. The federal constitution came to be regarded as a work that was divinely inspired and ordained. Men like Washington, Franklin, and Jackson were eulogized and elevated to semi-Godlike posture. To bring about an American nationalism, a sharp contrast with Europe was created. But a distorted picture was emerging of the ancient, grasping, aggressive, reactionary European nations opposing the young, generous, pacific, democratic United States. United States residents who did not conform to this view of American nationalism were denounced as un-American, as aliens with almost treasonable motives.

The War of 1812 had stirred the residents of western New York to scorn all aliens in general, and the Holland Land Company in particular. The settlers had relegated Ellicott, who represented the Company in western New York, to the ranks of the foreigners. Moreover, in accentuating American nationalism, the war had reduced the social and personal pressures on the settlers to honor their debts to foreigners. Thus, many residents did not meet their obligations, offering explanations, instead, in the form of "patriotic grievances" against their creditors. While an increasing number of residents continued to voice complaints, it was not until 1819 that a series of four articles, signed by "Agricola," appearing in the *Niagara Journal,* summarized succinctly what the settlers had been muttering incoherently. "Agricola" blamed the Holland Company for many injustices; it was foreign owned; it reserved choice land which it refused to sell; and it charged excessively high prices for the land that it did sell. The Company levied compound interest on debts, and it planned to keep the settlers in a state of perpetual debt. Over a five-week period, the newspaper printed the case of the settlers, each article covering from two to more than three columns. With the publication of the "Agricola" series, a systematic all-out attack against the Company was launched criticizing both the Agent-General and his Resident-Agent.[6]

To reduce Busti's great concern over these charges, Ellicott revealed to him the identity of "Agricola," and explained the cause of such blistering criticism. The pen name belonged to Albert H. Tracy, a lawyer in Buffalo who was a congressman and a leading Clintonian in western New York. Tracy's reasons for writing the articles, Ellicott stated, were primarily political, the actions of a congressman seeking additional support of the voters. After all, claimed Ellicott, "Agricola" was held high "in the confidence of the State Administration," and the "Agricola" series was probably part of a larger political plan against himself and his supporters. As additional evidence, the Resident-Agent linked Tracy with the struggle to undermine the Bank of Niagara. "He was," charged Ellicott, "the principal agent and director of the combination that ran down the Niagara Bank." [7]

Ellicott regarded Albert Tracy as a mere pawn in the political game, and he placed the blame for the over-all attack squarely on DeWitt Clinton. He claimed that Clinton had learned that the Big Family had lost much of its affection for the Governor. To keep Ellicott in line, Clinton had used Tracy to pressure Ellicott into continuing his support of himself, or, failing in that, to discredit the Big Family entirely. Clinton, Ellicott explained, "may have received from his spies and informers [information] that the people in the Land office do not idolize him as formerly." The Resident-Agent continued his appraisal of Clinton, noting shrewdly: "as nothing but the greatest adulation will continue him friendly, and probably having taken the idea that we are not altogether gratified with all his measures I think it probably has through the agency of others set this young man [Tracy] to work to write down the agents of the Holland Company." At the same time, Ellicott confessed that "I was once myself a perfect adorer of Mr. D.W.C. . . . but my ardour for him has become considerably cooled." The rationale for this change, explained Ellicott, was that Clinton "most unquestionably contemplates to govern the State through the agency of the bankrupt Jacobin, and the lower order of the people." Ellicott insisted that his position was not sudden but that he had "for more than a year been a silent spectator of events." [8] Sharing Ellicott's interpretation, Archibald S. Clarke blamed Clinton, as well as the politically powerful Ambrose Spencer, for "Agricola's" attack against the Company. "The fingers of Clinton & Spencer," accused Clarke, "are in all this business." [9]

While Busti considered ways in which to cope with the attacks on the Company, Ellicott advised that nothing should be done until the attackers had wearied and lost their aggressiveness. "My impressions are," counseled Ellicott, "that the writer if no notice was taken of him, would grow tired of the subject, and for the want of fuel cease his malignant hostility." [10] The Resident-Agent applied his own advice when he instructed William Peacock not to retaliate but to "lay perfectly quiet" for he felt "the least said the better." [11] Contrary to Ellicott's expectations that the attacks would cease, the criticisms spread. The *Chautauqua Gazette* was soon publishing the "Agricola" series.

The nativistic complaints that Tracy used in his "Agricola" series accounted only in part for the genuine hostility that many western New Yorkers felt against the Company and Ellicott. After the war, the stream of immigrants to western New York had dried to a trickle and thus reduced business activity on the purchase. In addition, the settlers west of the Genesee began to feel the effects of the panic of 1819 earlier than the rest of the nation, for the war prosperity had soon given way to an acute currency shortage. The settlers therefore censured Joseph Ellicott for shipping precious money off the purchase and blamed the Dutch owners, as aliens, for pocketing the currency so badly needed. As the postwar spirit for widening individual land-ownership spread throughout the western frontier, the settlers also vehemently denounced the large land holdings of the Holland Company as anti-democratic. It was just a short step, then, for the residents west of the Genesee to broaden their opposition to the Company to include Joseph Ellicott himself. As agent, they pointed out, he had gained for himself considerable wealth from land sales and speculation. Unable to redress their grievances by their own efforts, the settlers on the purchase now turned to the state legislature and demanded protective legislation. Thus, instead of placating the residents by remaining silent, Ellicott now faced a large number of malcontented settlers who girded themselves for a more serious battle.

Paul Busti was greatly disturbed at Ellicott's increasing melancholy. However, the Agent-General was a man of honor and integrity, without a disposition to embarrass Ellicott, much less fault him for his own mental illness. Busti tried to accommodate himself to the first problem. But the Agent-General blamed the Resident-Agent for the second issue: Ellicott's failure to pacify the western New Yorkers. Many residents on the purchase were organizing, openly attacking the Company and its two main agents, and carrying their grievances to the legislature. Whatever the justification, this movement could not be treated lightly.

Busti was seriously concerned, too, with a third controversial area —Ellicott's lobbying efforts at the state level. Ellicott's task here was twofold: to obstruct the passage of bills desired by the residents of the purchase that might reduce the Company profits; and to help to push through the legislature a bill that Busti desired—to sell the Company land to the State of New York. The Agent-General watched closely as his Resident-Agent and the settlers on the purchase shifted to the next scene of their combat at Albany.

In seeking a solution to their economic problems, the settlers west of the Genesee suggested to the state legislature that nonresidents, as well as residents, be taxed for construction projects. New York law compelled only the residents to pay the tax for the maintenance of roads and the construction of schools, and this disturbed the settlers because such legislation exempted the nonresident landowners whom the western New Yorkers felt were best able to pay. If the law could be changed, the residents felt that their financial condition would be greatly improved. Their taxes, for example, would decrease by transferring some of the burden to the shoulders of the Company, the largest absentee landowner. Furthermore, the money collected from the Holland Land Company would reduce the amount that Busti sent overseas, and the circulation of currency in western New York would also be increased. This might hasten the return of prosperity in the area west of the Genesee. Finally, such a change in the law would unify the residents on the purchase against the Company. This was the kind of legislation that Ellicott had to combat.

The Resident-Agent had a difficult problem to handle in the movement for tax reform. As early as 1815, petitions were circulated demanding that absentee-landowners be included in the "road-tax." Although the Batavia newspaper, the Republican *Advocate,* continued to defend Ellicott and the Holland Land Company, the Buffalo *Gazette* added its influence in support of these requests, and in 1816 a bill for such a measure appeared in the legislature. The proposed tax applied to all nonresident property owners in western New York who owned land where new roads would be built. Frightened by the implications of the proposed levy, Ellicott took action against the bill. For example, he urged Silas Hopkins, a supervisor of Niagara County, to protest formally: "I hope, Sir, you have or will be good enough to frame a remonstrance against those petitions, with such remarks and elucidations as will be calculated to prevent the effects such petitions in all probability would produce if not any opposition was made to them." [12] Hopkins did what Ellicott bid him. By using his influence with Hopkins and other influential citizens, Ellicott thus succeeded in defeating these early bills for tax reform.

However, the idea for a revised levy remained alive, and in 1817 some residents of Buffalo petitioned the legislature to permit its village to apply the road-tax to the nonresident landowners. Ellicott opposed the Buffalo bill and argued that the absentee landowners already paid far more than their share of the taxes. In support of this view, he cited the fact that empty lots owned by nonresidents were assessed "100 percent higher" than resident lots "with buildings erected." [13] Ellicott felt confident that the lawmakers would defeat the bill, for the legislature had granted similar powers in only one prior case. However, the ever-careful Ellicott took no chances and notified his influential friends that he was strongly opposed to the bill. As a result, the legislature refused to grant the village of Buffalo permission to use the road-tax against absentee lands.

Undaunted, the settlers in western New York continued to press for authority to tax nonresident landowners. In 1818, the assembly received a petition urging such legislation and routed it to the proper committee. Senator Jediah Prendergast, a friend of Ellicott and a representative of the western district, requested permission to come before this committee so that he could explain his reasons for opposing the bill. Ellicott furnished the Senator with additional arguments and data to be used at the committee hearings. In addition, Ellicott urged members of both houses to vote against the measure. In an effort to compromise, the lawmakers approved a road-tax on absentee landowners in western New York who owned land in sections where the new roads would run, but they limited such tax to one year.

Considering this measure as only a partial victory, the proponents of the road-tax redoubled their efforts to extend and broaden the law. Some of the residents of Cattaraugus County acted independently from the rest of western New York, and in 1819, they petitioned the legislature to permit a tax of five dollars for each square mile owned by nonresident landowners. This money would be applied to the construction of roads and the building of bridges. Had the legislature passed such a bill, the Company, which owned 1,400 square miles of land in that county, would have been forced to pay $7,000 a year in addition to its current taxes. However, through the efforts of Senator Evans, Ellicott's nephew, this bill died in committee. "Mr. Evans," Ellicott reported to

Busti, "prevailed upon the committee to whom the petition was re-
ferred to report against the prayers of the petitioners, and nothing
further was done with the petition." At the same time, Ellicott assured
Busti that Evans always had the interest of the Company at heart.
"You may rest satisfied," he confided, "that as far as Mr. Evans will
have influence to prevent any act or acts from being passed injurious
to our Principals it will be exerted." The Resident-Agent elaborated
that "Mr. E. being one of the Majority on the political Side of the
Senate, I do not apprehend the Company have much to fear that any
act will be passed very injurious to our principals." [14]

Despite the setback dealt the residents of Cattaraugus County, the
other settlers in western New York persisted in agitating for a permanent road-tax on absentee landowners. Starting in September, 1819,
the *Niagara Journal* printed the "Agricola" series that attacked the Holland Company. Its author, Tracy, dwelt on what he regarded as the
Company evils, but he offered no sweeping solutions. He simply suggested that the legislature permanently terminate the road-tax exemp-
tions of nonresident landowners in western New York. With this in
mind, Tracy called a meeting of the residents of Niagara County in
October of the same year. To this gathering came several prominent
politicians west of the Genesee: Oliver Forward, formerly a friend of
Ellicott, who served as chairman; Augustus Porter; and Porter's partner, Benjamin Barton. The members present voted unanimously to
petition the legislature for a law that would permanently tax the nonresident landowners for the building and maintenance of roads,
bridges, and schoolhouses.

The movement gathered momentum as the petitions that had been
agreed upon at the October meeting were circulated on the purchase.
The editor of the *Niagara Journal,* rabidly anti-Ellicott, trumpeted that
the formal requests were getting much support in the five counties
and praised the "unexampled degree of unanimity of opinion and con-
cert of action among the people." The newspaper openly attacked
Joseph Ellicott and his family for the "strenuous opposition, personal
invective and abuse levelled by them" against every one who favored
such a tax. Refusing to believe that the Big Family could block the
passage of such a bill, the *Niagara Journal* argued that the opposition
of the Ellicott family to this measure was "grounded on merely the
personal interest of Mr. Ellicott and supported solely by his family
connections and dependents." [15] The petitions attracted signers, and,
when 1,300 persons added their signatures, they were forwarded to
Albany.

Early in 1820, the road-tax petition, now taking the form of a bill, started through the legislature. First, the Speaker routed it to the proper committee for its scrutiny. As chairman of this committee, Oliver Forward wasted little time on committee hearings; instead, he presented it quickly to the assembly. Senator Evans, who hoped to obstruct the bill's progress in committee, was deeply disappointed and reported to his uncle: "Forward had made the report and presented the bill of his own mere motion without taking the opinion of any other member of the committee." [16] When the bill reached the assembly floor, Forward presented a strong case for its support. As Ellicott feared, the Clintonian-controlled assembly easily passed the road-tax bill.

Ellicott now mustered all his influence to get the senate to defeat the hated measure. Ogden, the Company lobbyist, was alerted, and Senator Evans exerted still greater pressure on his fellow senators. Busti watched the procedure apprehensively but felt some assurance in knowing that Evans would "combat" the bill.[17] Ellicott, however, refused to rely solely on these trusted aides. He allied himself with Robert Troup, the land agent for the nearby Pulteney Estate. In December, 1819, Ellicott and Troup had together employed Philip Church to lobby for a law that limited the taxing powers of the county board of supervisors. Church, whose mother was the daughter of the once politically powerful General Philip Schuyler, was now thrown into the battle to defeat the bill—and Ellicott did not haggle over the costs involved: "Any sum," agreed Ellicott, "which may be considered just and proper to allow Mr. Church for his services will be paid by my Principals with pleasure on the receipt of your Draft." [18] The Resident-Agent had done all that he could and it was enough. In April, 1820, the bill for the road-tax died in the senate.

Evans had done yeoman's work "in laying the ground of the heavy opposition to the bill," [19] Ogden had given considerable support to Evans, and Church had "increased the weight of the opposition to the bill." [20] The cleavage in the Republican ranks had also benefited Ellicott. Back in 1817, the Republicans had split into two factions, the followers of Clinton and the supporters of Tammany. The anti-Clintonians were called Bucktails, a name given to Tammany Society because the members wore tails of deer at patriotic gatherings. Led by Martin Van Buren, the Bucktails used this opportunity to oppose the road-tax bill because the Clintonians favored it. After 1820, the legislature discussed similar highway bills nearly every year for almost ten years, but every time the large landowners wielded sufficient influence to prevent their passage.

While Ellicott busied himself organizing the opposition to the road-tax, Busti also urged him to promote the sale of Company land to the State of New York. This proposal was not a new one, for the Dutch owners had advanced it as early as 1798 when great spending and negligible returns seemed "ruinous." The Company had offered to sell its 3.3 million acres for two dollars an acre and to take in return state bonds that paid 5½ percent annually and were "reimbursable in 20 years." If the state wanted more time, an alternate plan would defer interest payments until January 1, 1804, but would increase interest charges to 6 percent and the price per acre to $2.50.[21] Political leaders, who in 1791 had sold 4 million acres in northern New York for eight cents an acre, understandably had ignored the offer.

The Company directors had persisted and, in 1802, had renewed their proposition in modified form. The plan of 1802 had reduced the price of the land to $1.50 per acre on the condition that the Company would retain some four or five hundred thousand acres to be sold later when increased settlement would enhance land values. Loyal to his superiors, Paul Busti had taken his instructions seriously and had appointed Ellicott to handle this matter at Albany. Ellicott had not succeeded either, for the legislature had done nothing about this proposal during the spring session of 1803. "Continue your exertions," Busti had instructed Ellicott, "in procuring influential advocates to our plan." [22] Although Ellicott had not been "very Sanguine" about the success of the project, he had complied with Busti's orders.[23] The politicians whom Ellicott had consulted, however, had refused to risk their positions for such a venture, and the project had been dropped for many years.

In 1819, Busti revived this idea of selling the Company land to the State of New York. The sharp criticism of the Company and its representatives had upset him, and the vigorous efforts to impose the road-tax on the Company lands had frightened him into taking action. He considered the project of selling the land an extremely important one and urged Ellicott to work to his fullest capacity towards its achievement. Ellicott accepted the assignment and made Busti's desires known to those persons in Albany who could effect such a sale. Early in 1820, the Company lieutenants moved to achieve this objective: both David Ogden and his brother Ludlow lobbied in Albany; Evans against pressured his fellow senators; and Ellicott himself prepared "the minds of the people of the western counties" for the sale.[24] When all preparations were completed by March, Busti offered to sell all the Company lands, mortgages, and contracts in the state for a little over $6 million; he later reduced this figure to $5.5 million. The state could pay this money in 4 percent bonds. Busti made a good case for the sale as he pointed out that of the original purchase, the company still owned 1,770,369 acres, and were creditors for $4.5 million in future payments.

With prospects for an early passage quite favorable, Busti's petition moved into the legislature, but the bill was not destined to win approval. Ellicott, of course, urged his nephew David Evans to support the measure and to "use all his efforts consistent with his legislative duties towards accomplishing the Sale." [25] Agent-General Busti recognized Ellicott's influence on his nephew for he told Ellicott: "From your Nephew Evans . . . I expect to find a strong cooperation of my scheme; besides my insinuation, he [Evans] will have received the injunctions of his uncle." [26] Ogden also worked hard on behalf of the Company's cause, but the legislative term was too close to adjournment to allow sufficient time for the necessary discussion of such a sale. Moreover, the Bucktails and Clintonians fought each other so bitterly that they refused to effect a compromise on the plan. Thus ended the Company's efforts to sell its land west of the Genesee to the government, for Busti accepted the fact that the project had become too controversial for the legislators to handle. While Busti lauded Ellicott for blocking the passage of the road-tax, he felt that his Resident-Agent had not demonstrated sufficient flexibility in campaigning for the sale of Company land to the state. The Agent-General was never to forgive his Resident-Agent's failure in this project.

Joseph Ellicott's conduct in each of the three major issues had shaken Busti's great confidence in the Resident-Agent. His increasing melancholia had upset Busti, as had his failure to placate the western New Yorkers, and his inability to persuade the state legislature to buy the Company land. The gubernatorial election of 1820 was the Joshua-like blow that caused the final split between the two men.

The election of 1820 had special significance because it was the first time that Ellicott opposed DeWitt Clinton politically. Prior to this, in 1817, he had given Clinton his wholehearted support in his race against Peter B. Porter, and in the 1818 election, he had backed Clintonian candidates for offices in the state legislature. What is more, his nephew, David E. Evans, a member of the state senate, had generally supported Clinton during the legislative squabbles of the following year.

In the campaign for the governorship in 1820, however, Joseph Ellicott decided to break with the Governor and to support Daniel Tompkins, the Bucktail candidate. The split was the direct result of

Clinton's opposition to Ellicott's policies for the Bank of Niagara. The Governor's intervention in the affairs of the bank convinced Ellicott that Clinton lacked integrity. Thus, in the 1820 election he joined the opposition party and the Big Family followed its leader out of the Clintonian ranks. Ellicott's nephew, David Evans, also refused to support Clinton's associates and along with his uncle united with the Bucktails, while William Peacock, Ellicott's nephew by marriage and the Company subagent of Chautauqua County, used his political influence against Clinton. The Bucktails depended on this schism between the Governor and the Big Family to reduce Clinton's traditional pluralities in western New York and thus bring victory to Daniel Tompkins. "The Bucks agree," reasoned Forward, who was a Clintonian, "that the election depends on our Counties [Niagara, Genesee, Cattaraugus, Chautauqua] & they depend on Ellicott, Clarke & Wilson." [27] Archibald Clarke and Isaac Wilson were friends of Ellicott and had supported him loyally.

After a hard-fought campaign in which some 80 percent of the normally Republican newspapers favored the incumbent, the voters reelected DeWitt Clinton as governor by a scant majority. In nearly 93,500 votes cast, only 1,457 separated the two candidates. Ellicott and the Big Family failed in their mission. In western New York, Clinton received a plurality of 3,462 that helped to decide the election. The voters in the western section preferred Clinton because they wanted the canal, and Clinton had never wavered in his support of this waterway. Tompkins, on the other hand, carefully avoided committing himself on this issue. As a result, although Ellicott had given valiant support to the canal project, the voters refused to hand over the governorship to his candidate, Daniel Tompkins.

Both parties claimed the 1820 election results as a victory, and in part each could justify its assertions. The Clintonians won the gubernatorial election, and in the western district, senatorial candidates Forward, Hart, and Mills defeated their Bucktail opponents. The Bucktails, on the other hand, gained a majority in both houses of the legislature. No one disputed the fact that Clinton ran ahead of his party in all sections of the state.

The Bucktail-controlled assembly now proceeded to elect a Council of Appointment that included David Evans, Ellicott's nephew. Evans had gone a long way. Starting as a Clintonian, he had switched to the Bucktails, and now served on the omnipotent council. Van Buren, a master of political persuasion, recalled this pleasing conversation in his *Autobiography:*

Evans came to Albany, an honest and intelligent young man from the Western District as a Clintonian, but being disgusted with his Associates in the Legislature, he sought me out, in one of our Caucuses, before they separated from us and when their leaders were trying, against our opposition, to obtain an adjournment, and told me that he had lost all confidence in the men with whom he was acting, and asked me to consent to an adjournment, which I cheerfully did, from which time to the end of his life he was my fast and active friend politically and personally." [28]

Throughout his term, Senator Evans abided by the advice of Joseph Ellicott. He served as eyes and ears for his uncle and loyally transmitted what he saw and heard.

Paul Busti, Ellicott's employer, carefully followed the 1820 campaign from his office in Philadelphia and soon grew alarmed at the venomous manner in which the parties attacked each other. In this struggle, the press printed ugly, inflammatory stories about the candidates and their supporters. The attacks spread from Tompkins to Ellicott to the Big Family, and finally to the Holland Land Company. Busti was afraid that the bitterness engendered in this election would continue against the Company after the canvassers counted the ballots. He wrote to Evans seeking "the best means (if there any exists) of putting a stop to the evil consequences, that may result from the abuse [that] is made of the press." [29]

The over-cautious Busti, sensitive about any criticisms of himself or the Company, had always gone out of his way to avoid censure. In 1802, for example, he had decided against buying the Indians' land around Buffalo "to avoid the odiosity and jealousy so unjustly attached to them of being monopolizers." [30] Yet, at so early a date, some people already regarded the Company as a "menace" and indicated these feelings to Busti. In July, 1808, Louis LeCouteulx, a Company agent and a friend to Ellicott, reported that in Buffalo he overheard this comment: "If the Holland Company did own the land, they did not own the People." [31]

Busti was greatly disturbed, therefore, by Ellicott's participation in the 1820 elections, particularly since there had been a long record of earlier political involvement on the part of his Resident-Agent. In the 1807 elections, some one had blamed Ellicott for excessive exertions that included physical violence. Flatly denying that he committed any of these acts, the Resident-Agent explained: "We had carefully avoided putting our Names to a single electioneering Address, and during the

Election I made it a strict Point of keeping away from the Election Ground until the Election was nearly to a Close, and when I went to give my vote I turned immediately to the Land Office, and I am confident without exchanging a single word on the Subject of beating Brown, or any other person." [32]

In his explanation to Busti, Ellicott pointed out that the land agents of the nearby Pulteney Estate and the Hornby English Land Company had played prominent roles in the election. He then raised the questions with Busti concerning the political rights that employees of the Holland Company could exercise. "Shall the Persons," he asked, "who transact business for the Holland Land Company enjoy less Privileges, and even forfeit their Rights of Citizenship so far as not be allowed to give an Opinion in favour of their Candidates for Governor, Senate and Assembly [who] they have the Best Reason to believe are friendly disposed towards their Principals the Holland Land Company for fear of offending a few Characters who differ from them in Political Principles?" Ellicott, a strong Jeffersonian, answered his own inquiry with a ringing "No" and continued his active role in politics. Thus, in the election of 1820, Ellicott broke no personal precedents by his political involvement. He merely followed his established course of action.

Since the start of Ellicott's agency, Busti had clearly and frequently cautioned him to avoid political entanglements. He explained his "dislike" that Ellicott "meddle" in politics by this simple logic: "In case of success no favor can be favored by the company and much harm in case of a failure." [33] As Resident-Agent, Ellicott occupied a prominent position; therefore, Busti felt that he would have to conduct himself in a most discreet manner. For almost a score of years, though, Busti had also vaccilated on the issue of Ellicott's political actions. The two men had frequently wrangled over the question, yet it remained unresolved. Because the subject became crucial in their relationship, it is perhaps sensible to analyze the incident of 1805.

On April 11, 1805, Ellicott had written a circular taking a strong position on the coming elections to the assembly. The circular categorically indicted the Federalists as "a Set of designing knaves" who were using "every means that falsehood & intrigue can invent" to elect their nominees. "Every honest Man and friend to his Country," was therefore urged, "to frustrate" the Federalist "Schemes." Pushing the Republican cause, Ellicott "earnestly recommended" that the voters "warmly support" the anti-Federalist ticket. Specifically he proposed that meetings be called in all the neighborhoods to nominate the Republican candidates. The circular concluded with "Believe me your friend" and was signed Joseph Ellicott.[34]

This overt, blunt, frontier type of appeal for political support was common to the times, yet it offended the sensibilities of Paul Busti. He preferred the inconspicuous, behind the scenes, soft-glove approach, and upon receiving a copy of the circular was outraged. In a blistering three-page letter to Ellicott, Busti opened with the customary "Dear Sir" but followed with an exclamation point. He criticized "the outrageous language" that gave the impression Ellicott "must be ranked among those incendiaries" whose only aim was to overturn the American government. The Agent-General did not ask Ellicott "for an open recantation" or "a retraction." "Avow to me to have been in the wrong," proposed Busti, and "that your real sentiments are not those expressed in that circular." But Busti wanted more from Ellicott. He firmly insisted that in the future there must be no "political misconduct," adding pointedly: "'You should not meddle in any manner with the political intrigues about the Elections." Then in a more equivocal vein, he advised Ellicott to draw "near a reconciliation with your political oponents." The business-oriented Busti reminded his Resident-Agent that "self-preservation is the supreme law." The Company wanted peace, avoided political entanglements, and was unconcerned "whether the helm of the State is held by Adams or Jefferson, Clinton or Lewis." To make unquestionably clear his grave concern, Busti warned Ellicott that if the author of the circular could not promote peace on the purchase, "it would be a salutary measure to dismiss him." The letter concluded with a demand for Ellicott's explanation.[35]

In characteristic fullness, the Resident-Agent responded. As to the distribution of the circular, it was not designed "to be shown to more than two or three Characters." Far more crucial, reasoned Ellicott, was the election and more particularly the Federalist candidates who posed a threat to the Company. This was his main rebuttal. Defending himself against Busti's charge of being narrow and partisan, Ellicott asserted that his friends were divided equally in both parties. As proof he cited that the Federalists held about half of the political offices, adding a bit smugly: "the greater part of which I have the vanity to believe obtained their offices through my recommendation." For example, Richard Smith, a Federalist, held the office of surrogate "entirely through my recommendation." The same could be said, continued Ellicott, about Federalists in the offices of "the Senior Judge of the County, two assistant Judges, and divers Justices of the Peace."

Having disposed of the criticism of political bias, Ellicott detailed his objections to Cyrenius Chapin, one of the three Federalist candidates for the assembly. It was Busti who in an earlier letter was not disposed to sell certain lands to Chapin. And it was Jan Lincklaen, a trusted Company employee, who had informed Ellicott that Cyrenius Chapin "was one of the most vicious inhabitants in the County of Shenango" from which he came. From first-hand experience, the Resident-Agent recalled that Chapin had brought charges against a man named Johnston, accusing him of having "Stolen a pair of suspenders, & Some other trifling articles." Accepting Chapin's advice that confession would reduce the sentence, Johnston nonetheless was imprisoned six months and fined $25. Unable to pay the fine, he remained in jail. Johnston was finally released through the intervention of Ellicott and his friends who provided the needed money "to prevent a further expence to the County."

Ignoring the other two Federalist candidates running with Chapin, Ellicott now documented the position of another malcontent, Daniel B. Brown. When Federalist Brown first settled on the purchase, Ellicott had "patronized him, and recommended him to business." In a short time, Brown prospered but then "began to pry into all the secrets of this office" to determine "whether the Company's title to these lands were not defective." The two men quarreled. Soon after, Brown sought to buy land near the Batavia courthouse. According to Ellicott, he informed Brown that the lands had not yet been laid out, prices had not been fixed, and that "it was immaterial . . . who became the purchasers." The bitter feeling, nevertheless, deepened, and one day Brown "in a fit of intoxication" abused Ellicott "publicly in the Street." Still seeking trouble, Brown now cast suspicion on the Articles of Agreement given by the Company in lieu of granting full deeds until the entire purchase price had been paid.

Ellicott's refutation rested mainly on the danger to the Company from people like Chapin and Brown, who "were riding through the County propagating lies and falsehoods." It was under these conditions, explained Ellicott, that the circular was drafted. He admitted that it was "hastily wrote without that due Consideration, which would have been proper on that occasion." He conceded, too, that the language used in stigmatizing all the Federalists "was extremely intemperate and improper." For these infractions, he offered to apologize publicly. On his criticisms of Chapin and Brown, however, Ellicott stubbornly refused to retract a word.

In the last part of the letter, the Resident-Agent used arguments in his defense that a man of the world like Busti understood. He protested being labeled "Jacobin, or a dangerous Character," as being efforts at character assassination. Any man in his position, Ellicott reminded Busti, was bound to incur some enemies who "Stand ready Centinels to Communicate any information . . . that they conceive will have a tendency to bring me in disrepute in the opinion of the Agent-General." Adopting Busti's concern for peace, the Resident-Agent asserted that no other settlements had greater unity and harmony "between the People and the Agent" as on "this Purchase." And in a closing literary flourish, Ellicott accepted Busti's advice "as a Beacon for me to Steer by to avoid the Shoals that might otherwise occasion a Shipwreck" and promised to "be more cautious where I place my Signature." [36]

The 1805 incident is worth examining a bit further. The two letters between Busti and Ellicott demonstrated an underlying tone that resounded in most dealings of the Company. The Company was all important, the alpha and omega, a sacred cow, a glorified entity just short of being a deity. To paraphrase a contemporary cliché what was good for the Holland Land Company was good for all those involved with the Dutch-based syndicate. To this shibboleth Paul Busti, Joseph Ellicott, and their respective successors subscribed wholeheartedly.

The circular and the two letters also exposed basic differences between Ellicott and Busti. Ellicott was direct, brusque, and blunt, while Busti was diplomatic, compromising, and urbane. On the issue of political intervention, their differences were subtle, one of degree. Both men understood the value of political influence and the Company need for well-placed friends in government. So long as Ellicott wielded his political authority to gain company objectives without trouble, Busti applauded. Occasionally, as in the case of 1805, when Ellicott used a heavy-handed approach, Busti remonstrated.

Emerging sharply in the fight over Ellicott's political activities is the picture of the Agent-General as somewhat ambiguous but certainly ambivalent. While Busti admonished his Resident-Agent to keep out of political entanglements and embarrassing commitments, he was not averse to employing Ellicott's political influence in a respectable fashion. When the Company was involved in a problem that the Resident-Agent could solve through the use of political channels, Busti encouraged Ellicott to avail himself of circumspect political means. In the strongly contested election of 1820, for example, Busti confided to Evans: "I am far from believing [that] your good Uncle has acted in direct opposition of the old recommendation I made of avoiding to meddle and temper in State politics." Busti recognized that Ellicott

held great political influence in western New York, and that his political opponents would revile him, regardless of his tactics. The Agent-
General lamented over the entire situation: "Defamation in such cases
of party squabbles ought never to attain the proposed end with men
endowed with common sense." [37]

The unfavorable criticism of the Company and its Resident-Agent
reached a climax in the winter of 1820–21 when demands arose for
Joseph Ellicott's resignation. Until now, Busti had supported Ellicott
with unswerving loyalty. By 1820, opposition to the Resident-Agent
had become so formidable, however, that he began carefully to re-
assess Ellicott's over-all record. A cautious man, Busti was particularly
disturbed by the Clintonians' attitude because it seemed to indicate
that Ellicott had broken his rule of remaining clear of antagonistic
political involvement.

When the Clintonians lost control of the assembly in 1820, they
forfeited, at the same time, the political patronage of the Council of
Appointment; they blamed Ellicott's desertion for these failures. Thus,
the goal of the punitive Clintonians became the removal of Ellicott
as Resident-Agent and the substitution of a more loyal party follower.
They suggested that Samuel M. Hopkins replace Ellicott. Hopkins
came from Connecticut and had earned a good reputation, especially
for his work in developing some of the lands on the Genesee River
just east of the purchase. To advance Hopkins to the post of Resident-
Agent, the Clintonians organized their forces to bring pressure directly
on Paul Busti. Ambrose Spencer, Chancellor Kent, and even Governor
Clinton wrote to Busti and warmly praised Hopkins' qualifications as
Resident-Agent, in the event that the Agent-General dismissed Ellicott.
They indicated to Busti that they understood Ellicott's removal was
a distinct probability.

Additional support for replacing Ellicott with Hopkins came from
influential Buffalo residents headed by Samuel Wilkeson. In 1814,
Wilkeson had come to Buffalo where he started as a merchant and
quickly rose to prominence. In 1817 he accepted the then important
office of justice of the peace; a year later, the voters elected him
supervisor, and in 1819 he became an assessor. Wilkeson continued
to climb the political ladder as a Clintonian. He clashed with Ellicott
in 1819 by aggressively pushing for the early construction of a harbor
at Buffalo. This disagreement widened the following year when Ellicott withheld his full support for the harbor. Wilkeson and his friends
sought Busti's aid for this port, and at the same time, they bitterly
castigated Ellicott. In March, 1821, Wilkeson headed a petition of

fifty-seven persons who strongly urged Busti to remove Ellicott and employ Hopkins in his stead. This petition reviewed Ellicott's liabilities to the Company: the settlers would not pay their debts to the Company just to spite Ellicott; the Resident-Agent had made his office into a political party; and Ellicott was "ungentlemanly, morose, inaccessible, inhospitable and abusive." In contrast, Samuel M. Hopkins was "conciliatory and Gentlemanly," and striking a sensitive point, he had not "mingled at all for many years in the contentions and squabbles of party." [38] The petition concluded with a bargain: if Busti appointed Hopkins as Resident-Agent, the Clintonians would cease fighting for a road-tax on nonresident landowners such as the Holland Company.

When the Bucktails heard the rumor of the Clintonian effort to oust Ellicott and replace him with Hopkins, Van Buren and his friends quickly moved to prevent Joseph Ellicott's dismissal. The Bucktails, who for years had criticized DeWitt Clinton for party disloyalty, took a firm stand. In typical Van Buren sophistry, they suggested that "to prevent the subjection of the power of the Company to the purpose of party," [39] Busti should retain Ellicott. A letter signed by thirteen Bucktails, headed by Martin Van Buren, was sent to Busti on March 12, 1821. This note summed up the recent political history to prove that the Bucktails, and not the Clintonians, had remained loyal to the best interests of the Company.

While their letter was written in a temperate vein, the Bucktails took the matter of Ellicott's proposed ouster seriously. To Van Buren in particular, this case tested an important tenet of the Bucktails— party support for party loyalty. After Busti received the appeals from both parties regarding Ellicott's future, Hopkins visited the Agent-General at Philadelphia. When he returned to Albany, Hopkins announced that Busti had appointed him agent for part of the Company lands. Deeply upset, the Bucktails laid plans to retaliate in the event that Hopkins' claim were true. They asked Rufus King, at that time a United States senator, to inquire how far the Monroe administration would support the Bucktails in this fight. In reply, Secretary of State John Quincy Adams offered to send whatever reports were involved to the United States representatives in Holland with the request that these papers be given to the directors of the Holland Land Company. Adams also agreed to instruct the United States embassy in Holland to express the American government's displeasure at the behavior of Holland Company agents in the United States, and to urge the Company to remove both Hopkins and Busti from their posts.

Even before both parties pressured him concerning Ellicott's future,

Busti had realized the full dangers that the Company faced if the office of Resident-Agent became a political plum. Vividly he remembered his unhappy experiences in Pennsylvania when some of the politicians there had used the Company's program as a political football. Busti, moreover, had lately received impressive information in the Wilkeson petition that Ellicott was not treating the settlers in a civil manner.

The Agent-General had an agonizing decision to make. For twenty years, he had worked closely with his tall, portly Resident-Agent. Their relationship had been one of sincere mutual respect, and the two men had fully discussed with each other various Company matters. Busti had consulted Ellicott on numerous occasions and had followed his advice in most instances. He had come to value Ellicott's strengths: his industry, honesty, ability, and total dedication to the Company. What Busti could never fully understand were his Resident-Agent's experiences. Ellicott's two years of tramping through the forest during the Big Survey of 1798–1800 and his two decades of living in the wilderness of western New York were ways of life that were alien to the Agent-General. During Busti's first forty-nine years, he had resided in Europe in comfortable circumstances. While Ellicott was working in frontier Batavia, Busti was occupied in cosmopolitan Philadelphia. Only once, in 1805, had he visited Batavia; in 1821, he would go there a second time. Although he became an American citizen, Busti had never experienced the trials of frontier living.

A man of impeccable manners, personally kind and generous, the well-educated Agent-General had to determine whether his Resident-Agent had reached a point where his liabilities to the Company outweighed his assets. As individual problems, Busti could live with Ellicott's mental depression, could adjust to the frontier criticisms of the Company and its agents, and could even try to reconcile himself to legislative decisions not to buy the Company land. However, the election of 1820 had ramifications which, added to the other three problems, were more than Busti could bear. Today, a prominent executive who needed to be removed would be given a high sounding title and shifted to a harmless post. In those days, apparently, such changes were not made. Nor did Busti have the pressure of worrying about Ellicott's financial circumstances; the patroon of Batavia had become wealthy. After some painful soul-searching, the Agent-General concluded that the Resident-Agent had outlived his usefulness to the Holland Land Company.

By December, 1820, Paul Busti had decided to discharge Joseph

Ellicott. It was a serious decision that demanded proper timing and diplomatic handling. As he explained to the Company directors, to whom he always wrote in French, Ellicott had reached a position of influence that could be compared to the "Intendants des grands Seigneurs"; he needed to be treated discreetly (*"ménager"*).[40] Busti elaborated that he was waiting for a more opportune time to make this resolution known to Ellicott. To dismiss his Resident-Agent now before he could complete the lobbying activities that he was supervising in the state legislature of 1821 was dangerous. Nor did Busti permit the March, 1821, memorials from the Wilkeson-Clinton group and from the Bucktails to hurry him. With the patience of an experienced administrator, he waited for the proper time, meanwhile giving careful thought to how such a letter of dismissal should be written.

The proper time came after the state legislature had ended its session, and on April 9, 1821, Busti sent his long-considered communiqué to Ellicott. The Agent-General began the vital letter by expressing "mortification" that his proposal to the legislature asking the state to buy the purchase had not been called up either by Ellicott's political friends or even by his nephew and long-time Company employee, state Senator David Evans. For many months Busti had worked on the plan of sale, which he considered "the best possible remedy" for the Company, and its rejection was a great disappointment. He now summarized the situation concisely. Finding capitalists to buy the entire purchase, when property had depreciated so much, was unlikely. Were a buyer located, he could not be expected to risk money west of the Genesee where discontent could flare any moment into the open, endangering the peace. Many complaints, especially during the past two years, had come to the Agent-General; although he had fully supported Ellicott, the protests were portents that could not be ignored.

The Agent-General developed his thoughts further. Unable to sell the land in one block, the Company had to remain in western New York, and this gave Busti two choices: to keep Ellicott or replace him. He was in a quandary. He insisted that his preference was to keep Ellicott. However, by retaining him, Busti would endanger "the dear & best interests of the HLCy." Sacrificing his Dutch employers was unthinkable, almost sacrilegious. In further explanation, the Agent-General drew an analogy between himself and a king whom the people compelled to dismiss a trusted minister. Busti came now to the heart of the letter. To avoid deposing Ellicott, he diplomatically requested him: "give in Your demission yourself."

In picking the word *demission*, Busti chose aptly. He wanted Ellicott to relinquish the office of Resident-Agent as a voluntary act, insisting piously, on "word of honor," that no one knew of the decision. Idle rumors of a new Resident-Agent had abounded, but Busti had denied such gossip. Then playing up to Ellicott's pride, he added: "None of Your open or Secret enemies will be able to boast of having prevailed against you." Returning to the argument that the last hope of selling the purchase in one piece was gone, Busti was driven to make drastic changes. As a starter, he would choose a Resident-Agent who was "perfectly neutral to parties, who neither enjoys nor excites the animosity of a divided people." Reverting to another analogy, he pointed out that the Company, like a popular government, required the good will of the people to continue. It was not really an option, Busti concluded, but a necessity that Ellicott resign.

At the same time that he gave Ellicott notice of his decision, Busti sought to mitigate the blow. Rather than abrupt abdication, he asked the Resident-Agent to take his time and determine for himself "the epoch of your resignation." Such a time, suggested Busti, might well coincide with the submission of the annual report. To offset any impression of a long-time conspiracy, Busti indicated that he had not yet chosen a successor, and that none who had already applied would be elected. One criterion was certain: "the next Agent shall be a Stranger to the political squabbles by which the State is disturbed." To soften further the shock of "demission," Busti proposed that Ellicott grant concessions to the debtors on the purchase. The Company proposals would reduce financial pressures and help the industrious to pay their debts more easily. The good will offers would also enable Ellicott to retire from his agency with additional respect from the settlers.[41]

Busti's efforts to soften the effects of Ellicott's dismissal failed. The notification that he would be dropped from his post deeply upset Ellicott. His melancholy had by now deepened and Ellicott found himself "in almost constant excitement." He condemned those "who had insinuated themselves" in the Agent-General's confidence so that he would discharge him, and denounced the men who had petitioned for his removal.[42] To change Busti's mind, he analyzed in a detailed twenty-nine page letter each of the causes that the Agent-General had given for his dismissal. He reminded Busti that he had labored long in behalf of the Company and the Agent-General: "I shall always have the pleasing satisfaction in my retirement to conscientiously believe (as far as discretionary power was voted) that all my transactions have been with the single eye to the honor of the Agent-General's admiration, and with the most pure views for the promotion of the best and dearest interests of the Holland Company."[43]

Ellicott even threatened to take his case to the Company Directors in Holland. But Busti clung to his decision to appoint a new Resident-Agent. In desperation, Ellicott now countered by refusing to comply with Busti's request to resign. Instead, he insisted that Busti "dismiss" him if he wanted a new Resident-Agent.[44] In the end, Busti's reason and moderation prevailed, and Joseph Ellicott resigned as Resident-Agent of the Holland Land Company, effective October 26, 1821. As Ellicott's replacement, Busti had selected in May, 1821, a Philadelphia lawyer and business friend, Jacob S. Otto; he did not take office, though, until October 25 of that year.

Still undaunted, Ellicott made one more effort to regain his position, this time as owner rather than employee. In July, 1821, he asked Busti at what price the Company would sell its remaining land west of the Genesee. Promptly responding, Busti offered to dispose of virtually all the Company land for sixty cents an acre, payment to be made in cash or stock in the Bank of the United States. Reserved to the Company, however, would be single lots in Batavia, Buffalo, Mayville, and Ellicottville. The old Resident-Agent tried to get financial support from his monied friends but in vain, so he dropped the idea. Thus, with the official changeover in Resident-Agents a permanent reality, an eventful period in the history of western New York and the Holland Land Company had drawn to a close.

The bitterness engendered by the Busti-Ellicott quarrel left a sour residue between the supporters of each side. For all concerned, the transition period following Ellicott's departure was difficult. The main question, though, involved the members of Ellicott's Big Family, who continued to hold prominent positions in the Company hierarchy. During the tension-filled change, the Busti forces made accusations of corruption, special privilege, and divided loyalties. The newly installed Resident-Agent, Otto, charged Ellicott with having deeded 13.74 acres in Buffalo to David Evans and another nephew Joseph Ellicott, Jr., for $137.40 at a time when the same land could have brought $50 an acre. More serious was Otto's blanket denunciation that, in Buffalo alone, Joseph Ellicott held "the best property," brother Benjamin owned "corner Lots, water Lots, and all the prominent Spots which overlook the Lake," and nephews Evans and Peacock likewise possessed choice parcels of land.[45] Busti, normally urbane and impartial, caustically regarded three members of the Big Family—David Evans, William Peacock, and David Goodwin—as "continuing to fatten on the

carcass of the Holland Land Company as worms do on corpses." [46]
Yet, these were key personnel, veterans of many years experience in
selling land: Evans, a chief clerk in the Batavia office since 1803; Peacock, a subagent of Chautauqua County since 1810; and, Goodwin,
a subagent of Cattaraugus County since 1817. Combined, the three
cousins had thirty-three years of seasoning, and what to do with them
was no small problem.

Something different happened to each of the three men. In the most
prickly position was David Evans, who wavered, then decided to remain with the Company as first clerk until 1825 when he resigned. In
1827, he returned, this time as Resident-Agent to replace Otto, who
had died that year. During the decade that Evans held office, the
Company sold its remaining holdings west of the Genesee. William
Peacock, Ellicott's nephew-in-law, kept his position of subagent until
1836 when he retired. Of the trio, David Goodwin, another nephew-
in-law, was most vulnerable. Accused of "habitual intemperance" and
"dishonest conduct in office," [47] he even forfeited the support of David
Evans, and Otto forced Goodwin to resign in December, 1821.

Meanwhile, worried about his health, Joseph Ellicott prepared a
comprehensive will that covered more than thirteen ledger-sized pages.
The will contained no major surprises. Characteristic of Ellicott, it
confirmed his strong family ties, his partiality for nephew David Evans,
and his gratitude to brother Andrew. It did reveal, though, the extent
of his large land holdings and the problems of their disposal. To his
sisters, Ann, Letitia, and Rachel, and to Sara Ellicott, wife of his deceased older brother Andrew, Joseph allocated $250 annually. To three
churches in Batavia, he donated land, and to David Evans, John B.
Ellicott, Lewis B. Evans, and Jonathan Brown, Ellicott granted in
perpetuity the lots they were already using. Of the residual estate, he
bequeathed one-fifteenth to brother Benjamin; the remaining fourteen-
fifteenths he divided among the children and their lineal descendants
of brother Andrew and sisters Ann, Letitia, and Rachel. Joseph favored
Andrew's children, who would receive one-eighth more than the other
cousins, because his older brother had set him on the path to success.
As executors, he appointed five men: brother Benjamin, nephews David
Evans and Andrew Ellicott, William Peacock, and Nathaniel Griffith.
In addition, he selected Evans and Peacock as "special Trustees" to
dispose of land not now under contract. This was the will to which
Ellicott affixed his signature on December 31, 1823.

Dissatisfied with certain terms, Joseph added three codicils. In
the first modification, he withdrew the one-fifteenth grant to Benjamin

"in consideration of the large estate he now owns." Instead, he transferred to his brother two lots and the Batavia mansion with many of
the buildings "thereon." Another change reflected Joseph's deep feelings for primary relatives. He removed executors Peacock and Griffith
as "not being related by blood," replacing them with William Evans
and Benjamin Evans. Similarly, he dropped Peacock as a special
trustee and kept Evans as the only one. In the first codicil, too, he
distributed land more specifically. The valuable lot number 104 in
Buffalo was partitioned into three equal parts: to the sons of Andrew
Ellicott, to four other nephews, and to David Evans. The esteemed
Evans received, also, lands and houses in Batavia, and with the children of brother Andrew, shared all of Joseph's land in the Counties
of Niagara and Erie owned jointly with his brother Benjamin; Evans
acquired one-third, the children two-thirds.

The undated first codicil was written before December 20, 1824,
the date of the second change. In the second codicil, Ellicott distributed
shares of stock of the Bank of the United States to more distant relatives: one cousin, twenty-five; five unmarried nieces, fifteen each;
an aunt of the late wife of David Evans, twenty-five; and, to an orphan
child who had lived several years with the family, fifteen. The third
and final codicil, signed March 15, 1825, specified that sisters Ann,
Letitia, and Rachel and sister-in-law Sara Ellicott would inherit equally
the household furniture and all his stock in the Ontario Bank.[48]

In its final form, Joseph Ellicott left over half of his estate to
special bequests and the residual portion to eighty-seven legatees.
When Ellicott drew up his will, his estate was valued roughly at six
hundred thousand dollars. It was almost twice the size of Benjamin's
whose holdings were appraised at about three to four hundred thousand dollars.

After his retirement, Ellicott's health, already poor, deteriorated
rapidly. Accepting the advice of his physicians that he go to New York
City where specialists could attend him, Ellicott in November, 1824,
made the journey in the company of relatives and friends. When the
analysis disclosed that he was suffering from severe mental depression,
as well as a physical breakdown, the New York City doctors urged
him to enter the asylum at Bloomingdale, at that time situated near the
present site of Columbia University. This he did, but his condition
grew so critical that David Evans was legally empowered to act in
behalf of his uncle.

While his health was failing at Bloomingdale, many of the projects
that Ellicott had initiated came to fruition. One hundred thousand set-

tlers were now developing the land that he had helped to survey. Several desirable counties were emerging from the original Genesee county as a result of the campaign that he had started. The canal whose route he had helped to plan was transporting increasing numbers of people to the west to start New York on its road to becoming the Empire State. Ellicott's dreams had become realities, hardly marred by the ironic turn of events that had led to the alliance in 1826 of his friend, Van Buren, with his opponent, Clinton, for "political expediency."

Joseph Ellicott, however, was in no condition to rejoice over his achievements or to lament the hypocrisies of political conduct. His life had become a twisted world of tormented thoughts, whirling confusion, and deep moroseness. Occasionally, his mind would flash back to the rich and warm moments of the past, but the blackness of the present would soon overwhelm him once again. Unable to control himself any longer, Ellicott made several attempts at suicide. Finally, he escaped his attendants and on August 19, 1826, took his life, hanging himself by a handkerchief.[49]

Thus at the age of sixty-five Joseph Ellicott ended a vigorous and useful life. He was interred in the Friends burial ground. A few months later, he was laid to his final rest in Batavia in the same plot with the family twins whom he had always loved, sister Rachel and brother Benjamin. Over his grave, a towering granite obelisk now stands; and across the street, facing the graveyard, a large Massey-Harris factory produces farm tractors to work the land that he had sold.

Joseph Ellicott was not a great man—not if he is measured on the basis of his contributions to economic theory or political philosophy. If, however, he is judged by specific contributions to the economic and political development of western New York from 1800 to 1821, he emerges as an important figure in the history of this area. A frontier leader by dint of practical economic and political common sense, rather than by military prowess, a planner who planned for others as well as for himself, Joseph Ellicott was largely responsible for accomplishments that are still worthy of recognition today.

Appendix

TABLE I

POPULATION OF WESTERN NEW YORK, 1800 [1] AND 1810 [2]

	1800		1810		
MALES	Ontario [3]	Alleghany	Ontario	Genesee	Niagara
under 10	3,023	378	8,239	2,459	1,713
10 to 16	1,143	164	3,484	987	656
16 to 26	1,502	163	3,617	1,355	1,132
26 to 45	1,991	208	4,235	1,482	1,134
45 and up	592	100	2,263	540	414
TOTAL	8,251	1,013	21,838	6,823	5,049
FEMALES					
under 10	2,630	385	7,812	2,273	1,504
10 to 16	964	137	2,964	806	552
16 to 26	1,195	168	3,328	1,152	825
26 to 45	1,487	161	3,756	1,123	755
45 and up	525	57	1,823	386	247
TOTAL	6,801	908	19,683	5,740	3,883
GRAND TOTAL	15,052	1,921	41,521	12,563	8,932

Total in western New York in 1810   23,416
Total in New York State in 1800   484,065
Total in New York State in 1810   959,220

[1] *Second Census of the United States* (Washington, D.C.: Duane, 1802), p. 29.

[2] *Aggregate Amount of Persons within the United States in the Year 1810* (Washington, D.C.: Luther Cornwall Company, 1811), p. 28A.

[3] In 1800, Ontario County included all of western New York and some land on the east side of the Genesee River. After 1802 with the creation of Genesee County, Ontario County kept its land east of the Genesee but lost the area west of that river.

TABLE II

Population of Western New York, 1820 [1]

	Alleghany	Cattaraugus	Chautauqua	Genesee	Niagara
MALES					
under 10	1,718	726	2,367	11,092	4,345
10 to 16	687	262	921	4,312	1,639
between 16 and 18	185	89	211	1,206	494
16 to 26, heads of families also	996	571	1,241	5,677	2,354
26 to 45	1,049	579	1,497	6,550	2,810
45 and up	469	112	564	2,636	1,051
TOTALS	5,104	2,339	6,801	31,473	12,693
FEMALES					
under 10	1,687	753	2,399	10,650	4,144
10 to 16	662	242	867	4,015	1,523
16 to 26	864	413	1,071	5,183	2,073
26 to 45	829	352	1,164	5,662	2,118
45 and up	340	74	464	2,171	851
TOTALS	4,382	1,834	5,965	27,681	10,709
GRAND TOTALS	9,486	4,173	12,766	59,154	23,402

Total in western New York 108,981
Total in New York State 1,372,812

[1] *Census for 1820, Fourth Census, Book I* (Washington, D.C.: Gales and Seaton, 1821), 12. Ontario County was excluded because it technically did not belong to western New York in 1820.

TABLE III

NUMBER OF ELECTORS IN WESTERN NEW YORK,[1] 1800–1821
I—electors worth one hundred pounds
II—electors worth from twenty to one hundred pounds
III—electors renting tenements of annual value of forty shillings

	On-tario	Gen-esee	Alle-ghany	Nia-gara	Chau-tauqua	Catta-raugus	Erie	Total[2]
1801 I	1,691							1,691
1801 II	247							247
1801 III	923							923
	Grand total for western New York including Ontario County							2,861
1807 I		477	66					543
1807 II		128						128
1807 III		1,318	278					1,596
	Grand total for western New York							2,267
1814 I		745	135	418	430			1,728
1814 II		43	11	78	115			247
1814 III		3,197	473	955	95			4,720
	Grand total for western New York							6,695
1821 I		1,813	325	276	629	147	871	4,061
1821 II		223	66	16	137	59	104	605
1821 III		4,052	1,292	689	1,141	477	1,690	9,341
	Grand total for western New York							14,007

[1] Hough, *Census of the State of New York* (Albany: Charles Van Benthuysen, 1855), pp. ix, x.

[2] The legislature created Genesee in 1802, Alleghany in 1806, Niagara in 1808, Chautauqua in 1811, Cattaraugus in 1817, and Erie in 1821.

Notes to the Chapters

I. THE GREAT SURVEY

1. Joseph Ellicott to Theophile Cazenove, Sept. 11, 1794, Holland Land Company Papers, hereafter cited as HLC, Sundries Unclassified. Original spellings are retained throughout, and editorial interjection made only where confusion might result.

2. Robert Morris to Thomas Morris and Charles Williamson, Aug. 1, 1797, HLC, Ea #59.

3. Theophile Cazenove to William Bayard, July 19, 1797, HLC, Ea #59.

4. Robert Morris to Theophile Cazenove, Oct. 6, 1795, HLC, Ea #59.

5. Robert Morris to George Washington, Aug. 25, 1796, HLC, I O 367.

6. Theophile Cazenove to William Bayard, July 19, 1797, HLC, Ea #59.

7. LeRoy and Bayard to the Holland Land Company, Oct. 2, 1797, HLC, Ed 220. Theophile Cazenove to Van Eeghen, Sept. 28, 1797, HLC, Ea 218 #62.

8. Theophile Cazenove to P. & C. Van Eeghen, undated, probably Sept., 1797, HLC, Ea 218, #60.

9. *American State Papers,* Class 2, Indian Affairs (Washington, D.C.: Gales and Seaton, 1823–1861), I, Treaty between Robert Morris and the Seneca Nation of Indians, Sept. 15, 1797.

10. James McHenry to the Senecas, May 14, 1798, *American State Papers,* Class 2, Indian Affairs.

11. Robert W. Bingham, ed., *Reports of Joseph Ellicott,* 2 vols. (Buffalo: Buffalo Historical Society, 1937), I, 15, 16, 33, 34; hereafter cited as *RJE.*

12. *RJE,* I, 15. Joseph Ellicott to Theophile Cazenove, Oct. 19, 1797, HLC, Ea 118, #63.

13. *RJE,* I, 21, 22, 25.

14. *RJE,* I, 21, 29.

15. *RJE,* I, 42, 47.

16. *RJE,* I, 48.

II. MANY APPLICANTS, FEW BUYERS

1. James Wadsworth to the Board of Directors, undated but between Sept. 2, 1797 and Oct. 11, 1797, HLC, Written Copybooks.

2. James Wadsworth to Paul Busti, June 18, 1799, HLC, II, 152.

3. John Maude, *Visit to the Falls of Niagara in 1800* (London: Longman, Reese, Orme, Brown, & Green, 1826), pp. 24, 25.

4. *Ibid.,* p. 32.

5. *Ibid.,* p. 38.

6. *Ibid.*, p. 95.

7. Charles Williamson, "Narratives of Eighteenth Century Visitors to Niagara" (Buffalo: Buffalo Historical Society Publications, XV, 1911), 399. Rev. D. M. Cooper, ed., "Rev. David Bacon's Visits to Buffalo in 1800 and 1801" (Buffalo: Buffalo Historical Society Publications, VI, 1903), 185. Maude, *Visit to Niagara*, p. 122. Timothy Dwight, *Travels in New-England and New-York* (New Haven: Timothy Dwight, 1821–22), IV, 56.

8. William Ketchum, *An Authentic and Comprehensive History of Buffalo* (Buffalo: Rockwell, Baker & Hill, 1865), II, 132.

9. *RJE*, I, 105. Originally, Ellicott had wanted to name Batavia Bustia or Bustiville in honor of the Agent-General. When Busti objected, Ellicott called it the Bend. Later, Busti suggested the name of Batavia which Ellicott adopted.

10. Jan Lincklaen to Paul Busti, Oct. 25, 1802, HLC, P 368.

11. Jan Lincklaen to Paul Busti, Oct. 25, 1802, HLC, P 368.

12. David A. Ogden to Joseph Ellicott, Nov. 20, 1800, Joseph Ellicott Collection, Buffalo and Erie County Historical Society. The Joseph Ellicott Collection will hereafter be cited as JEC.

13. Joseph Ellicott to Paul Busti, Feb. 16, 1802, JEC.

III. RELUCTANT POLITICIAN

1. Paul Busti to Joseph Ellicott, Dec. 6, 1803, JEC.

2. Marcus Cunliffe, *The Nation Takes Shape: 1789–1837* (Chicago: University of Chicago Press, 1959), p. 168.

3. *Ibid.*, p. 163.

4. Frank Monaghan, *John Jay Defender of Liberty* (New York: Bobbs-Merrill, 1935), p. 325.

5. Benjamin Ellicott to Joseph Ellicott, March 8, 1802, JEC.

6. Paul Busti to David A. Ogden, March 11, 1802, JEC.

7. David A. Ogden to Joseph Ellicott, March 3, 1802, JEC. Although the description fits Elkanah Watson, the author lacks conclusive proof that E. Watson was Elkanah Watson. All quotations used in the paragraph were taken from this letter.

8. Paul Busti to Joseph Ellicott, March 1802, JEC.

9. David A. Ogden to Joseph Ellicott, June 18, 1802, JEC.

10. Paul Busti to Joseph Ellicott, March 1802, JEC.

11. Joseph Ellicott to Paul Busti, Jan. 22, 1802, JEC.

12. Joseph Ellicott to Paul Busti, April 2, 1803, JEC.

13. *New York State Constitution Annotated*, New York State Convention Committee (New York: Burland Printing, 1938), I, part II, 15. Article XXIII reads: "That all officers, other than those who by this Constitution, are directed to be otherwise appointed, shall be appointed in the manner following, to wit: The Assembly shall, once in every year, openly nominate and appoint one of the Senators from each great district, which senators shall form a Council for the appointment of the said officers, of which the governor for the time being, or the lieutenant governor, or the president of the senate (which they shall respectively administer the government), shall be president, and have a casting voice, but no other vote, and, with the advice and consent of the said council, shall

appoint all of the said officers; and that a majority of the said council be a quorum; AND FURTHER, the said Senators shall not be eligible to the said council for two years successively."

14. *Council of Appointment Minutes, 1777–1821,* I.

15. *New York State Constitution Annotated,* I, part II, 23. Article V reads: "the right to nominate all officers, other than those, who, by the Constitution, are directed to be otherwise appointed, is vested concurrently in the person administering the government of this state for the time being, and in each of the members of the Council of Appointment."

16. *New York State Constitution Annotated,* Article XXIII.

17. Joseph Ellicott to Paul Busti, April 2, 1803, JEC.

18. *RJE,* I, 322.

19. Joseph Ellicott to Richard Stoddard, May 8, 1801, JEC.

20. *RJE,* I, 130.

21. Paul Busti to Joseph Ellicott, Dec. 6, 1803, JEC.

22. Joseph Ellicott to Paul Busti, June 22, 1804, JEC.

23. Joseph Ellicott to Paul Busti, June 22, 1804, JEC.

24. Joseph Ellicott to Paul Busti, June 22, 1804, JEC.

25. Joseph Ellicott to Paul Busti, June 4, 1802, JEC.

26. Joseph Ellicott to Paul Busti, June 4, 1802, JEC.

27. *Transcript of the Original Records of the Town of Batavia* (Buffalo: Buffalo and Erie County Historical Society), p. 26.

28. Lemuel Chipman to Joseph Ellicott, March 18, 1802, JEC.

29. Paul Busti to Joseph Ellicott, June 5, 1804, JEC.

IV. THE BIG FAMILY

1. Andrew Ellicott to Joseph Ellicott, March 12, 1804, JEC.

2. *Laws of the State of New York,* 19th Sess., Chap. 58, April 11, 1796.

3. *Laws of the State of New York,* 20th Sess., Chap. 36, March 17, 1797.

4. *Laws of the State of New York,* 21st Sess., Chap. 72, April 2, 1798.

5. Evans, *The Holland Land Company,* p. 212.

6. Nathan Schachner, *Aaron Burr* (New York: Frederick A. Stokes, 1937), pp. 157, 158.

7. Joseph Ellicott to Paul Busti, March 9, 1804, JEC.

8. Paul Busti to Joseph Ellicott, Feb. 20, 1804, JEC.

9. Joseph Ellicott to Paul Busti, June 22, 1804, JEC.

10. Joseph Ellicott to Paul Busti, June 22, 1804, JEC.

11. *Western Repository,* July 17, 1804.

12. *Transcript of the Original Records of the Town of Batavia,* p. 31.

13. James Mower to Joseph Ellicott, May 27, 1804, JEC.

14. Henry Dearborn to Paul Busti, Jan. 16, 1804, JEC.

15. Paul Busti to Joseph Ellicott, Feb. 8, 1804, JEC.

16. Alexander Rea to Joseph Ellicott, Jan. 10, 1801, JEC.

17. Alexander Rea to Joseph Ellicott, Dec. 22, 1804, JEC.

18. Alexander Rea to Joseph Ellicott, Feb. 3, 1804, JEC.

19. David Evans to Joseph Ellicott, Feb. 5, 1819, JEC.

V. ROADS AND THE UNHAPPY TAXPAYER

1. *RJE*, I, 144. The Batavia–Connewagus Road did not appear on the map which Ellicott enclosed with his annual report. For other roads built, *RJE*, I, 214–16, 248, 249, 271–74, 308, 310, 311, 330–38, 362–64, 397–99.

2. David Eason to Joseph Ellicott, 1808, JEC. No exact date given.

3. Lemuel Chipman to Joseph Ellicott, Feb. 24, 1805, JEC. Joseph Ellicott to Alexander Rea, Feb. 14, 1805, JEC.

4. Joseph Ellicott to Alexander Rea, Feb. 14, 1805, JEC.

5. Joseph Ellicott to Paul Busti, Oct. 27, 1806, JEC.

6. Joseph Ellicott to Paul Busti, July 15, 1812, JEC.

7. *Pomfret Assessment Rolls, 1810–1823.* When the legislature created Chautauqua County in 1808, the town of Pomfret was formed from the Town of Chautauqua. These rolls spelled out in detail the road building of the settlers and are kept at the Town Clerk's Office, Fredonia, New York.

8. Joseph Ellicott to Paul Busti, Nov. 17, 1803, JEC.

9. Joseph Ellicott to Paul Busti, Nov. 17, 1803, JEC.

10. Joseph Ellicott to Paul Busti, Dec. 5, 1805, JEC.

11. *RJE*, I, 287.

12. *RJE*, I, 289.

13. *RJE*, I, 286.

14. *RJE*, I, 287.

15. The author was unable to locate what the Company had paid in taxes for 1806. According to Ellicott's Annual Report of 1807 in the *Reports of Joseph Ellicott*, I, 345, Ellicott explained without citing figures that the 1807 tax exceeded that of the previous year. Since this increase amounted to about $100 over the 1805 figure, the 1806 taxes were probably similar to those of 1805.

16. *RJE*, II, 140.

17. *RJE*, I, 390–92. The State of Pennsylvania taxed the Company lands the monied equivalent of the highway tax.

18. *RJE*, II, 58.

VI. AN EXPANDING POPULATION

1. John Melish, *Travels in the United States of America in the Years 1806 & 1807, and 1809, 1810 & 1811* (Philadelphia: John Melish, 1812), II, 420.

2. Melish, *Travels in the Unitel States*, II, 364.

3. Margaret Louise Plunkett, "The Upstate Cities and Villages," in *History of the State of New York*, Alexander C. Flick, ed., 10 vols. (New York: Columbia University Press, 1933–37), VIII, 56.

4. G. Hunter Bartlett, "Andrew and Joseph Ellicott" (Buffalo: Buffalo Historical Society Publications, XXVI, 1922), 28, 29n. The Ellicott building was demolished in 1887 to make room for constructing a new street, Dellinger Avenue.

5. Dwight, *Travels in New-England and New-York*, IV, 57.

6. Le Comte de Colbert Maulevrier, *Voyage dans L'Intérieur des Etats-Unis et Au Canada* (Baltimore: The Johns Hopkins Press, 1935), p. 50. "Mr. Ellicott sentant que la Cie Hollandaise pourrait un jour tirer un grand advantage de cette situation, a persuadé aux Indiens de ne pas comprendre cet endroit dans le terrain qu'ils se sont réservés." Translated, it would read: "Mr. Ellicott, feeling that the Holland Company could one day gain a great advantage from this situation, persuaded the Indians not to include this place in the territory that they have reserved."

7. Robert W. Bingham, *The Cradle of the Queen City* (Buffalo: Buffalo Historical Society Publications, XXXI, 1931), p. 183. Using the same order, those streets in Buffalo are today named Main (to Shelton Square), Main (north of Shelton Square), Niagara, Erie, Church, Genesee, and Court.

8. Dwight, *Travels in New-England and New-York*, II, 67.

9. *RJE*, II, 42.

10. *Laws of the State of New York*, 21st Sess., Chap. 72, April 2, 1798.

11. Joseph Ellicott to Paul Busti, July 31, 1802, JEC.

12. Joseph Ellicott to Paul Busti, May 17, 1804, JEC.

13. Joseph Ellicott to Paul Busti, May 14, 1804, JEC.

14. *Laws of the State of New York*, 28th Sess., Chap. 21, March 2, 1805.

15. Joseph Ellicott to Paul Busti, May 17, 1805, JEC.

16. Joseph Ellicott to Paul Busti, May 22, 1806, JEC.

17. Joseph Ellicott to Paul Busti, May 22, 1806, JEC.

18. Joseph Ellicott to Paul Busti, Aug. 15, 1806, JEC.

19. Joseph Ellicott to Paul Busti, Jan. 9, 1807, JEC.

20. Joseph Ellicott to Paul Busti, Jan. 9, 1807, JEC.

21. *RJE*, I, 373.

22. Joseph Ellicott to Paul Busti, July 9, 1807, JEC.

23. Joseph Ellicott to Paul Busti, Feb. 6, 1808, JEC.

24. Joseph Ellicott to Alexander Rea, Feb. 1808, JEC.

25. Joseph Ellicott to Alexander Rea, Feb. 1808, JEC.

26. Alexander Rea to Joseph Ellicott, Feb. 2, 1808, JEC.

27. Joseph Ellicott to Alexander Rea and William Rumsey, Feb. 13, 1808, JEC.

28. Joseph Ellicott to ?, Feb. 27, 1808, JEC. Probably addressed to Alexander Rea and William Rumsey.

29. Daniel Tompkins to Joseph Ellicott, June 29, 1808, JEC.

30. Joseph Ellicott to Asa Ransom, July 12, 1808, JEC.

VII. THE WAR OF 1812

1. Henry Steele Comager, *Documents of American History* (New York: Appleton-Century-Crofts, 1949), p. 202.

2. Joseph Ellicott to Paul Busti, June 9, 1810, JEC.

3. *RJE*, I, 394.

4. Joseph Ellicott to Paul Busti, June 9, 1810, JEC.

5. Joseph Ellicott to Paul Busti, Aug. 26, 1809, JEC.

6. Henry Adams, *History of the United States of America during the Administrations of Jefferson and Madison* (New York: Charles Scribner's Sons, 1889–91),

IV, 278. Adams quoted from John Lambert, *Travels through Canada and the United States in the Years 1806, 1807, 1808,* II, 64, 65.

7. Jeremiah Munson to Benjamin Ellicott, April 16, 1806, JEC.

8. A. Dox to Peter Porter, March 26, 1812; John C. Spencer to Peter Porter, Feb. 23, 1812; Jonathan Woodbury to Peter Porter, July 6, 1812; Daniel Tompkins to Peter Porter, May 29, 1812; Daniel Goodwin to Peter Porter, May 14, 1812. All these letters are in the Peter B. Porter Papers, Buffalo and Erie County Historical Society.

9. Dixon Ryan Fox, *The Decline of Aristocracy in the Politics of New York* (New York: Columbia University, 1919), p. 186.

10. Joseph Ellicott to Paul Busti, Sept. 19, 1809, JEC.

11. Joseph Ellicott to Paul Busti, Aug. 7, 1811, JEC.

12. *Annals of the Congress of the United States* (Washington, D.C.: Gales and Seaton, 1853), 12 Cong, 1 sess., Nov. 29, 1811, 416. Henry Adams, who described the debate in detail in his *History of the United States,* VI, 133–53, had small respect for Peter Porter and pictured him thus: "Such ideas were not unbecoming to Porter, who began life as a Federalist, and had no philosophical theories or recorded principles to explain or defend," VI, 137.

13. *Annals of the Congress of the United States,* 12 Cong, 1 sess., Jan. 10, 1812, 719.

14. Joseph Ellicott to Paul Busti, April 1812, JEC.

15. Joseph Ellicott to Paul Busti, May 20, 1812, JEC.

16. Bingham, *The Cradle of the Queen City,* p. 257.

17. Joseph Ellicott to the inhabitants of Alleghany County, June 30, 1812, JEC.

18. Joseph Ellicott to Paul Busti, July 7, 1812, JEC.

19. William Peacock to Joseph Ellicott, Oct. 27, 1812, JEC.

20. Joseph Ellicott to Alexander Rea, June 29, 1812, JEC.

21. Joseph Ellicott to Paul Busti, March 23, 1813, JEC.

22. Joseph Ellicott to Paul Busti, July 15, 1812, JEC.

23. Joseph Ellicott to Paul Busti, March 23, 1813, JEC.

24. Adams, *History of the United States,* VI, 358.

25. All quotations in the paragraph were drawn from Joseph Ellicott to Paul Busti, March 25, 1813, JEC.

26. Joseph Ellicott to Paul Busti, June 3, 1812, JEC.

27. Louis Babcock, *The War of 1812 on the Niagara Frontier* (Buffalo: Buffalo Historical Society Publications, XIX, 1927), p. 118.

28. All quotations in the paragraph were taken from Joseph Ellicott to Paul Busti, Jan. 5, 1814, JEC.

29. Orsamus Turner, *Pioneer History of the Holland Purchase,* p. 603.

30. Joseph Ellicott to George Izard, Nov. 18, 1814, JEC.

31. George Izard to Joseph Ellicott, Nov. 21, 1814, JEC.

VIII. THE BANK OF NIAGARA

1. *RJE,* I, 130.

2. Bray Hammond, *Banks and Politics in America from the Revolution to the Civil War* (Princeton, N.J.: Princeton University Press, 1957), p. 66.

3. *Laws of the State of New York,* 22nd Sess., Chap. 84, April 2, 1799, 433.

4. *Laws of the State of New York*, 22nd Sess., Chap. 84, April 2, 1799, 436, 437.

5. Nelson M. Blake, *Water for the Cities* (Syracuse: Syracuse University Press, 1956), p. 44. Blake has an excellent chapter on the subject, thoroughly researched, judiciously appraised.

6. Paul Busti to Joseph Ellicott, July 18, 1810, JEC.

7. Joseph Ellicott to Paul Busti, July 15, 1812, JEC.

8. Joseph Ellicott to Paul Busti, March 25, 1813, JEC.

9. Chauncey Loomis to Joseph Ellicott, Feb. 27, 1815, JEC.

10. Joseph Ellicott to Paul Busti, Oct. 21, 1814, JEC.

11. Joseph Ellicott to Paul Busti, Nov. 14, 1814, JEC.

12. All the quotations in this paragraph come from Joseph Ellicott to Chauncey Loomis, Feb. 14, 1816, JEC.

13. Jonas Harrison to Joseph Ellicott, May 28, 1816, C. W. Evans Papers, Buffalo and Erie County Historical Society.

14. Joseph Ellicott to Chauncey Loomis, Feb. 14, 1816, JEC.

15. Parnell St. John Sidway, "Recollections of the Burning of Buffalo" (Buffalo: Buffalo Historical Society Publications, IX, 1906), 315.

16. Peter Porter to Augustus Porter, June 2, 1816, Augustus Porter Papers, Buffalo and Erie County Historical Society.

17. Joseph Ellicott to Paul Busti, May 19, 1819, JEC.

18. Joseph Ellicott to Paul Busti, Jan. 31, 1817, JEC.

19. Joseph Ellicott to William Peacock, March 7, 1817, JEC.

20. William Peacock to Joseph Ellicott, July 10, 1818, JEC.

21. Joseph Ellicott to Paul Busti, May 19, 1819, JEC.

22. All the quotations in this paragraph were drawn from Archibald S. Clarke to Joseph Ellicott, July 26, 1818, JEC.

23. Board of Directors to Joseph Ellicott, July 3, 1818, JEC.

24. Joseph Ellicott to Paul Busti, Aug. 24, 1818, JEC.

25. Archibald S. Clarke to Joseph Ellicott, Sept. 2, 1818, JEC.

26. William Peacock to Joseph Ellicott, Sept. 25, 1818, JEC.

27. Archibald S. Clarke to Joseph Ellicott, Oct. 2, 1818, JEC.

28. William Peacock to Joseph Ellicott, Nov. 24, 1818, JEC.

29. Joseph Ellicott to Ebenezer Johnston, Jan. 12, 1819, JEC.

30. Joseph Ellicott to David Evans, Jan. 13, 1819, JEC.

31. William Peacock to Joseph Ellicott, Jan. 26, 1819, JEC.

32. Samuel Russell, Augustus Porter, Archibald S. Clarke, James Brisbane, John G. Camp to ?, probably Joseph Ellicott, Jan. 29, 1819, C. W. Evans Papers.

33. Joseph Ellicott to David Evans, Feb. 1, 1819, JEC.

34. David Evans to Joseph Ellicott, Feb. 5, 1819, JEC.

35. Joseph Ellicott to William Peacock, March 26, 1819, JEC.

36. Joseph Ellicott to Paul Busti, March 19, 1819, JEC.

IX. THE GRAND CANAL

1. *Laws of the State of New York*, 15th Sess., Chap. 40, March 3, 1792, 316.

2. Nathan Miller, *The Enterprise of a Free People: Aspects of Economic Development during the Canal Period, 1792–1838* (Ithaca, N.Y.: Cornell University Press, 1962), p. 20.

3. Gouverneur Morris to John Parish, Dec. 20, 1800, in the Appendix of David Hosack's *Memoir of DeWitt Clinton* (Ann Arbor: University Microfilms, 1967), p. 257.

4. Ronald E. Shaw, *Erie Water West: A History of the Erie Canal 1792–1854* (Lexington: University of Kentucky Press, 1966), p. 25.

5. Carter Goodrich, Julius Rubin, H. Jerome Cramner, Harvey H. Segal, *Canals and American Economic Development* (New York: Columbia University Press, 1961), p. 31.

6. Simeon De Witt to Joseph Ellicott, June 13, 1808, in the *Correspondence on the Holland Land Company and Canal Construction in Western New York,* ed. by Frank H. Severance (Buffalo: Buffalo Historical Society Publications, XIV, 1910), p. 4. Hereafter cited as *Canal Correspondence.*

7. Joseph Ellicott to Paul Busti, July 16, 1808, JEC.

8. Joseph Ellicott to Simeon De Witt, Nov. 19, 1808, JEC.

9. Joseph Ellicott to Paul Busti, March 30, 1812, JEC.

10. Thomas Eddy to Joseph Ellicott, July 10, 1812, *Canal Correspondence,* pp. 24n, 25, 26. Thomas Eddy wrote to Joseph Ellicott: "The amount in Land that other large proprietors may be induced to grant to the State, will depend very much on what your Company may agree to contribute. If *the whole* should amount to something considerable, there is no doubt the Legislature would agree to commence the work—but it is, in truth, so materially and decidedly your interest to make a handsome & liberal offer, that there can be no doubt of your doing equal to our expectation—if unfortunately *you should fall short of what might reasonably be expected from you, the whole plan would be frustrated.*"

11. Jabez D. Hammond, *The History of Political Parties,* I, 426. Hammond explained Ellicott's appointment thus: "Joseph Ellicott was the agent of the great Holland Company, residing in Batavia; of course a zealous friend to the canal, and a man of wealth and influence."

12. Joseph Ellicott to Paul Busti, May 13, 1816, *Canal Correspondence,* p. 63.

13. DeWitt Clinton to Joseph Ellicott, April 4, 1816, DeWitt Clinton Papers, Columbia University. Clinton had marked this letter "confidential."

14. DeWitt Clinton to Joseph Ellicott, March 15, 1816, *Canal Correspondence,* p. 51.

15. DeWitt Clinton to Joseph Ellicott, Sept. 20, 1816, JEC.

16. Joseph Ellicott to Thomas Eddy, May 6, 1816, JEC.

17. Joseph Ellicott to Samuel Young, Oct. 24, 1816, *Canal Correspondence,* p. 73.

18. Joseph Ellicott to Paul Busti, June 21, 1817, *ibid.,* p. 126.

19. Joseph Ellicott to Samuel Young, Oct. 24, 1816, *ibid.,* pp. 75, 76.

20. Joseph Ellicott to Paul Busti, June 21, 1817, *ibid.,* p. 127.

21. Paul Busti to Joseph Ellicott, May 17, 1811, *ibid.,* p. 19.

22. Paul Busti to Joseph Ellicott, May 4, 1812, *ibid.,* p. 22.

23. Paul Busti to Joseph Ellicott, Oct. 31, 1816, *ibid.,* p. 78.

24. Paul Busti to Joseph Ellicott, Jan. 23, 1817, *ibid.,* p. 98.

25. Paul Busti to Joseph Ellicott, Feb. 22, 1817, *ibid.,* p. 120.

26. Joseph Ellicott to Micah Brooks, Dec. 30, 1816, JEC.

27. DeWitt Clinton to Joseph Ellicott, April 16, 1817, *Canal Correspondence,* p. 124.

28. Joseph Ellicott to Paul Busti, June 21, 1817, *ibid.,* p. 128.

29. DeWitt Clinton to Joseph Ellicott, Sept. 25, 1818, *ibid.*, p. 144.

30. Joseph Ellicott to DeWitt Clinton, April 2, 1818, JEC.

31. DeWitt Clinton to Joseph Ellicott, May 2, 1818, *Canal Correspondence*, p. 138.

32. *Laws of the State of New York*, 29th Sess., Chap. 110, April 2, 1806, 465, 466.

33. DeWitt Clinton to Joseph Ellicott, Feb. 3, 1816, JEC.

34. All quotations in this paragraph came from William Peacock to Joseph Ellicott, Jan. 18, 1819, *Canal Correspondence*, pp. 149, 151, 154.

35. Joseph Ellicott to William Peacock, Feb. 15, 1819, JEC.

36. *Laws of the State of New York*, 42nd Sess., Chap. 104, April 7, 1819, 121.

37. Both quotations in the paragraph were taken from Oliver Forward, Samuel Wilkeson, George Coit, Charles Townsend to Paul Busti, April 30, 1820, C. W. Evans Papers.

38. "Buffalo and Black Rock Harbor Papers, 1816–1825," ed. by Frank H. Severance (Buffalo: Buffalo Historical Society Publications, XIV, 1910), 311.

X. "GIVE IN YOUR DEMISSION YOURSELF"

1. Orsamus Turner, *Pioneer History of the Holland Purchase*, pp. 321, 322.

2. David M. Ellis, "The Yankee Invasion of New York, 1783–1850," *New York History*, XXXII (Jan., 1951), 3.

3. John Brannan to Paul Busti, March 3, 1823, HLC, II, #136.

4. H. J. Huidekoper to Paul Busti, Dec. 14, 1809, HLC, II, #159.

5. Philip Church to Paul Busti, April 13, 1822, HLC, II, #134.

6. *Niagara Journal*, Sept. 28, 1819; Oct. 2, 1819; Oct. 19, 1819; Nov. 2, 1819.

7. Joseph Ellicott to Paul Busti, Nov. 2, 1819, JEC.

8. Joseph Ellicott to Paul Busti, Nov. 2, 1819, JEC.

9. Archibald S. Clarke to Joseph Ellicott, Nov. 2, 1819, JEC.

10. Joseph Ellicott to Paul Busti, Nov. 2, 1819, JEC.

11. Joseph Ellicott to William Peacock, Oct. 5, 1819, JEC.

12. Joseph Ellicott to Samuel Hopkins, Jan. 15, 1816, JEC.

13. Joseph Ellicott to Chauncey Loomis, Jan. 27, 1817, JEC.

14. All quotations in the paragraph were drawn from Joseph Ellicott to Paul Busti, Dec. 13, 1819, JEC.

15. The three quotations in the paragraph came from the *Niagara Journal*, the first, Dec. 7, 1819; the other two, Dec. 14, 1819.

16. David Evans to Joseph Ellicott, Feb. 17, 1820, JEC.

17. Paul Busti to David Evans, March 2, 1820, C. W. Evans Papers.

18. Joseph Ellicott to Robert Troup, Dec. 13, 1820, JEC.

19. Robert Troup to Joseph Ellicott, April 19, 1820, C. W. Evans Papers.

20. Robert Troup to David Evans, April 19, 1820, C. W. Evans Papers.

21. Directors to Cazenove and Busti, Oct. 16, 1798, HLC, Written Copybooks, 253.

22. Paul Busti to Joseph Ellicott, June 30, 1803, JEC.

23. Joseph Ellicott to Paul Busti, July 29, 1803, JEC.

24. David Evans to Joseph Ellicott, Feb. 17, 1820, C. W. Evans Papers.

25. Joseph Ellicott to Paul Busti, March 7, 1820, JEC.

26. Paul Busti to Joseph Ellicott, March 21, 1820, JEC.

27. Oliver Forward to James Sheldon, April 2, 1820, James Sheldon Papers, Buffalo and Erie County Historical Society.

28. Martin Van Buren, *The Autobiography of Martin Van Buren*, ed. by John C. Fitzpatrick (Washington, D.C.: Government Printing Office, 1920), II, 103.

29. Paul Busti to David Evans, Feb. 2, 1820, C. W. Evans Papers.

30. Paul Busti to Joseph Ellicott, Nov. 3, 1802, JEC.

31. Louis LeCouteulx to Joseph Ellicott, April 17, 1808, JEC.

32. Joseph Ellicott to Paul Busti, Aug. 21, 1807, JEC.

33. Paul Busti to Joseph Ellicott, Feb. 2, 1804, JEC.

34. Circular, April 11, 1805, HLC, Eb 191 #106.

35. Paul Busti to Joseph Ellicott, Jan. 26, 1806, HLC, Eb 191 #106.

36. Quotations in this and the previous four paragraphs were drawn from Joseph Ellicott to Paul Busti, Feb. 21, 1820, HLC, Eb 191 #107.

37. Both quotations in the paragraph came from Paul Busti to David Evans, Feb. 2, 1820, C. W. Evans Papers.

38. Memorial to Paul Busti, March 10, 1821, HLC, Sundries, #13.

39. Martin Van Buren to Paul Busti, March 12, 1821, HLC, Miscellaneous, II.

40. Paul Busti to Van Eeghen & Co., Dec. 15, 1820, HLC, Eb 193 #84.

41. Quotations in this and the previous four paragraphs were taken from Paul Busti to Joseph Ellicott, April 9, 1821, HLC, Copybooks 35.

42. Joseph Ellicott to William Peacock, June 1, 1821, JEC.

43. Joseph Ellicott to Paul Busti, May 9, 1821, JEC.

44. Joseph Ellicott to William Peacock, June 1, 1821, JEC.

45. Jacob Otto to John J. Vanderkemp, Jan. 27, 1825, HLC, II, 171.

46. Paul Busti to Jacob Otto, Dec. 6, 1821, HLC, Letterbooks 77.

47. Jacob Otto to John J. Vanderkemp, Nov. 25, 1821, HLC, Copybooks 73.

48. Genesee County Wills, I, 308–23, Surrogate's Office, Batavia, New York.

49. Jacob Otto to John Vanderkemp, Aug. 30, 1826, HLC, II, 173.

Bibliographical Essay

The Bibliography offers over-all comments on the large manuscript collections and the most frequently used sources; and annotated citations for topics discussed within each chapter.

The Holland Land Company Papers, abbreviated HLC in Notes to the Chapters, is amazing, with the seventy-five-year life of the Holland Land Company crammed into forty-three yards of primary sources. Housed in the City Archives of Amsterdam, Holland, the collection is currently being inventoried, most of the work having been completed. The Holland Land Company archives are divided into three major parts: Management in Amsterdam, Management in America, and Maps. The first two sections contain, among other items, Resolutions of the Directors, Journals of income and expenditure, Copybooks of letters between directors and Company employees, and vital correspondence among Busti and Ellicott, Otto, and Ogden, and also between Evans and his subordinates. The third part has 141 maps, some of American states but most showing Company-owned areas in New York and Pennsylvania.

The records that involved the Dutch proprietors directly are written mainly in Dutch. Cazenove and Busti corresponded with their employees in French. Otherwise, the collection is in English. Despite two world wars and an incredible occupation, the HLC Papers have remained undamaged, their contents intact and in good condition. For more detail, see William Chazanof, "The Van Eeghen Collection," *Niagara Frontier*, Autumn 1968, 80–85.

The manuscript material at the Buffalo and Erie County Historical Society was valuable indeed. The Joseph Ellicott Collection, cited in the Notes to the Chapters as JEC, consisted of more than six thousand pieces and was indispensable for the entire study. The Peter B. Porter Papers and the Dr. Cyrenius Chapin Papers discussed certain aspects of the War of 1812. On the subject of the Erie Canal, the *Correspondence on the Holland Land Company and Canal Construction in Western New York* (Buffalo: Buffalo Historical Society Publications, XIV, 1910) was pertinent; it contains letters between Paul Busti and Joseph Ellicott discussing the canal as well as the William Peacock Report on the construction of the port of Buffalo. The Black Rock Harbor Papers concentrated on the disputes over the western terminus, while the DeWitt Clinton Papers at Columbia University dealt with the entire canal. For the gubernatorial election of 1820, the C. W.

223

Evans Papers, the Erastus Granger Papers, and the James Sheldon Papers had information of a regional nature.

The legislative history of the period was delineated in the *Journal of the Assembly of the State of New York* and in the *Journal of the Senate of the State of New York*. *Laws of the State of New York* provided a surprising amount of detail on the legislation. The *Council of Appointment Minutes, 1777–1821* recorded faithfully the multitudinous appointments, both civil and military. The *Annals of the Congress of the United States* contained interesting information on the debate that led to the declaration of the War of 1812.

The newspapers had to be used with discrimination. They were more biased in terms of individuals than issues. The Buffalo *Gazette*, founded in 1811, was the first newspaper to appear in Buffalo and later changed its name to the *Niagara Patriot* and then to the *Buffalo Patriot*; it switched from support to criticism of Joseph Ellicott. The *Niagara Journal*, started in 1815, was Buffalo's second newspaper and altered its name to the *Buffalo Journal*; it favored Peter B. Porter and opposed Joseph Ellicott. The Buffalo *Emporium and General Advertiser* endorsed DeWitt Clinton and differed with Peter B. Porter. The *Black Rock Gazette* staunchly supported Peter B. Porter and his desire for the harbor and canal terminus to be at Black Rock. The *Albany Gazette* sympathized with DeWitt Clinton and fought the Bucktails.

The Buffalo Historical Society Publications had many contemporary articles that were admirable. In his autobiography, "Early Life of Augustus Porter" (VII, 277–322), Porter discussed his education, surveys, and especially his mercantile interests. Samuel Wilkeson, in "Recollections of the West and the First Building of Buffalo Harbor" (V, 147–214), supplied useful information on the struggle to erect the port of Buffalo. The two-volume *Reports of Joseph Ellicott*, cited in the notes as *RJE*, provided detailed statements and comments in his annual reports on all matters affecting the purchase.

Only one book and one article treat Ellicott's life biographically. The book, written by Clara L. T. Williams, is *Joseph Ellicott and Stories of the Holland Purchase* (Batavia: Clara L. T. Williams, 1936); it relies mainly on secondary sources and does not probe the subject deeply. G. Hunter Bartlett wrote an article called "Andrew and Joseph Ellicott" that appeared in the Buffalo Historical Society Publications (XXVI, 3–48); seven pages are given to Joseph Ellicott, mainly in defense of the Resident-Agent. On the early history of western New York, Orsamus Turner, in the *Pioneer History of the Holland Purchase of Western New York* (Buffalo: Jewett, Thomas & Co., 1849), offered much local color but rambled excessively and omitted the political-economic relationship. Paul Evans, in *The Holland Land Company*, gave a full and penetrating analysis of the Company holdings in New York and in Pennsylvania, but his concern was primarily with the social and economic phases.

Chapter I

For genealogy and information on the Ellicott family, the best source is Charles W. Evans, *Biographical and Historical Accounts of the Fox, Ellicott, and Evans Families* (Buffalo: Baker, Jones & Co., 1882). Less valuable on the Ellicott background but not to be ignored are: Catharine V. Mathews, *Andrew Ellicott His Life and Letters* (New York: Grafton Press, 1908); Clara L. T. Williams, *Joseph Ellicott and Stories of the Holland Purchase* (Batavia: Clara L. T. Williams, 1936); Wilhelmus Bogart Bryan, *A History of the National Capital* (New York: Macmillan, 1914); G. Hunter Bartlett, "Andrew and Joseph Ellicott," *Recalling Pioneer Days*, ed. by Frank H. Severance (Buffalo: Buffalo Historical Society Publications, 1922), XXVI, 3–48; and Martha E. Tyson, "Settlement of Ellicott's Mills with Fragments of History therewith Connected," *Maryland Historical Society* (Maryland: Fund Publication, 1865). Andrew Ellicott's engineering achievements are described in the following: fully in the Mathews volume cited above; interpretively by Charles B. Stuart, *Lives and Works of Civil and Military Engineers of America* (New York: Van Nostrand, 1871); and broadly in Warren S. Ely, "Andrew Ellicott, the Great Surveyor," *Bucks County Historical Society* (Meadville, Pa.: Tribune Publishing, 1926), V.

The land squabbles are described carefully in Paul D. Evans, *The Holland Land Company* (Buffalo: Buffalo Historical Society Publications, 1924). Insights into Cazenove's expensive tastes appear in Theophile Cazenove, *Journal 1794*, ed. by Rayner W. Kelsey (Haverford, Pa.: Pennsylvania History Press, 1922). Details on the Treaty of Big Tree, replete with the major figures and bribery details, can be found in the HLC Papers in Amsterdam, Holland, especially Ea 218, #58, #60, and #62. Documents and correspondence on the Treaty are published in the *American State Papers*, Class 2, Indian Affairs.

For the fascinating details of the Big Survey of western New York, the *Reports of Joseph Ellicott*, 2 vols., ed. by Robert W. Bingham (Buffalo: Buffalo Historical Society Publications, 1937), I, are, to use Ellicott's favorite word, "indispensable." Charming but meandering descriptions of the Big Survey appear in Orsamus Turner, *Pioneer History of the Holland Purchase of Western New York* (Buffalo: Jewett, Thomas & Co., 1849).

Chapter II

How the Company selected the Resident-Agent can be followed in the HLC Papers, especially the Written Copybooks. The role of James Wadsworth is examined in Neil Adams McNall, *An Agricultural History of the Genesee Valley 1790–1860* (Philadelphia: University of Pennsylvania Press, 1953), while that of Charles Williamson is traced in Helen I. Cowan,

Charles Williamson Genesee Promoter—Friend of Anglo-American Rapprochement (Rochester: Rochester Historical Society Publications, XIX, 1941). Ellicott's plans and contract are included in the *Reports of Joseph Ellicott,* I.

Published descriptions of life in 1800 are numerous. For Philadelphia, see John Allen Krout and Dixon Ryan Fox, *The Completion of Independence 1790–1830* (New York: Macmillan, 1944), and Carl Bridenbaugh, *Cities in Revolt Urban Life in America, 1743–1776* (New York: Capricorn Books, 1964). The best volume on New York is Sidney I. Pomerantz, *New York an American City 1783–1803* (Port Washington, N.Y.: Ira J. Friedman, 1965). Also useful are Thomas A. Janvier, *In Old New York* (New York: Harper and Brothers, 1894), and Charles M. Wiltse, *The New Nation 1800–1845* (New York: Hill and Wang, 1961). Travel in western New York is most ably described by John Maude, *Visit to the Falls of Niagara in 1800* (London: Longman, Reese, Orme, Brown, & Green, 1826). Other informative volumes are the frequently cited Timothy Dwight, *Travels in New-England and New-York* (New Haven: Timothy Dwight, 1821–22), IV; Jane L. Mesick, *The English Traveler in America, 1785–1835* (New York: Columbia University Press, 1933); and, especially good for geology, housing, and food prices, Robert Munro, *A Description of the Genesee Country, in the State of New-York* (New York: Robert Munro, 1804).

Ellicott's major problems as Resident-Agent can be found in a source that is absolutely essential to any study of his work: the Joseph Ellicott Collection at the Buffalo and Erie County Historical Society. Additional information appears in the *Reports of Joseph Ellicott,* I.

Chapter III

The political situation about 1800 is presented refreshingly by an Englishman, Marcus Cunliffe, in *The Nation Takes Shape: 1789–1837* (Chicago: University of Chicago Press, 1959), p. 168. For New York, the most dependable and often a primary source continues to be Jabez D. Hammond, *The History of Political Parties in the State of New York* (Cooperstown: H. & E. Phinney, 1844), I. Also illuminating New York's complex political picture are Alvin Kass, *Politics in New York State 1800–1830* (Syracuse: Syracuse University Press, 1965); Frank Monaghan, *John Jay Defender of Liberty* (New York: Bobbs-Merrill, 1935); M. R. Werner, *Tammany Hall* (Garden City, N.Y.: Garden City Publishing Company, 1932); and Howard Lee McBain, *DeWitt Clinton and the Origin of the Spoils System in New York* (New York: Columbia University Press, 1907).

Ellicott's entry into politics can best be followed through the Joseph Ellicott Collection. Good insight into Ellicott's motives can be found in Paul Evans, *The Holland Land Company.*

Ellicott's part in the organization of Genesee County is best understood by reading the Joseph Ellicott Collection for those years; it should be supplemented by the *Reports of Joseph Ellicott*, I. Because the Council of Appointment is vital to Ellicott's control, it is helpful to examine the *New York State Constitution Annotated* (New York: Burland Printing Company, 1938), especially Article XXIII. Useful for civil and militia appointments is the *Council of Appointment Minutes, 1777–1821*.

How Ellicott used political influence to subdivide Batavia into four separate towns can be understood through the Joseph Ellicott Collection. For his use of associates, it is rewarding to study *A Transcript of the Original Records of the Town of Batavia*, kept at the Buffalo and Erie County Historical Society.

Chapter IV

The bitter gubernatorial election of 1804 is well presented in either Jabez Hammond, *The History of Political Parties*, I, or DeAlva S. Alexander, *A Political History of the State of New York* (New York: Henry Holt, 1906), I. Aaron Burr's relations with the Holland Land Company are fully described in Nathan Schachner, *Aaron Burr* (New York: Frederick A. Stokes, 1937). The political positions of Ellicott and Busti can be found in the Joseph Ellicott Collection, 1804. A gem of an autobiography is that of Augustus Porter, "Early Life of Augustus Porter," Buffalo and Erie County Historical Society, 1848; reprinted in the Buffalo Historical Society Publications, VII. A thorough biography of Peter Porter is an unpublished doctoral dissertation of I. Frank Mogavero, "Peter B. Porter, Citizen and Statesman," University of Ottawa, 1950. A feel for the mutual recrimination during the election can be gained by perusing the contemporary newspapers as geographically apart as the New York *Evening Post* and the *Western Repository*.

The evolution of other rising political figures in western New York can be found in Orsamus Turner, *Pioneer History of the Holland Purchase*. Erastus Granger's role in Buffalo is traced in Robert W. Bingham, *The Cradle of the Queen City* (Buffalo: Buffalo Historical Society Publications, XXXI, 1931). Evidence of Ellicott's relations with his political satellites— for example Alexander Rea and Joseph Annin—is practically restricted to the Joseph Ellicott Collection.

Material on the Big Family can be extracted by industrious use of the Joseph Ellicott Collection. A valuable source on David Evans is the HLC Papers. Four precious volumes on William Peacock are also in the HLC Papers. Shrewd appraisals of Peacock may be found in Orsamus Turner, *Pioneer History of the Holland Purchase* and in an exceptionally good county history by Andrew W. Young, *History of Chautauqua County, New York* (Buffalo: Mathews and Warren, 1875).

Chapter V

The road situation in the nation is well covered in George R. Taylor, *The Transportation Revolution, 1815–1860* (New York: Rinehart and Company, 1958). Additional information can be found in Curtis P. Nettels, *The Emergence of a National Economy, 1775–1815* (New York: Holt, Rinehart and Winston, 1962), and Krout and Fox, *The Completion of Independence, 1790–1830.* The situation in eastern New York is covered with exceptional care in David M. Ellis, *Landlords and Farmers in the Hudson-Mohawk Region, 1790–1850* (Ithaca: Cornell University Press, 1946). For western New York, the conditions are fully described in Helen I. Cowan, *Charles Williamson Genesee Promoter—Friend of Anglo-American Rapprochement,* and Paul D. Evans, "The Pulteney Purchase," *Quarterly Journal of the New York State Historical Association,* III (Jan., 1922). Ellicott's ideas can be found in the *Reports of Joseph Ellicott,* I, II. The story of the turnpikes can be followed in the Joseph Ellicott Collection, while the local color can be seen in the Buffalo *Gazette,* 1811, 1812.

Essential to the subject of taxation are the statistics found in the *Reports of Joseph Ellicott,* I, II. Ellicott's efforts to cope with the problem can be traced in the Joseph Ellicott Collection. A balanced, interpretive view appears in Paul Evans, *The Holland Land Company.*

The two best sources for the Company land sales are the *Reports of Joseph Ellicott,* I, and Paul Evans, *The Holland Land Company.*

Chapter VI

The statistical growth of New York State and its small political units is published in the decennial reports of the *Federal Census.* The 1810 *Federal Census* is amazingly thin for New York State with two pages, while Pennsylvania has thirty-eight, and even little New Jersey rates seven. Additional statistical material appears in Franklin B. Hough's excellent volume, *Census of the State of New York, for 1855* (Albany: Charles Van Benthuysen, 1857), and in J. H. French, *Gazetteer of the State of New York* (New York: Collins, 1860).

The development of various communities can be found in specialized monographs. The best volume on the port of New York, especially on business innovations, is Robert G. Albion, *The Rise of New York Port 1815–1860* (New York: Charles Scribner's, 1939). Colorful details on Albany, Utica, and Canandaigua can be read in John Melish, *Travels in the United States of America in the Years 1807 & 1808, and 1809, 1810 & 1811* (Philadelphia: John Melish, 1812). Easily the best source on Rochester is Blake McKelvey, *Rochester, the Water-Power City 1812–1854* (Cambridge: Harvard University Press, 1945). The architecture, old photograph, and some articles of the Ellicott home can be seen at the Holland Land Company Office Museum in Batavia, New York. How Ellicott gained access to Buffalo Creek for the Company is told in Robert W. Bingham, *The Cradle of the Queen City* (Buffalo: Buffalo Historical Society Publications, XXXI, 1931). Further details on this acquisition appear in Le Comte de Colbert Maulevrier, *Voyage dans L'Intérieur des Etats-Unis et Au Canada* (Baltimore: Johns Hopkins Press, 1935); Orsamus Turner's *Pioneer History of the Holland Purchase;* and the Joseph Ellicott Collection. The full story of the survey of Buffalo can be found in Robert W. Bingham, *The Cradle of the Queen City.*

Ellicott's efforts to expand the suffrage in western New York can best be followed in the Joseph Ellicott Collection. On this subject, a judicious appraisal can be found in Paul Evans, *The Holland Land Company.*

The key role played by Ellicott in the creation of Genesee County is fully revealed in the Joseph Ellicott Collection. More details on this topic can be located in Paul Evans, *The Holland Land Company,* Orsamus Turner, *Pioneer History of the Holland Purchase,* Andrew W. Young, *History of Chautauqua County,* and of course the *Laws of the State of New York.*

Chapter VII

The over-all effects of the Embargo Act on the nation are well described in Bradford Perkins, *Prologue to War* (Berkeley: University of California Press, 1961). Despite an anti-Jefferson bias, Volumes IV–VI of Henry Adams, *History of the United States of America during the Administrations of Jefferson and Madison* (New York: Charles Scribner's, 1889–91), are fruitful reading. Additional information can be found in the imaginative monograph of Julius W. Pratt, *Expansionists of 1812* (New York: Macmillan, 1925) and in Louis M. Sears, *Jefferson and the Embargo* (Durham, N.C.: Duke University Press, 1927). The impact of the Embargo Act and its repeal on the state's Republican party are well handled in Jabez D. Hammond, *The History of Political Parties,* and in the Joseph Ellicott Collection. Insights on the personal economic ambitions of Peter Porter can be found in Henry R. Howland, "Robert Hamilton, the Founder of Queenstown" (Buffalo: Buffalo Historical Society Publications, VI, 1903).

The War of 1812 can be analyzed from many aspects. The role of the War Hawks can be studied from three valuable sources: Julius Pratt's exciting thesis in *Expansionists of 1812;* Henry Adams' thorough study in the *History of the United States of America,* VI; Bradford and Perkins' findings in the British archives in *Prologue to War.* To catch the feelings of 1811 and 1812, one needs to read relevant sections in the *Annals of the Congress of the United States* (Washington, D.C.: Gales and Seaton, 1853). The reactions of the settlers in western New York to the war declaration is recaptured in Orsamus Turner, *Pioneer History of the Holland Purchase.* On the same topic, good supplementary material can be located in Robert W. Bingham, *The Cradle of the Queen City* and in Louis L. Babcock, *The War of 1812 on the Niagara Frontier* (Buffalo: Buffalo Historical Society Publications, XIX, 1927). Ellicott's personal responses to the war can best be followed in the Joseph Ellicott Collection. The fiascoes on the invasions of Canada from Buffalo are fully treated in Henry Adams' *History of the United States of America,* VI. For eye-witness recall of the occasions, see Archer Galloway, "The First Shot, Reminiscences of Archer Galloway" (Buffalo: Buffalo Historical Society Publications, V, 1902). Details on the military phases are well treated in Louis Babcock, *The War of 1812 on the Niagara Frontier,* especially the senseless burning of Newark. The British invasion of western New York is described in Orsamus Turner *Pioneer History of the Holland Purchase.* Excellent vignettes of the retreat of soldiers and civilians in western New York can be read in "Militia Service of 1813–1814. Correspondence of Amos Hall," ed. by Frank H. Severance (Buffalo: Buffalo Historical Society Publications, V, 1902). Ellicott's vivid descriptions of the withdrawal can be found in the Joseph Ellicott Collection, particularly Jan. 5, 1814 and Jan. 13, 1814. Ellicott's role in the handling of the refugees is treated objectively in the Joseph Ellicott Collection.

Chapter VIII

The fullest and best history of banking in America during this period can be found in Bray Hammond, *Banks and Politics in America from the Revolution to the Civil War* (Princeton: Princeton University Press, 1957). Material on New York banking in particular appears in Margaret G. Myers, *The New York Money Market* (New York: Columbia University Press, 1931); Robert G. Albion, *The Rise of New York Port, 1815–1860;* and Sidney I. Pomerantz, *New York An American City 1783–1803.* The influence of New Englanders is illuminated in David M. Ellis, "The Yankee Invasion of New York, 1783–1850," *New York History,* XXXII (Jan., 1951). An exceptional analysis of Burr and the Bank of Manhattan can be read in Nelson M. Blake, *Water for the Cities* (Syracuse: Syracuse University Press, 1956). Interpretations more favorable to Burr can be located in Bray Hammond, *Banks and Politics in America,* and in Nathan Schachner, *Aaron Burr.*

The needs of western New York for a bank on the purchase are fully demonstrated in the Joseph Ellicott Collection. The Company office can be seen today in the Holland Land Company Office Museum in Batavia, New York, while details on building costs are published in the *Reports of Joseph Ellicott,* I. How the Company was caught in the sharp competition between the two banks in Canandaigua can be followed in the Joseph Ellicott Collection. The shortage of specie is explained in the Joseph Ellicott Collection. On this subject see also James L. Barton, "Early Reminiscences of Buffalo and Vicinity" (Buffalo: Buffalo Historical Society Publications, I, 1879); Truman C. White, *Our Country and Its People* (Boston: Boston Historical

Company, I, 1898); and, Samuel M. Welsh, Home History. *Recollections of Buffalo during the Decade from 1830–1840* (Buffalo: Peter, Paul and Brothers, 1891).

Ellicott's pivotal role in the creation of the Bank of Niagara can be found in the Joseph Ellicott Collection. Ellicott's dominant position is discussed in Paul Evans, *The Holland Land Company* and in Orsamus Turner, *Pioneer History of the Holland Purchase.* The rivalry between Ellicott and the Porter brothers can be found in the Joseph Ellicott Collection. Valuable on this subject, too, are the Porter Papers and the Letterbook of Jonas Harrison, 1813–19, both at the Buffalo and Erie County Historical Society.

The acrimonious quarrel for control of the bank can be followed best in the Joseph Ellicott Collection. The deep animosities toward Ellicott appear in the *Niagara Patriot,* the C. W. Evans Papers, and the Porter Papers. The shadowy position of DeWitt Clinton can be located in the Joseph Ellicott Collection and in Jabez D. Hammond, *The History of Political Parties,* I. For a description of Ellicott's period as bank president, the Joseph Ellicott Collection is vital. The Kibbe machinations appear in the C. W. Evans Papers and in the Joseph Ellicott Collection. Ellicott's great disillusion with DeWitt Clinton, so important in the break between the two men, can be found in the Joseph Ellicott Collection. For additional material on the subject, see Verna G. Walker, "Banking in Buffalo before the Civil War," an unpublished master's thesis, Department of History, University of Buffalo, 1933.

Chapter IX

The history of the earliest proposals for a projected canal from New York City to the Great Lakes, predating the Erie one, is fully covered in an excellent monograph by Ronald E. Shaw, *Erie Water West: A History of the Erie Canal 1792–1854* (Lexington: University of Kentucky Press, 1966). An exceptionally good article on the Western Inland Navigation Company is that of Nathan Miller, "Private Enterprise in Inland Navigation," *New York History,* XXXI (Oct., 1950). The extensive correspondence between David Hosack and contemporaries of Gouverneur Morris, and the fourteen essays of the Hercules series are published in the Appendix of David Hosack, *Memoir of DeWitt Clinton* (Ann Arbor: University Microfilms, 1967). The economic aspects are stressed in Carter Goodrich, Julius Rubin, H. Jerome Cranmer, Harvey H. Segal, *Canals and American Economic Development* (New York: Columbia University Press, 1961); and Nathan Miller, *The Enterprise of a Free People: Aspects of Economic Development during the Canal Period, 1792–1838* (Ithaca: Cornell University Press, 1962). Ellicott's characteristic thoroughness is demonstrated in his interesting ten-page letter of July 30, 1808, to Simeon De Witt in the *Correspondence on the Holland Land Company and Canal Construction in Western New York,* ed. by Frank H. Severance (Buffalo: Buffalo Historical Society Publications, XIV, 1910), cited in the notes and hereafter as *Canal Correspondence*. The Holland Land Company's official position on the canal can be found in the *Canal Correspondence*, a source essential to the topic.

The legislature's shifting position on the canal is very sketchy in the *Laws of the State of New York*. The classic story of the canal is told by Noble E. Whitford, *History of the Canal System of the State of New York*, 2 vols. (Albany: Brandow Publishing Company, 1906). More recent research can be found in Ronald Shaw, *Erie Water West*; Carter Goodrich, *et al.*, *Canals and American Economic Development*; and Nathan Miller, *The Enterprise of a Free People*. Porter's proposal to terminate the canal at Lake Ontario is described in John T. Horton, *et al.*, *History of Northwestern New York* (New York: Lewis Historical Publishing Company, 1947), II. Details on proposed routes can be read in the *Canal Correspondence*, Noble Whitford, *History of the Canal System*, and Ronald Shaw, *Erie Water West*. An excellent source for the work of the canal commissioners before 1812, the Company offer, and Ellicott's use of political influence to gain support for the canal is the *Canal Correspondence*. The harmonious working relationships between Ellicott and DeWitt Clinton—illuminating especially because of the later split—can be easily followed in the *Canal Correspondence* and the DeWitt Clinton Papers at Columbia University. Ellicott's efforts to combat Busti's skepticism over the canal can be read in the *Canal Correspondence*.

The construction of the canal is well described in Ronald Shaw, *Erie Water West*. Additional details can be located in Noble Whitford, *History of the Canal System*; and in Elkanah Watson, *History of the Rise, Progress, and Existing Condition of the Western Canals in the State of New-York* (Albany: D. Steele, 1820). The struggle between Buffalo and Black Rock and the tiff between Ellicott and the Buffalo residents are covered in the Joseph Ellicott Collection, the *Canal Correspondence*, and the C. W. Evans Papers at the Buffalo and Erie County Historical Society. Colorful, exciting, but often slanted are the newspaper articles in the *Niagara Journal*, the *Niagara Patriot*, and the *Black Rock Beacon*.

Chapter X

The reasons for Ellicott's removal as Resident-Agent can be followed best in the Joseph Ellicott Collection. Economic life in western New York during the transition period from Indian to white man's control can be found in Orsamus Turner, *Pioneer History of the Holland Purchase*; Andrew Young, *History of Chautauqua County, New York*; and Robert Bingham, *The Cradle of the Queen City*. For more information about the early settlers, the Chautauqua County Historical Museum in Westfield, New York, has eighteen volumes of material that Elial T. Foote had collected; volumes 2, 15, 19, 27, and especially 6 include letters about the early settlers. Examples of the deterioration of Ellicott's mental health can be located in the HLC Papers; Orsamus Turner, *Pioneer History of the Holland Purchase;* and the local newspapers, particularly the *Niagara Journal* and the *Black Rock Gazette.* The "Agricola" articles are printed in the *Niagara Journal* while Ellicott's reactions can be read in the Joseph Ellicott Collection. The roadtax episode can be found in several sources: the Joseph Ellicott Collection, the C. W. Evans Papers, Paul Evans, *The Holland Land Company,* and in the local press of the Republican *Advocate,* the Buffalo *Gazette,* and the *Niagara Journal.* Ellicott's efforts to sell the Company land to the State of New York appear fully in the Joseph Ellicott Collection.

The gubernatorial election of 1820 has been described in various publications: reliable and judicious is Jabez D. Hammond, *The History of Political Parties,* I; urbane and sophisticated is Martin Van Buren, *The Autobiography of Martin Van Buren,* ed. by John C. Fitzpatrick (Washington, D.C.: Government Printing Office, 1920), II; and wisely discriminatory is Milton W. Hamilton, *The Country Printer, New York State, 1765–1830* (New York: Columbia University Press, 1936). Additional information can be gleaned from the C. W. Evans Papers and the James Sheldon Papers, both collections at the Buffalo and Erie County Historical Society. Busti's ambivalent feelings about Ellicott appear clearly in the Joseph Ellicott Collection. Ellicott's defense of his political actions is fully given, especially in the HLC Papers, Feb. 21, 1820, Eb 191 #107. The political pressures on Busti to remove Ellicott as Resident-Agent can be read in the HLC Papers, the C. W. Evans Papers, and in Paul Evans, *The Holland Land Company.*

Ellicott's dismissal as Resident-Agent is well covered in the HLC Papers, especially in the Copybooks and Eb 193. Busti's key letter urging Ellicott to resign is in the HLC Papers, Copybook 35, dated April 9, 1821. Ellicott's twenty-nine-page answer to Busti can be found in the C. W. Evans Papers, June 18, 1821. The charges against the Big Family of abusing their positions can be located in the HLC Papers. Ellicott's will is kept at the Surrogate's Office, Batavia, New York. Ellicott's suicide is reported in the HLC Papers. From the Municipal Archives and Records Center, New York City, the author obtained a copy of what the Death Register of 1826 contained. Additional information about the death of Ellicott may be found in the New York *Commercial Advertiser,* Aug. 21, 1826; the New York *Evening Post,* Aug. 21, 1826; the *Black Rock Gazette,* Aug. 31, 1826; and the Buffalo *Emporium* and *General Advertiser,* Sept. 2, 1826.

Sources for the Maps

Land Holdings in Western New York, 1804. In the preparation of this map, three sources were used. One was the *Map of Morris's Purchase of West Geneseo in the State of New York* drawn by Joseph and Benjamin Ellicott in 1800; it appeared in Paul D. Evans, *The Holland Land Company.* A second source was the *Map of the State of New York Showing the Loca-*

tion of the Original Land Grants Patents and Purchases and was included in
the *Atlas of the State of New York,* by Joseph R. Bien (1895); it was reproduced in *Expansion in New York with Special Reference to the Eighteenth
Century,* by Ruth Higgins. The third was Orsamus Turner, *Pioneer History
of the Holland Purchase of Western New York;* it was depended upon to
settle the question of the eastern boundary line of the purchase.

County Organization, 1800. Three maps and two gazetteers were the
main sources for preparing this drawing. Preserved in the New York State
Library at Albany, the three maps were the following: William McAlpin,
*Section of a Map of the State of New York Compiled from the Latest Au-
thorities, Including the Turnpike Roads Now Granted as Also the Principal
Common Roads,* 1808; Amos Lay, *Section of a Map of the State of New
York with Part of the States of Pennsylvania and New Jersey, etc. Compiled,
Corrected and Published from the Most Recent Authorities and Accurate
Surveys,* 1817; and, A. Finley, *Section of a Map of New York,* 1826. The
gazetteers were Horatio Gates Spafford, *Gazetteer of the State of New York,*
1826, and J. H. French, *Gazetteer of the State of New York,* 1860. This map
was used as a blueprint in laying out three others: County Organization,
1802; County Organization, 1806; and County Organization, 1808.

County Organization, 1802. This map relied on the five sources that had
been used in preparing the drawing of County Organization, 1800. New
Amsterdam was the name chosen by Joseph Ellicott. The settlers preferred
Buffaloe Creek, and it eventually became just Buffalo.

Roads in Western New York, 1804. In preparing this map, two sources
were used. One was the map drawn by Amos Lay, *Section of a Map of the
State of New York with Part of the States of Pennsylvania and New Jersey,
etc. Compiled, Corrected and Published from the Most Recent Authorities
and Accurate Surveys,* 1817. The other was a map drafted by Joseph and
Benjamin Ellicott, *Map of Morris's Purchase of West Geneseo in the State
of New York,* 1800; it was taken from Paul D. Evans, *The Holland Land
Company.*

County Organization, 1806. The same five sources were depended upon
in preparing this map as those used to draw County Organization, 1800.

County Organization, 1808. The five sources used in preparing the map
of County Organization, 1800 were also relied upon in drawing this one.

War of 1812. This map depended on the one drawn by Joseph and
Benjamin Ellicott, *Map of Morris's Purchase of West Geneseo in the State
of New York,* 1800; it was included in Paul D. Evans, *The Holland Land
Company.* The main areas where the fighting occurred were designated.

The Grand Canal, 1825. Three sources were used in preparing this map.
One was the Amos Lay map, *Section of a Map of the State of New York
with Part of the States of Pennsylvania and New Jersey, etc. Compiled,
Corrected and Published from the Most Recent Authorities and Accurate
Surveys,* 1817. A second was the map by A. Finley, *Section of a Map of
the State of New York,* 1828. The Lay and Finley maps were kept in the

New York State Library in Albany. The third source was *A New Map and Profile of the Proposed Canal from Lake Erie to Hudson River in the State of New York Contracted by Direction of the Canal Commissioners from the Maps of the Engineers,* 1821; there were two maps, print 1 and print 2.

Index

G2